Real Estate

D0088302

Traditional studies of the property market have tended to focus solely on commercial and legal issues, but the growing importance of the issue of sustainability means that a different approach is needed.

This new textbook provides an overview of property within a market context, examining the complex nature of property rights and issues related to both investors and occupiers. At the same time it assesses property from the perspective of financial, social and environmental sustainability. Topics covered range from the characteristics of property and depreciation, to ownership and development through to investments and sustainability reporting. The book concludes with key skills in sustainable knowledge needed by those working in the real estate industry.

Written by an author team of experienced property professionals, this essential introductory textbook is well suited for property, planning and architecture students on undergraduate, graduate and conversion courses, as well as those on CPD and training programmes in related areas.

Peter Dent is a Fellow of the Royal Institution of Chartered Surveyors. He has held various posts at Oxford Brookes University, most recently as the Comerford Climate Change Fellow in the Department of Real Estate and Construction. He has had considerable experience of managing both academic development and research projects both in the UK and overseas.

Michael Patrick is a chartered surveyor and has over 30 years' experience in the real estate fund management industry in the UK and Canada. He has an MBA from the Cranfield School of Management and is currently lecturing in valuation and investment at Oxford Brookes University. Prior to joining Brookes he had held roles with a number of major fund managers including Henderson, Legal & General, Morgan Grenfell and Grosvenor.

Ye Xu is a chartered surveyor and is currently a senior lecturer in the Department of Real Estate and Construction, Oxford Brookes University. With more than ten years' research and advisory experience in the property industry as well as the academic field, she has gained a wide knowledge of quantitative modelling and property market research. Ye's recently completed doctoral thesis examined property market performance through both traditional and behavioural theories.

The Natural and Built Environment Series

Editor: Professor John Glasson
Oxford Brookes University

Real Estate: Property Markets and Sustainable Behaviour
Peter Dent, Michael Patrick and Ye Xu

Introduction to Environmental Impact Assessment, 4th edition
John Glasson, Riki Therivel and Andrew Chadwick

The Environmental Impact Statement after Two Generations
Michael Greenberg

Building Competences for Spatial Planners
Anastassios Perdicoulis

Spatial Planning and Climate Change
Elizabeth Wilson and Jake Piper

Water and the City
Iain White

Urban Planning and Real Estate Development
John Ratcliffe and Michael Stubbs

Transport Policy and Planning in Great Britain
Peter Headicar

Introduction to Rural Planning
Nick Gallent, Meri Juntti, Sue Kidd and Dave Shaw

Regional Planning
John Glasson and Tim Marshall

Strategic Planning for Regional Development
Harry T. Dimitriou and Robin Thompson

Methods of Environmental Impact Assessment
Peter Morris and Riki Therivel

Public Transport
Peter White

Landscape Planning and Environmental Impact Design
Tom Turner

Controlling Development
Philip Booth

Partnership Agencies in British Urban Policy
Nicholas Bailey, Alison Barker and Kelvin MacDonald

Development Control
Keith Thomas

Expert Systems and Geographic Information Systems for Impact Assessment
Agustin Rodriguez-Bachiller and John Glasson

Real Estate

Property markets and sustainable behaviour

Peter Dent, Michael Patrick and Ye Xu

Routledge
Taylor & Francis Group

LONDON AND NEW YORK

First published 2012
by Routledge
2 Park Square, Milton Park, Abingdon, Oxon OX14 4RN

Simultaneously published in the USA and Canada
by Routledge
711 Third Avenue, New York, NY 10017

Routledge is an imprint of the Taylor & Francis Group, an informa business

British Library Cataloguing in Publication Data
A catalogue record for this book is available from the British Library

Library of Congress Cataloging in Publication Data
Dent, Peter.
Real estate : property markets and sustainable behaviour / Peter Dent,
Michael Patrick, and Ye Xu.
p. cm. – (The natural and built environment series)
Includes bibliographical references and index.
1. Real estate business. 2. Real property. 3. Right of property. I. Patrick,
Michael. II. Xu, Ye. III. Title.
HD1361.D46 2012
333.33–dc23
2011047697

ISBN: 978-0-415-59143-0 (hbk)
ISBN: 978-0-415-59144-7 (pbk)
ISBN: 978-0-203-11794-1 (ebk)

Typeset in Stone Serif and Akzidenz Grotesk
by Saxon Graphics Ltd, Derby.

Contents

Section I – Introduction and Concepts   1

1 Introduction   3
   Introduction   3
   The theme of the book   3
   The structure of the book   4

2 Background and orientation   9
   Introduction   9
   Value issues   11
   Knowledge and experience   12
   Institutional wealth   13
   Responsibility   14
   Sustainable thinking   15
   Transdisciplinary thinking   17
   Sustainability literacy   18
   Summary   22

3 Culture, markets and institutions   23
   Introduction   23
   Culture   24
   Buildings   29
   Urban space   30
   Markets   30
   Market changes over time   31
   The institutional framework of the property market   31
   Summary   34

Section II – Background to Real Estate and Financial Markets 37

4 Real estate market mechanisms 39
Introduction 39
Characteristics of property 40
Regulatory framework of the property market 47
Summary 53

5 Methods of ownership in the property market 54
Introduction 54
Overview of property ownership 54
Ownership and control 55
Types of owners in the market 55
Types of indirect ownership of property 57
Summary 68

6 Sustainability 69
Introduction 69
Changing patterns 69
Sustainable development 71
Sustainable development case study 77
Summary 79

7 Property investment decisions 81
Introduction 81
Risk and return 81
Efficient market hypothesis 83
Price, value and worth 84
Property indices and performance benchmarks 85
Sustainability tools 86
Further thoughts and summary 92

8 Decision making and sustainability 94
Introduction 94
The basics of decision making 94
Behavioural finance techniques 101
Behavioural studies in the property discipline 104
Decision making and sustainability 106
Behavioural barriers towards sustainability 107
Summary 110

9 Responsible property investment 113
Introduction 113
Sustainability plans 114
Sustainability reporting 116
The Better Buildings Partnership and the Greenprint Foundation 117

Sustainable approach to business 118
Case study 118
Investment process 124
Public commitments 125
Implementation issues 127
Summary 129

Section III – Sustainable Real Estate and Business Tools   131

10 Real estate and shear zones   133
Introduction 133
The triple bottom line 133
Shear zones 133
Seeking sustainable solutions 135
Occupation decision making 139
Aligning real estate with business operations 140
Case study 142
Reflection on the case study 144
Summary 148

11 Portrait of place   150
Introduction 150
Case study background 150
Project framework 152
Summary 161

12 Sustainability balanced scorecard that aligns real estate
with business   164
Introduction 164
Real estate's five dimensions 164
Organisational change 166
A balanced sustainability scorecard 167
Case study 172
Reflection from the case study 175
Summary 178

13 Introduction to the big conversation   179
Introduction 179
The Big Conversation case study 179
Summary 190

Section IV – Sustainability Leadership and Reflection 193

14 Sustainable leadership 195
Introduction 195
Learning 195
Leadership 198
The leader's journey 200
Case study 201
Summary 205

15 Sustainability skills 206
Sustainable literacy skills and knowledge 1 206
Sustainable literacy skills and knowledge 2 208
Sustainable literacy skills and knowledge 3 209
Sustainable literacy skills and knowledge 4 209
Sustainable literacy skills and knowledge 5 211
Sustainable literacy skills and knowledge 6 211
Sustainable literacy skills and knowledge 7 212
Sustainable literacy skills and knowledge 8 212
Final thoughts 213

Bibliography 215

Index 227

Illustrations

· ·

Figures

1.1	Structure of the book	5
2.1	Relationship between attitude, knowledge, behaviour and value	10
2.2	Four levels of discipline in transdisciplinary learning	18
2.3	Stabilisation wedges (Socolow *et al.* 2004: 11)	19
3.1	Relationships between language, building and culture	24
3.2	A moral philosophy model of cross-cultural societal ethics (Robertson *et al.* 2003: 387)	25
3.3	Relationship between values, beliefs, behaviour and action	28
3.4	The institutional hierarchy of property markets (Keogh *et al.* 1999: 2407)	32
4.1	All UK commercial property initial yield versus swap rate (IPD data)	47
4.2	City of London office rent 1980–2010 (IPD 2010)	49
5.1	IPD quarterly property derivatives trading volumes (IPD 2010: 2)	65
8.1	A portfolio as a layered pyramid (Shefrin 2002: 122)	99
8.2	Behavioural relationships in financial markets	102
8.3	Identifying irrational space	103
8.4	Responding to irrational space	104
8.5	Basic model of pro-environmental behaviour (Kollmuss *et al.* 2002: 241)	108
8.6	Barriers between environmental concern and action (Blake 1999: 267)	109
8.7	Model of pro-environmental behaviour (Kollmuss *et al.* 2002: 257)	110
9.1	Strategic and tactical sustainable principles (RREEF 2011a)	119
10.1	The shear zones of corporate sustainability (Hockerts 2001: 5)	134
10.2	Some of the benefits of working at Brockwood	143
10.3	Social capital dimensions	144
11.1	Location of Central Lincolnshire (AECOM 2011: 18)	151
12.1	Five dimensions of real estate analysis tool (RICS 2009c: 24)	165

12.2	Balanced scorecard (strategic perspectives) (Procurement Executives' Association 1999: x)	168
12.3	Sustainability balanced scorecard (strategic perspectives)	169
12.4	Illustrative example for an eco-efficiency balanced scorecard (Hockerts 2001:17)	171
12.5	Strategic core issues	172
14.1	Developing the moral component of authentic leadership (May *et al*. 2003: 250)	199

Tables

4.1	Assets total (ONS 2011: 247)	39
7.1	Decomposition of property risk into systematic and specific risk (adapted from Brown *et al*. 2000: 268)	83
7.2	Recommended environmental benchmarks: existing buildings (CRC 2004: 33)	90
7.3	Proposed social benchmarks: existing buildings (CRC 2004: 89)	91
9.1	Public statements of selected companies	115
9.2	Sustainable activities in business	118
10.1	A four-way matrix for social capital aligned with real estate (MacGillivray 2004: 123)	148
11.1	The seven roles of communities in Central Lincolnshire (AECOM 2011: 10)	153
11.2	The sustainability domains (AECOM 2011: 52)	155
11.3	Scoring system (AECOM 2011: 56)	157
11.4	Sustainability domains comparison to SCSs (AECOM 2011: 54)	159
11.5	Summaries of opportunities to improve sustainability (AECOM 2011: 59–150)	161
12.1	Real estate in the business process	168
14.1	Situational types (Head *et al*. 2008: 8)	197
14.2	Strategies for increasing authentic leadership (Ilies *et al*. 2005: 389)	200

Illustrations

6.1	Photos of Central St Giles in London	78
7.1	An example showing sustainability impact on calculation of worth	88
9.1	Photos of RREEF case studies (RREEF 2011b)	122
11.1	Stakeholder participation (AECOM 2011: 55)	156
14.1	Case Study 1	204

Acknowledgements

· ·

The authors would like to acknowledge the help and support of the following:

John Comerford, for his cartoons, his support and his passion for promoting the climate change agenda to the surveying profession.

Paul Roach for challenging the way we think about real estate. Milena Tasheva-Petrova for sharing her ideas on Chapter 3.

Caroline Pang, Andrew Nelson and Patricia Connolly from RREEF for their help and guidance in putting together the case study material contained in Chapter 9.

Staff and students at Brockwood Park School who participated in the focus groups which helped to form part of the case study material used in Chapter 10.

Paul Comerford and Michael Henderson from AECOM Design + Planning who provided the material for Chapter 11.

Paul Winter from CORPRA for the case study material in Chapter 12 and other material in that Chapter which formed the basis of a paper which appeared in the *Corporate Real Estate Journal*. Also for his contribution of the case study material in Chapter 13.

Paul McNamara from PRUPIM who provided the case study material for Chapter 14.

Section I

Introduction and Concepts

NEW GUERNICA

1   Introduction

Introduction

Property markets and sustainable behaviour? Surely, everything that needs to be said about these two has already been said. There are a wealth of books on markets and market mechanisms. Every other book that we pick up seems to have 'sustainability' somewhere in the title. So, why is this book different? The answer is that we believe that this book covers ground that has not appeared in others nor has it been covered in the way that we cover it here. We hope that it stimulates discussion, reflection and ultimately action based on knowledge and understanding rather than knowledge alone.

We tend to think that once we have given something a name (e.g. sustainable development), discovered how it fits into our world, so that we can describe it, then we understand it (Loori 2007). In this whole process, however, we argue that it may be necessary to reflect on our attitudes and behaviours in order to get closer to understanding the complexities of sustainable development or sustainability. We do not necessarily prescribe changes of behaviour. We simply make the point that we can all influence, as individuals, the nature of property (both physical and financial), the markets within which it is transacted (both local and global), the way it is financed (direct or indirect) and the way it is used (as a part of strategy or apart from strategy).

Oskamp (2000) asks the extent to which behavioural change is needed towards sustainability. His answer: a value system that moves away from human mastery over nature to one of harmony with nature. However, it is not so much change that is needed but '...a complete mutation of consciousness' (Krishnamurti 2007: 37).

The theme of the book

The essential theme running through this book is the behaviour of individuals as professionals, and organisations as part of the institutional framework of markets. The emphasis of the book is on real estate markets but, of necessity, it will cut across other markets as well. If we believe that we are living and working unsustainably, then current behavioural patterns, and how they have emerged, need to be understood and set against the need for change and the introduction of new business models.

The book takes a transdisciplinary approach, integrating, horizontally, disciplines such as economics, psychology, education, technology and social science, and, vertically, at empirical, pragmatic, normative and value levels. The book addresses both reflection in modes of thinking and reflexivity in courses of action. Acknowledging ambiguity in the concept of sustainability, the authors do not attempt to add it as a layer in decision making. Instead, the reader is encouraged to recover what might have been perceived to have been lost or, at least, overlooked over the centuries through industrialisation and latterly globalisation. This approach is not intended to undermine the benefits of industrialisation, but simply to see these in a post-industrial setting and identify the tensions created around the concept of sustainability. Some of the issues surrounding this concept and its meaning will be addressed later.

Our approach therefore seeks to consider a more participatory response that could lead to longer term sustainable solutions rather than what appears to be the current vogue for short termism in much of the actions of commerce, government and individuals. This involves *responsible* actions on the part of professionals who advise clients on real estate matters principally through different forms of *dialogue* to communicate *sustainable* ideas to meet *sufficient* needs.

The structure of the book

The book is divided into four parts as shown in Figure 1.1. A starting point for the book is to establish a ground on which this participatory response is based. Accordingly, the first part of the book includes an examination of the concepts of 'value', 'sustainability', 'transdisciplinarity', 'sustainability literacy' and 'knowledge' and their impact on behaviour and the way we might think about markets as complex systems generally and real estate specifically. This then leads onto a chapter that considers culture as an evolving process of collective knowledge and its implicit and explicit social construction. It is important to see the built environment within a cultural setting, not just as the physical symbol of a society, but as an integral part of the social fabric. Real estate is a tangible representation of meaning for many organisations. It is also the ground on which much sustainability discussion takes place (buildings representing a major contributor to carbon emissions). From this, the chapter questions the gaps that exist between values and actions specifically as they relate to sustainable behaviour and real estate. Finally, some examination of markets and their ability to evaluate sustainable variables is included in preparation for more detailed consideration later in the book.

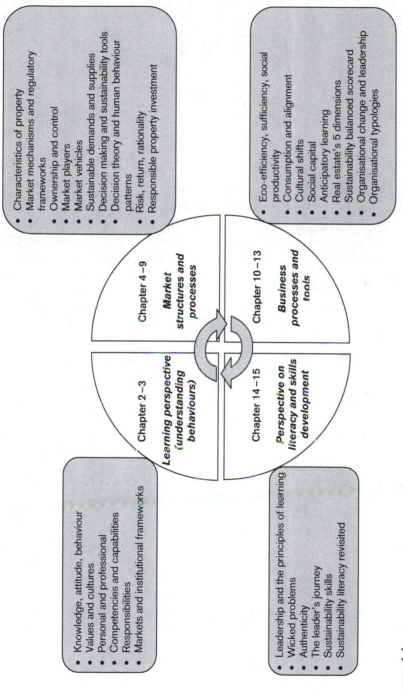

Chapter 4–9
Market structures and processes

Chapter 10–13
Business processes and tools

Chapter 2–3
Learning perspective (understanding behaviours)

Chapter 14–15
Perspective on literacy and skills development

- Characteristics of property
- Market mechanisms and regulatory frameworks
- Ownership and control
- Market players
- Market vehicles
- Sustainable demands and supplies
- Decision making and sustainability tools
- Decision theory and human behaviour patterns
- Risk, return, rationality
- Responsible property investment

- Eco-efficiency, sufficiency, social productivity
- Consumption and alignment
- Cultural shifts
- Social capital
- Anticipatory learning
- Real estate's 5 dimensions
- Sustainability balanced scorecard
- Organisational change and leadership
- Organisational typologies

- Knowledge, attitude, behaviour
- Values and cultures
- Personal and professional
- Competencies and capabilities
- Responsibilities
- Markets and institutional frameworks

- Leadership and the principles of learning
- Wicked problems
- Authenticity
- The leader's journey
- Sustainability skills
- Sustainability literacy revisited

Figure 1.1

Structure of the book

Following on from the consideration of these underlying concepts, the book has three further sections. The first of these sections sets out to examine the background to real estate markets, finance, ownership and market mechanisms. It considers the nature of property and the markets within which it operates. The emphasis in this section of the book is more on investment and ownership of property as opposed to occupation. It is divided up into six chapters.

Chapter 4: Real estate market mechanisms. The complex nature of property is identified alongside the institutional framework, which includes legal and planning regulations, that exists to inhibit or enhance its use. The uniqueness of the asset and the different financial vehicles that exist to enable property to be held as an asset class are introduced to demonstrate its complex nature and the pivotal role that property has in the sustainability agenda and the responsibility inherent for those who own interests in property assets.

Chapter 5: Methods of ownership in the property market. This chapter considers in more detail the different levels of ownership, the legal rights and responsibilities of freehold, leasehold, direct and indirect owners. In the indirect market, property companies and REITs are used to increase liquidity and to address tax considerations. This then leads into a discussion of other indirect vehicles used for property investment. Finally, issues around securitised loans are highlighted. In all, the chapter shows the wide nature of property ownership and the differing motivations. This adds to the complexity as an asset class. It can also make consideration of sustainable behaviour beyond achieving acceptable financial returns difficult.

Chapter 6: Sustainability. This chapter looks at the move towards all aspects of sustainability in real estate using both coercive and incentive tools. Market demand and risks are considered together with the regulatory framework that underpins supply and demand. It questions the emphasis on energy efficiency, identifying that sustainability is much more than that. The property lifecycle is complex and risky and will represent different risks to different players at different times. Concentrating solely on energy efficiency may, therefore, add to the risks if it does not meet overall market expectations, particularly in the area of ongoing depreciation of assets.

Chapter 7: Property investment decisions. This chapter outlines the relationship between risk and return showing how, using capital market theory, decisions can be made. The use of indices is considered as guides to assessing relative performance and decision making. The chapter also reviews possible methodologies to incorporate all aspects of sustainability into the valuation process, particularly in investment worth calculations.

Chapter 8: Decision making and sustainability. This chapter examines different aspects of behaviour from the point of view of financial decision making. Behavioural finance is a relatively new area of study and it is, to an extent, a controversial area. With the growing theoretical base, however, it is gaining acceptance as an area worthy of inclusion within decision-making processes. This chapter starts from a theoretical base to help the reader to understand the logic of behavioural finance generally. General behavioural techniques applicable to investment decisions are then introduced, which could prove to be useful in trying to understand sustainable behaviour. Questions of rationality are included along with work that has been undertaken in the property discipline specifically. Finally, the theories of behavioural finance are related to sustainability together with some of the barriers to overcome.

Chapter 9: Responsible property investment. This chapter looks at some of the criteria used by investing institutions when making decisions to invest. It highlights their public statements about corporate social responsibility and comes to some conclusions about these statements. The chapter outlines some of the activities that go towards a sustainable approach to business, and this includes a case study example to illustrate some of the categories considered important by a fund manager. This leads onto the sustainable investment process and implementation together with ideas on green leases.

The next section of the book considers, in more detail, some of the tools that could be used as part of the sustainability evaluation of real estate. These include the adaptation of existing tools and the development of new ones. In most cases, actual examples are used to demonstrate how sustainable practices and behaviour are working and can be adapted to a variety of situations.

Chapter 10: Real estate and shear zones. The triple bottom line (TBL) has been identified by many as an appropriate way in which business could make environmental and social concerns an integral part of the business process. This chapter, whilst considering the three pillars of TBL, concentrates on the shear zones between these pillars. These zones (i.e. eco-efficiency, ethical sufficiency and social productivity) help to gain a better understanding of the linkages between economic, environmental and social concerns in the context of real estate decision making. A case study is used to demonstrate how to understand at a deeper level the needs of occupiers through processes such as dialogues and focus groups. Issues of organisational change and cultural shifts are also considered.

Chapter 11: Portrait of place. This chapter consists of a study of a region of the UK. It is used to show how the economic, environmental and social activities of a whole region can be integrated into a holistic, sustainable solution that seeks to achieve growth and well-being for all stakeholders. This is achieved through strategic partnerships between consultants, public bodies, communities and citizens. The way in which the case study is presented seeks to demonstrate the level of participation that took place to arrive at effective solutions. The commentary also links into the shear zones and the framework of anticipatory learning that were introduced in the previous chapter.

Chapter 12: Sustainability balanced scorecard. This chapter develops a traditional balanced scorecard into a sustainable real estate model and uses this in conjunction with a real estate dimensional tool to explore an organisational change case study. The chapter also introduces the importance of leadership in the process of moving organisations towards more sustainable practices.

Chapter 13: The big conversation. Leading on from the previous chapter, the notions of leadership and organisational adaptability are explored here using extracts from a series of conversations used in a report for the British Council of Offices in 2010, 'Towards a Zero Carbon Office'. These are used to illustrate where different organisations might be on their sustainability journey. The chapter as a whole also acts as an introduction to the final section.

The final section reflects back on the context for sustainability and the tools that could be applied for investors, occupiers and advisers of real estate. Specifically it revisits the principles of sustainability literacy and some of the leadership skills that would be useful in developing a sustainable agenda for real estate. This applies to either individual properties or as part of a portfolio or region.

Chapter 14: Sustainability leadership. This chapter considers learning as a process that requires flow, balance and clarity. These are applied to learning in the context of sustainability and the problems that might be encountered trying to understand what it means to be sustainable. This then leads onto issues around authentic leadership and the leader's journey. To illustrate some of the issues raised in the chapter (and the book as a whole) a case study example is provided.

Chapter 15: Sustainability skills. This final chapter takes a step back to view sustainability skills and how the sections of the book interlink. It uses the principles of sustainability literacy as a framework and shows how each principle relates to a specific element of the book. It highlights the main aspects of the real estate market and maps out the essential features to consider when creating sustainability in financial, social and environmental terms.

2 Background and orientation

· ·

Introduction

Economics has been defined as the discipline that deals with the production, distribution and consumption of wealth. It seeks to assess what is valuable at any given point in time by studying the relative exchange values of goods and services (Capra 1982). Models and theories in economics are always going to be based on a particular value system and a particular view of human nature. The value system adopted in the West for the last 400 years has tended, principally, to be based on monetary value as a means to achieving overall well-being. This has, as a consequence, limited consideration of the more qualitative elements of decision making for investment. Yet it is this very area that is important for an understanding of the environmental and social implications of investment decisions. Until recently, social and ecological interdependence have tended to be largely ignored, and it has been the monetary market value of goods and services that have tended to be the principal measure of relative value (Capra 1982). Monetary value in turn is influenced by the political, legal and economic framework within which transactions take place.

In order to include consideration of environmental and social sustainability, as well as financial sustainability in decision making, there has had to be therefore a fundamental change; a change not so much in technology, nor modelling, nor distribution of resources, but in ourselves. The question is: how do we motivate ourselves to make that change, and what are the incentives for making such changes? More specifically, under what conditions do we develop new fundamental behaviour patterns, as opposed to simply moving between the already well-established patterns that epitomise our social position and status (Bonta *et al.* 2004).

In order to consider this question, this book looks at both internal and external factors that can influence people's real estate decision making, especially towards sustainability issues. This chapter concentrates on and explores some of the concepts that may help in the process. It introduces ways in which people might handle knowledge and use knowledge sustainably through their behaviours rather than just apply the knowledge as if it were external to themselves.

The chapter starts with a section that includes an examination of some issues around the concept of value. This is not so much a question of value in monetary terms, but more about fundamental background issues to value embracing social and environmental considerations. This then leads into aspects of knowledge and experience, institutional wealth and responsibility. These sections question the manner in which knowledge is acquired and used. It is followed by a section on sustainable thinking generally. Here sustainability is examined as a concept (or not) and the limits to thought as a means of understanding. It questions whether the issue is being approached in the most effective way or if there is some other means by which the complexity of the concept could be addressed. There follows a consideration of transdisciplinary learning and sustainability literacy. These sections highlight the need to consider whether thinking should be broadened out beyond the traditional 'surveying' discipline to arrive at decisions in a much wider context. The final sections in this chapter touch on professional education and change of mindset.

Figure 2.1 shows the linkages between the sections in the chapter. Within a particular value system we acquire and evaluate information that we then interpret as knowledge. With this knowledge should come responsibility that feeds into institutional wealth, the moral compass that guides our journey.

In this way, we develop an attitude towards our place in society. In order to turn this attitude into a behaviour pattern we need to acquire skills in thinking and literacy. If, as is the case here, we seek sustainability, both professionally and privately, then these skills should be developed in that direction.

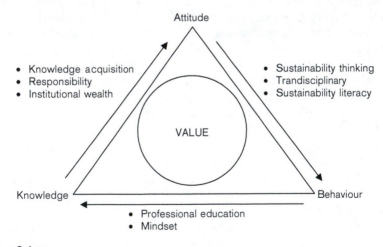

Figure 2.1

Relationship between attitude, knowledge, behaviour and value

The whole process represents a dynamic transformation continually growing and developing through education and an active mindset that is constantly alert to the present moment.

Value issues

It seems that the mindset that caused environmental problems is not going to solve environmental problems. That mindset is based around the notion of the rationality of economic man, or in other words the rational assumptions of human beings embedded in classic economic theories. This rationality tends to be dominated by the masculine orientation towards individual short-term financial profit, status and the market. Unfortunately this same mindset has tended to demote sustainability as a concept that is long term not immediate, generational not individual and nebulous not hard currency. Thus equations seeking equilibrium between risk and return tend to eschew the longer term externalities. In private markets (regulated or unregulated), the common good is not prioritised. 'In a sustainability context, this means that to promote less harmful behaviour, prevailing attitudes, beliefs and values need to be challenged at all levels, personal, cultural and institutional' (Murray *et al.* 2007: 288).

Unfortunately, in recent times, despite regular financial crises, it is difficult to promote anything that may be perceived as undermining the status quo of the financial system. Knowledge tends to be sanitized to create an illusion of *positive unconscious* or *irrational exuberance* such that even fictions in the market place are rarely challenged, but simply accepted as natural consequences of freedom. Chapman (2004) describes this as an underlying psychosis created by cultural myths that fill our collective consciousness. One such cultural myth using cognitive behavioural theory (CBT) is built around *an optimistic bubble of positive illusions* (James 2007) to improve emotional well-being. In reality, this may just be papering over the cracks and disguising the meaning of data available in the process of knowledge accumulation. This is the *illusion of certainty*, which is often used in health care to allay fears about particular diagnoses, but it can equally be presented in financial markets to disguise risks and uncertainties.

For example, it is important for those professionals working in the real estate market advising clients to share some of the responsibility for the way in which the profession takes stock of the impacts of climate change in the built environment. The RICS (2007: 26) have identified that 'the two most important barriers to the use of sustainability tools, techniques and information continue to be lack of knowledge and lack of expertise'. As such, it is therefore important to address these issues and find workable solutions. For those advising on real estate matters, it is important to consider whether they set the market or merely reflect it, or do both at the same time.

Knowledge and experience

The way in which we acquire knowledge is, according to Hume (1999), based on memory and imagination (Marciano 2006). Memory is a backward-looking function of the mind. It is useful for technical knowledge but less so when seeking innovation and change (particularly when that change is away from an entrenched hegemony such as exists in Western market mechanisms). It frames cognition within the dominant culture. Psychologically, therefore, to transcend memory when it comes to dealing with global issues, such as the nature of sustainability, the mind needs to develop a sense of spacelessness and timelessness (i.e. outside of cultural *norm* space and freed from the constraints of past accumulations of knowledge).

On the other hand, imagination plays a forward-looking role. Unfortunately, objectives tend to be set in the business and financial markets that have sought to perpetuate and, where possible, enhance the present. These objectives have tended to become defined in shorter timescales, so that longer perspectives are largely ignored even in strategic planning. Imagination as 'a reasoned choice of novelty' (Loasby 2001: 11), in a sense, has been replaced by identification that seems to be the conditioning by which problems are solved. Both individuals and institutions have developed routines 'to classify phenomena, simplify complexities, dissolve uncertainties and constrain choice' (Loasby 2001: 12).

Now the truth is that in global markets, looking back and learning from the past gives little insight into the 'next big thing' of the consumer-driven society or the 'little surprises' that are waiting to emerge from global economic activity. Individuals tend to 'frame' their decisions in the sense that a particular choice is associated with the way in which an individual perceives the current and future states of that choice. So choices involving judgement 'rather than mere calculation' are needed (Augier *et al.* 2000: 665). These, however, may be illusory, based on certain standards or interpretations of reality defined by past experience or upbringing. Pohl (2004) categorises these 'cognitive illusions' associated with the human information processing system as follows:

- *Illusions of thinking.* These involve the application of certain rules, which are derived from normative models, and the results from these models would normally be treated as standards.
- *Illusions of judgement.* These examine people's subjective view to a specific aspect of a given stimulus, such as its pleasantness and frequency. Some specific features, such as feelings of familiarity or confidence, might bias people's judgement under certain situations.
- *Illusions of memory.* These study how people recall or recognise earlier encoded materials.

These illusions will, to a greater or lesser extent, influence choices in individuals and institutions. It could thus be argued that the fundamental change taking place in the natural organic (and sustainable) growth of markets lies in time and space. People now seem to have a fantasy (and, potentially, unsustainable) culture of immediacy where they want it now and want it to come to them. So, instead of timelessness and spacelessness, individuals and institutions find both time and space gaining greater value. Time speeds up and space contracts.

These fantasy desires are reinforced by techno-economic dynamics at the expense of other psychical possibilities. This makes it harder to retrieve a sustainable position as the system creates its own momentum both in the actual circulation of virtual wealth creation and in the psychology of the market makers. However, it is interesting to note that greater wealth does not necessarily lead to greater well-being.

As far back as Socrates, wealth was seen to have its darker side. A wealthy city, for example, implied also a city of great poverty. It is not possible to have one without the other. Such a city potentially diminishes the power and status of neighbouring communities (social capital) and it also exploits natural resources (natural capital), as the desire for luxury beyond sufficiency requires additional land resources. These suggestions of 'the unsustainability of the luxurious city shore up Socrates' claim that it is a city with a fever, sick at its heart' (DeWeese-Boyd *et al.* 2007: 122).

Institutional wealth

One potential consequence of this apparent impatience or fantasy desire is a breakdown in ethical and moral codes. For example, professionalism may come under attack in order to complete the deal and to achieve targets, thus often distorting the pricing mechanism. Paradoxically, this is where political, social and financial institutions could play an important part. Unfortunately it is those very institutions (albeit with some notable exceptions) that are now tending to push the market forward. This potentially creates an environment where motivations and determinants for action (i.e. fixed energy points) tend to be seen in terms solely of money or commodities and not social and inter-generational capital.

In the property investment markets, for example, the risk and return of real estate for investors is traded rather than the building itself. As such the control of the performance of the building can become separate from the actual management of it (see Chapter 5 for more details). But not only does this appear to be potentially unsustainable, it is, in the end, an irrational decision because even in a situation where costs (both short and long term) outweigh benefits, an action is still likely to be pursued for the perceived short-term material benefits alone.

Whilst in this instance, it may still be the case that rationality is seen as seeking short-term monetary gain, in the wide business world. Rational economic man is now becoming a broader concept, and means 'collective-based sources of utility or welfare and dynamic preferences, linked to social norms' (Daniels 2005: 257).

In this sense, it could be that the self exists only as a consciousness of a succession of objects and we only really know ourselves in relationship to people, ideas, nature, material objects, etc. Self here could apply equally to the institutional self as to the individual self. In either case, there is no enduring self, no fixed thinking entity. This relationship between us and our world is evolving as life. As such there is no separation between objects (whether human or otherwise). This may imply a *middle way* or an *included middle* with new social definitions seeking 'a maximum of well-being with minimum consumption' (Daniels 2005: 249).

Responsibility

Here may be a way forward for the sustainable mind, because, as a consequence, the evaluation of any action or behaviour will depend on the perceived approval of others. Accordingly, it does not rest only on a private decision. Thus, in the case of sustainable property investment for example, such behaviour relies on market sentiment to sustain it. To readdress the issue as to whether real estate advisers set markets or merely reflect them it could be argued here that markets are not just reactive indicators of value or activity. Market players and their advisers also have the ability to anticipate and influence behaviours. There is therefore an opportunity, with sufficient will, to induce deep sustainable thinking in the market.

Recently, in the case of real estate investment, there is an obvious or substantial move towards responsible property investing (RPI) by major institutional investors, who invest directly in real estate assets. RPI properties are those that fit into 'property investment or management strategies that go beyond compliance with minimum legal requirements in order to address environmental, social and governance issues' (UNEP 2008: 3). These investors see RPI properties as adding positively to income and/or appreciation through tenant demand, expenses, perceived risk, capital improvement and management programmes (Pivo *et al.* 2008). This enables institutional investors to follow RPI criteria within their regulatory environments.

Alongside these types of initiatives in the field of property investment, other approaches to wider issues of evaluating economic activity are being explored. One such approach that receives some attention is material flow analysis (MFA), a means by which flows of materials and energy between nature and the economy can be measured and minimised with sufficient political will (Fischer-Kowalski *et al.* 1999). Such approaches do not necessarily lead to lower economic welfare (Daniels 2003). But they can raise awareness of the real impact on natural resources through economic activity.

Interestingly, Brennan (2000) picks up the issue of energy and use value in the context of reworking Marx's theory of capital. She makes the point that capital, lured by short-term profit, believes that 'energy reproduction time' is a more appropriate measure of use value. As far as real estate advisers are concerned, this could be achieved by applying the principles underlying lifecycle costing as a significant variable in the process to arrive at a calculation of worth to an investor, just as much as the level of annual outgoings are important to the level of rent acceptable to an occupier.

There is evidence therefore that changes are taking place in the way that the market views property. However, to change mindsets, it is necessary to work backwards through the chain of reactions and forces to redefine each in the context of a more altruistic outlook on the social and economic fabric of society in its widest sense. In other words, through the education system, individuals learn the 'ethics' that underpin the norms and values of the social relations of production. If these represent wealth as including well-being, social enterprise and environmental enhancement, then progressively financial wealth will be seen to have limited value without a social and environmental dimension. As such, an issue such as sustainability can only be understood in totality, along both vertical (historical) and horizontal (synchronic) axes. To break the problem down into constituent parts (for example, social, economic, environmental or scientific, technical, biological) will be illusory.

Sustainable thinking

Too often the term sustainability is just beyond the individual's grasp. At one level it is a simple concept, easily defined but not so easily enacted. How sustainable is it? Is it to sell an existing vehicle and buy a fuel efficient one, or a central heating boiler, or a building? On the face of it, these are sustainable solutions because the running of each will have less of an impact on the social and ecological environment and should improve financial positions. However, the embedded energy in capital formation is significant in each case and will impact on both the ecological and financial footprints of an individual or an organisation. Equally, advanced technology will improve sustainability only if use and continuing behavioural change take place at the same time.

The concept of sustainability is not therefore an island set in a becalmed sea. It is an underlying disturbance beneath the surface of an unpredictable ocean whose influence travels far and wide. So, sustainability sometimes would be seen as a concept, but, as a reality, it becomes much less comprehensible because of the limits to people's thinking. Priest (2002) has identified some of the limitations that we have as human beings and how we create concepts and symbols to deal with anything that is beyond our comprehension. These are not so much about subjective consciousness but more concerned with limits to what we are able to conceive and limits to the intensions (i.e. the internal contents) of the mind. More specifically these limits are: (1) limits of expression, (2) limits of iteration, (3) limits of cognition and, finally, (4) limits of conception. In the context of this chapter, each of these limits will have an impact on consideration of the evaluation of sustainable behaviour and the built environment. Outlines of these four limits are as follows:

- *Limits of expression.* Expression is the way we are able to use language to explain something. It denotes the boundaries within which concepts or objects and their attributes are communicated. Limits are not only imposed by experience and understanding but also by the nature of language and the brain itself.
- *Limits of iteration.* We can look back to find causes that created the present and we can project forward to forecast the impact of events today on the future. However, in the human mind, there is a limit to such iteration, such that we have to set boundaries by applying heuristics to our thinking. Otherwise we would be confronted by the notion that everything causes everything across an infinite period of time.

Relating these two limits of thought to the concept of sustainability, it is apparent that, in a selective use of causes and effects, it is possible to support any number of actions to achieve sustainability in response to pressures from an economic, environmental or social point of view whether as individuals, organisations or governments.

- *Limits of cognition.* The word cognition is originally derived from the Greek word *gnosco* and Latin word *cogito*, which means *to know* and *I think* respectively. So, for example, cognitive psychology is mainly concerned with 'how we think and create knowledge' (Tvede 1999: 84). This limit to thought, therefore, concerns the relationship between *representations and the thing represented*. Its primary concern is knowledge, truth and rational belief. But still there is a gap between the *thing* and the representation. This is a limit to the way human beings think about the world.
- *Limits of conception.* Human beings tend to respond to outside stimuli. As noted earlier, identification has replaced imagination in our thinking processes. In this way, we explain the world around us by using labels (which are second hand) rather than maintaining a creative sense of wonder. We go through a process of sensation, contact, identification and finally desire or aversion (Khare 1988: 151). What something means is related to a 'person's internal *system* of representations, his cognitive economy' (Churchland 1989: 344). Within a dominant culture based on financial wealth creation, this 'cognitive economy' tends to mean short-term financial gains.

The limits to thought identified above suggested that, in the context of sustainability, there may be limits to the actuality of the concept. Unless we can see the non-space between the observer and the observed (Krishnamurti's notion of *you are the world*) or the signifier and the signified (Derrida's *unmentionable difference*) or Max-Neef's *included middle*, then it will be difficult to understand the space to be sustainable whether as private individuals or as agents in the market place. Perhaps a fundamental change is needed in the way that the world is perceived, where there is much less separation between the act and the actor. Within the limits to thought outlined above, broadening out perspectives from 1) purely economic, 2) purely environmental, 3) purely social, to a way of thinking that, naturally, incorporates all three, may help towards sustainable thinking.

Transdisciplinary thinking

In its strong form, transdisciplinarity is complex and beyond the scope of this book. It involves an understanding of different 'levels of reality', the notion of 'the included middle' and the 'complexity' of non-linear processes. It offers a way of seeing the world in a 'more systemic and more holistic' way (Max-Neef 2005: 15).

However, it is necessary and important to have some understanding of the concept and its relationship to sustainable learning. The problem with transdisciplinarity is that, on the one hand, it can be very unsettling and on the other hand it can lead to vagueness and superficiality. Any examination must therefore be aware of these dangers at the outset.

It may be unsettling because transdisciplinary thinking questions the robustness of individual disciplines that have tended to identify themselves as architectures in their own right. To suggest that they are not freestanding but need to be seen within a landscape coloured by others, similarly discrete disciplines, somehow may be perceived as undermining the fundamental integrity of the vision of an individual discipline. Of course, there have been crossovers but, particularly in built environment studies, there has been a tendency to stick to the core of the discipline and the influence of the respective professional body. Where work has been undertaken across disciplines, it has tended to be interdisciplinary (i.e. coordinating individual disciplines around a higher level concept) rather than transdisciplinary (i.e. common set of axioms related to, but existing beyond and complementing traditional disciplines).

In considering transdisciplinary thinking, Max-Neef (2005) identifies four levels of discipline that get integrated into a whole and are described by him at four hierarchical levels. These levels are, first, the *empirical* level, which exists at the base of the pyramid, through the *pragmatic* level covering what we are capable of doing and the *normative* level showing what it is we want to do. At the apex of the pyramid is the *value* level where we question how we should do what we want to do (Figure 2.2).

Much of the learning on professional built environment programmes tends to take place at the first two levels (i.e. empirical and pragmatic). Concepts of sustainability could be addressed as part of the disciplinary mainstream (rather

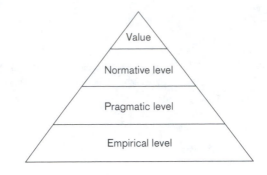

Figure 2.2

Four levels of discipline in transdisciplinary learning

than apart from the core). If that is the case then the starting point ought to be founded on the inclusion of all four levels. But, not only this, learning across disciplines should also not be constrained by traditional subject boundaries. For example, economics and finance are as much about behaviour and sentiment and ways of thinking as they are about demand and supply curves. Not only are they interlinked, but they are part of the same process. This transdisciplinary approach to learning is a crucial element in the achievement of long-term sustainable environments.

Sustainability literacy

It is quite interesting that it has been argued that we already have the technological know-how to address issues of energy conservation and reductions in CO_2 emissions to meet UN requirements. Pacala *et al.* (2004) have developed a stabilisation triangle consisting of a number of wedges (Figure 2.3). These cover efficiency, conservation, carbon capture, carbon storage, low carbon fuels, renewable and bio-storage. Each wedge represents 'an activity that reduces emissions to the atmosphere that starts at zero today and increases linearly until it accounts for 1 GtC/year of reduced carbon emission in 50 years' (Pacala *et al.* 2004: 968).

However, as yet, we do not appear to have the mind or the inclination to implement the solutions. The barriers set up are complex and embrace economic, social, political as well as psychological and financial considerations. To overcome these, it would require greater circulation of the concept of sustainability literacy.

'Literacy' as a term in the *Oxford English Dictionary* simply means 'the ability to read and write' (Fowler *et al.* 1961: 709). As such 'sustainability literacy' is a means of expressing an individual's ability to interact with the social, environmental and economic aspects of sustainable development (Parkin *et al.* 2004). It could be construed as knowledge of, and the ability to, articulate

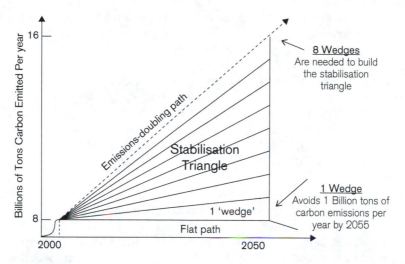

Figure 2.3

Stabilisation wedges (Socolow *et al.* 2004: 11)

sustainability. What is missing here is the ensuing action developing out of sustainable behaviour. Adapting terms used by Vare *et al.* (2007) the learning process therefore should embrace three essential elements for 'sustainability' to have meaning and impact on our decisions.

First, the process should not only *promote and facilitate changes* in what we do but should also *promote behaviours and ways of thinking*. This helps towards learning for sustainable development. Second, *build capacity* to think critically about (and beyond) what experts say and *explore the contradictions* inherent in sustainable living. This level of freedom *encourages learning* as sustainable development.

As such 'our freedom is to see through "personal meaning" to the random and meaningless world beyond – our responsibility is to create a meaning for ourselves, of which we are the sole and authentic authors, whether as individuals or societies' (Langford 2002: 106).

So the real issue is not so much the level of technical knowledge accumulated through study but the depth of the mind that meets knowledge (Forbes 1997). A change of mindset 'to bring about ecologically sustainable practices' is probably not sufficient in itself as 'thought has to be translated into action' (Engel-Di Mauro 2008: 91). Sustainability literacy might go some way to achieving this. In this respect, there has to be some negotiation between the private and the social, between the individual client and the global implication of particular courses of action.

The concern here is how professionals become aware of the multi-faceted aspects of sustainability in order to make sense of integration into their decision making. It is clear that changes in behaviour are required to deliver sustainable development. But, attitude and behaviour change is a complex subject. Information alone does not lead to behaviour change or close the so-called attitude–behaviour gap (DEFRA 2005).

As with any decision, information is gathered as codes and then interwoven into patterns. These patterns are preconceived notions that have often been built up through a combination of upbringing, education and experience (Dent *et al.* 1998). It is therefore not entirely the role of any one educator to bring sustainability into the mix. If there is not already an appropriate code in a person's upbringing, it is hard to influence. As Freire (1973: 67) states 'to teach is not *to transfer knowledge* but to create the possibilities for the production or construction of knowledge'.

Professionals in the built environment have to recognise that 'climate change ... is no longer simply an environmental problem but a wider issue affecting economic stability' (TCPA/FoE 2006: 1). This being the case, then why do 'most existing building performance assessment methods fail to assess buildings in use, fail to contribute to improving the performance of buildings, fail to link the performance to appraisal and valuation methods and practice and also do not sufficiently account for the existing building stock' (RICS 2008a: 5). Is this a failing in the education system leaving students illiterate in the area of sustainability? If it is, as it seems it might be, then, 'sustainability literacy' needs to become a core competency for professionals and for graduates (DEFRA 2005). The question is how can this best be achieved?

For graduates – sustainability and professional education

The report 'Sustainable Development in Higher Education – Current practice and future development' (Dawe *et al.* 2005) identifies the following skills and knowledge as representing sustainability literacy:

- an appreciation of the importance of environmental, social, political and economic contexts for each discipline;
- a broad and balanced foundation knowledge of sustainable development, its key principles and the main debate within them, including its contested and expanding boundaries;
- problem-solving skills in a non-reductionist manner for highly complex real-life problems;
- ability to think creatively and holistically and to make critical judgements;
- ability to develop a high level of self-reflection (both personal and professional);
- ability to identify, understand, evaluate and adopt values conducive to sustainability;
- ability to bridge the gap between theory and practice – in sustainable development, only transformational action counts;

- ability to participate creatively in interdisciplinary teams;
- ability to initiate and manage change.

These skills and knowledge sets will be referred to in this book for the identification of sustainable real estate solutions.

For real estate professionals – change of mind

As suggested in a previous section of this chapter, what is needed in order to incorporate sustainable thinking into decision making is a different mindset to that which has gone before. This is partly due to the tensions of the different time horizons and the globalisation of space (actual and virtual), but it is also due to the complexity of the systems that surround real estate decisions. Real estate advice is unlikely to be wholly effective if it is given solely on the basis of the legal ownership of the physical form. It needs also to embrace the organisation's culture, symbolism and 'unconscious' to provide sustainable business solutions that align real estate holdings with the business model. It has been shown that decisions regarding an organisation's real estate can exceed the direct financial effects. Krumm *et al.* (2003) for example, highlight increasing revenues, increasing employee profitability, smart purchasing, reducing reconstruction times as means by which the overall performance of the organisation can be enhanced through decisions regarding corporate real estate.

Real estate professionals can be inventive in their advice to clients (*creative imagination*). They can look beyond the building envelope (*identification*) to see hidden opportunities and to anticipate unforeseen consequences. 'The real issue is the quality of our mind; not its knowledge but the depth of the mind that meets knowledge' (Forbes 1997: 10). This suggests that, in seeking sustainable solutions, we should not rely in the longer term on technological fixes coupled with traditional learning either in higher education or the workplace. It may mean that we have to approach our learning differently. This is not only relevant in the debate about climate change and environmental sustainability but it also applies to the financial sustainability of global real estate investment (see Chapter 8) and the resilience of organisational assets (including real estate holdings) to structural change. Perhaps it requires a different level of intelligence.

Orr (2004) identifies certain key characteristics of intelligence. These are an ability to separate cause from effect and an understanding of the different application of 'know how' from 'know why' together with forbearance, a sense of limits and morality. It may, therefore, be difficult to be parochial in addressing the 'know why' issues of sustainability. On the one hand, for example, students will examine in detail statutes, legal principles, locally adopted methodologies, etc., pertinent to their area of jurisdiction. These have an immediacy about them because these are the operational tools necessary to gain employment. However, it is harder to get across strategic concepts and shifting mindsets necessary to accept 'the crafting of new identities in the process of globalization' (Leff 2005: 8). One of the problems therefore facing professionals in the built environment is how to incorporate broad (often remote) generic issues such as globalisation and climate change. In themselves, they are outside of the frame of professional or technical knowledge.

Summary

To improve sustainability literacy, the real issue seems to concern the nature of the problem. It does not appear to be an environmental one. If so, it could be solved by science alone. Nor is it simply a social problem that could be cured through changing behaviour. It does not even appear to be just a combination of these two. At heart, the problem that we face is complex and seems to require a more fundamental approach. As an analogy, an organisation (a complex adaptive system) would be unwise to seek more real estate without first reviewing its existing working practices, its organisational structure and its anticipated future. These go hand in hand.

To be sustainability literate, an individual should not only be aware of the right course of action now but, perhaps, more importantly, have a capacity to analyse and question alternatives in anticipation of unexpected outcomes. Agility, reflexivity and reflectivity are all required in an uncertain complex environment. Formulae and statistics will only go so far; without creativity and lateral thinking, old structures (with old problems) may simply persist. What is needed is a new way of seeing and a new way of doing that does not rely on contradiction and conflict between old dualities (good and bad, sustainable and unsustainable, etc.).

In reality, they co-exist as one and, as such, they complement each other or rather they exist in each other. 'When the people of the world know the beautiful as beauty, there arises the recognition of the ugly. When they know the good as good, there arises the recognition of the evil' (Wang 1998: 221). This requires a total awareness and attention to the now.

In addition, sustainability literacy cannot be learnt. It is not a discipline in itself. It is not a string of facts or even opinions. There are probably as many illiterate greens as there are sceptics. Sustainability literates keep their room in order for itself, neither as a virtue nor for what it will bring, 'never taking sides, never opposing, never agreeing, never justifying, never condemning, never judging – which means watching ... without any choice' (Krishnamurti 2010: 29).

3 Culture, markets and institutions

· ·

Introduction

Real estate provides a backdrop to our lives. It is fundamental as shelter, for production, for exchange and for a wide range of human activities. As such it becomes an important signifier of something more than its physical, financial or legal status. It is part of the culture of place. It is invested with meaning within that culture whether considered from an individual's point of view or from the perspective of the institutional framework of society. In this sense, needless to say, real estate is not just bricks and mortar, it is an environment. The importance of real estate lies in its ability to be an active participant in the exchange of ideas, goods and services together with the more fundamental intercourse between individuals.

Real estate is highly codified and can be seen as a semiological system that communicates meaning in the same way as language. In fact, it could be that the link between language, buildings and culture is the basis for an understanding of the institutional structure of real estate investment and its markets. Figure 3.1 shows the process linking into Jung's four basic personality types of sensation, thinking, intuition and feeling (Pascal 1994). The vertical axis indicates a perceptual function (i.e. they rely on objective stimuli) and the horizontal axis represent a judgemental function (i.e. they rely on internal, mental processes). So, simplistically, in seeing a structure such as a building, we first give it meaning within our individual frame of reference. This is then fitted into a cultural context intuitively. From this comes the way in which we articulate our feelings about it (consciously or unconsciously) through language.

Any decisions to invest or occupy will be influenced by these linkages as part of an appraisal of performance. In the context of this book, it is necessary to understand something about the nature of the culture within which decisions are made, as this culture creates the environment and values that will enable sustainable activities to happen. Mapping buildings as cultural symbols, Wines (2003: 20, cited in Guy 1997) makes the interesting observation that 'the focus of the tallest building has changed as society has changed –

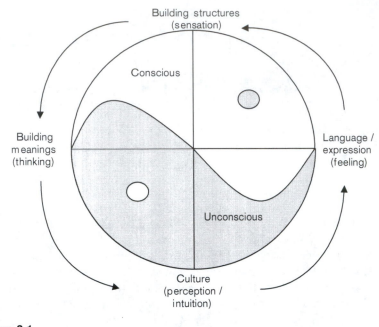

Figure 3.1

Relationships between language, building and culture

from church steeple to capital dome and currently, the corporate high-rise. Now we need a new paradigm and appropriate symbol'. The dominant player in cultural identity has, in this case, shifted from the church to the state to the multinationals.

If the overall objective is to create a cultural change in society (i.e. to become more sustainable, for example) then it is, therefore, necessary to examine the culture, and the institutions (particularly the institution of the market) in order to appreciate the ground on which sustainability needs to rest. This chapter attempts to specifically define culture in a built environment context first, then to consider the institutional framework of the property market.

Culture

Culture is a term that has been defined in many ways. The classic definition of culture quoted in McGrew (1998: 303) is 'that complex whole which includes knowledge, belief, art, law, morals, custom, and any of the capabilities and habits acquired by man as a member of society'. It is the foundation on which a society exists and the framework that we often unconsciously acknowledge in the way we conduct our lives. This is not to say that culture is a static monolith that controls and constrains. It is much more a fluid process that reflects an age. Figure 3.2 shows how the macro influences the individual moderated by externalities that cut across and mediate attitudes and behaviour.

As far as mature built environments are concerned, these have developed, in the main, within a culture of some form of market mechanism. Whether this mechanism exists within a capitalist or a socialist political system is less important than the outcome of the production. Due to globalisation, there is a need for intelligent reflection on the existence of certain conditions in the current economic and social circumstances more than ever (Gramsci 1971). Two significant reasons for this are that, first, change is the main driver in today's society more so than ever before in human history. This is mainly because of the speed of change and the nature of the political, social and economic change. Second, and emanating from the first, we have progressively been living unsustainable lives, financially, socially and environmentally. The *old* and the *new* worlds have coalesced into short-term consumption economies using personal wealth as the measure of well-being and success. Social construction and reconstruction in many emerging economies has generally been a process of borrowing values from more mature economies and redeploying indigenous influences and cultures. 'Buildings in this discourse

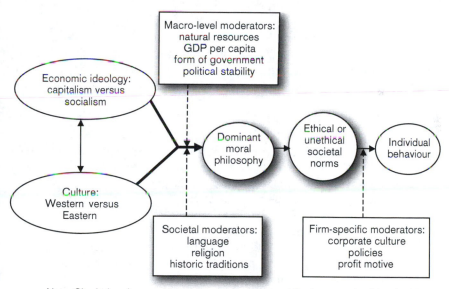

Note: Shaded regions represent current model's contribution to societal-level ethics scholarship

───── Focus of research propositions

- - - - Moderating variables

Figure 3.2

A moral philosophy model of cross-cultural societal ethics (Robertson *et al.* 2003: 387)

are symbols of societal values and the emblematic issue is how to represent the new millennium' (Guy 1997: 8). The shopping mall, the theme park and the pleasure dome could be appropriate symbols. But there is also growing evidence of *green* business parks, zero carbon housing and eco-town initiatives.

For the purposes of the theme for this book, culture can be seen as an evolving process that can develop through a series of stages. McGrew (1998) lists six steps in the process:

1. A new pattern of behaviour is invented, or an existing one is modified.
2. The innovator transmits this pattern to another.
3. The form of the pattern is consistent within and across performers, perhaps even in terms of recognisable stylistic features.
4. The one who acquires the pattern retains the ability to perform it long after having acquired it.
5. The pattern spreads across social units in a population. These social units may be families, clans, troops, or bands.
6. The pattern endures across generations.

In the current discussion, the six stages described by McGrew (1998) are pertinent as they can show how a concept such as sustainable thinking can be introduced into a society as follows:

- behaviour is modified to be more 'sustainable';
- an 'enlightened' real estate adviser transmits this behaviour to an institutional property investor client;
- the 'hard' material aspects of sustainability of buildings and environments become more recognised;
- the 'enlightened' real estate adviser continues to develop ideas on how to enhance business, communities and environments;
- improved environmental and social features are seen to enhance financial returns and therefore attract other investors and their advisers;
- sustainability becomes part of the 'collective unconscious' of those investing in, and advising on, real estate.

Culture can be seen in both material and non-material artefacts (Ellis *et al.* 1979 cited in Barthorpe *et al.* 2000). Geertz (1973) separates these into implicit – the features of social life – and explicit – the social construction that is accepted as a global framework.

Culture as implicit social construction

Culture as implicit social construction is a system of perceptions and taboos. It is 'the collective programming of the mind which distinguishes the members of one human group from another' (Hofstede 1984: 21). Human beings are self-interpreting and invariably they attach meanings to what they do.

In the sustainability debate, for example, not only will the approach and solution be different across cultures, but also the ground on which sustainability is based may differ fundamentally. In other words, meaning in one cultural setting may be no meaning in another environment. So, understanding of sustainability in Western countries, such as the UK, will be very different to Eastern countries, say, China. Equally and even within the same country, the interaction with the term will differ between the principal producers (i.e. developers and funders of real estate) and consumers of space (i.e. investors and occupiers). There will also be differing perceptions between leaders and followers. These sub-cultures will attribute different connotations to the generic label of sustainability thus creating their own reality of problem and solution.

The boundaries between different groups (i.e. the parameters within which each subculture works) are defined by 'internal causal conditions', and what really happens during times of change or upheaval is often 'hidden, lived by all and perceived by none' (Jung 1961: 139). This could be the case in professional disciplines as well as defined markets. For example, in the property market, it is possible to identify subcultures not only as developers, investors, occupiers, etc., but also surveyors, planners, engineers, architects, etc.

Even within a cultural group, attitudes, beliefs and values influence behaviour and relations (Figure 3.3). These can be defined as:

- Attitudes – test an individual's prime urge against another. Attitudes reflect opinions, beliefs and outlook on life. They give individual lives a rhythm of development and maturity. Certain attitudes are common to everyone of a specific age group or generation, but most often the quest for identity is unconsciously demonstrated through sticking to national, professional or peer group traditions.
- Beliefs – represent unconscious habits of perception, thought and feeling. They are the ultimate source of values and action.
- Values – compromise strategies, goals and philosophies. They are inner characteristics underlying all important choices, decisions, interests, preferences and intentions. Values in a national culture are held preconsciously and are fundamental. They influence beliefs and attitudes in national and organisational culture. Different cultures encourage different patterns of motivation in their members. This can be seen not only at national level, but also, for example, at organisational level. Motives contain the goals that members are predestined to pursue. Therefore, for example, national values can also contain compatibility with other people within multicultural interactions.
- Actions – signify meaningful behaviour (Huczynski *et al.* 1991). Culture also provides people with a meaningful context, as culture itself is man-made, confirmed by others, conventionalised and passed on for younger people or newcomers.
- Behaviour – concerns 'the things that human beings do that can be directly detected by the senses of others' (Huczynski *et al.* 1991: 22)

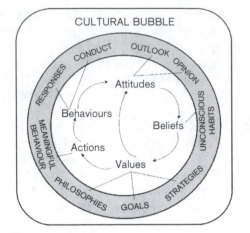

Figure 3.3

Relationship between values, beliefs, behaviour and action

Culture as explicit social construction

Culture as explicit social construction generates structures and meanings (Lotman 1990). These may change over time. Thrift (2004) suggests that industrialisation and globalisation have shifted those meanings, through remodelling the basic conditions of life. This has led to a move from a 'social, atomic structure to full-blown standardisation of space' (Thrift 2004: 177). The local has, in many cases, become the global, financed symbolically by global finance, designed by international architects and located in global cities. Unfortunately, this has often created junk space (Jameson 2003), which becomes part of the disposable urban landscape. It can also be argued that, if globalisation encourages the production of simultaneous space, it also accelerates the production of smooth space, that is, of space without any real differences. For example, shopping malls tend to be scientifically designed and tend towards standardisation.

The potential outcome from this is that, over time, structures such as buildings lose their local meaning and become global icons. The limit of all previous historical phases was logistical. Time, being compressed, resurfaces in reproduction of supply lines not just the reproduction of fixed capital. But when globalised space gets to go all the way around the planet then there is no logistical problem. Thus, time becomes exhausted by smooth space (Jameson 2003) fuelled by global finance. Indigenous culture tends to be subsumed as a subculture within some greater global culture, whose drivers are often narrowly defined and much less understood. Consequently, it is sometimes difficult to remember where you are. In one sense it may not matter as space has also become compressed.

What is now beginning to happen is

> a different kind of repetition, which allows things to show up differently with different kinds of opportunities associated with them. Through the application of a set of technologies and knowledges (the two being impossible to separate), a style of repetition has been produced which is more controlled and also more open-ended, a new kind of roving empiricism which continually ties up and undoes itself in a search for the most efficient ways to use the space and time of each moment.
>
> (Thrift 2004: 186)

This potentially opens a back door to sustainability as it means that the use of space (and its related carbon consumption) becomes compressed through *rationalisation, just-in-time*, etc. However, it might be sustainability at a cost – the mundane, the monotonous and the functional. Value becomes measured solely in quantitative terms as monetary worth rather than in any attributive or axiological sense.

Whether this is perceived as good or bad is not an issue here. What is interesting, however, is the fact that there are global players (financial institutions, multi-national corporations, international consultants) who, in the production and use of buildings, have the power to make a difference globally – more so than any national government or multi-government organisation. However, far from simplifying systems, these global structures make understanding and influencing transactions very complex. For example, it is often impossible to trace the actual real estate asset on which a particular securitised vehicle performs.

Buildings

The previous section discussed the definition of culture as well as its applications. This section attempts to look at how culture can be reflected or represented in buildings. At first glance, a building has the ability to reveal different aspects under different cultural environments. However, putting technologies and knowledges aside, it is not only the ideology of the architecture itself that will differ. Many of the legal and social constructs will also influence the form and use of buildings. For example:

- Tenure is a complex subject related to the culture of accommodation within the borders of societal value systems. This refers to the form in which domestic and commercial property is held and is often identified with status.
- Space standards, domestic equipment and the immediate surroundings of buildings. These are, in many countries, controlled by statute and case law. Updates and changes in laws can also reflect the changes taking place in the culture and in people's behaviours and values.

- The manner in which accommodation is provided. This relates to design, procurement and production as well as funding arrangements.

There is a correlation between the nature of buildings and the ways of approaching occupation and ownership. This is particularly evident in the residential sector, for example, where, in most West European countries, high rates of ownership are considered an important goal of government policy. Here, this is seen as a social objective and measure of the quality of life (Werczberger 1997). It is a *natural* aspiration.

On an individual level, therefore, the perception is that wealth and income correlate with the prosperity to own. No longer is a house simply a shelter. It has become a signifier of social interrelationships. This applies not only to the individual and housing but can also relate to the corporate organisation and the office or industrial unit. The way in which property is held (freehold or leasehold) is only one form of differentiation, which signifies status.

There are, of course, other signifying differences beyond the building's legal and physical form. Ontologically, a space becomes a place when it is named or identified. This is when the concrete (i.e. architectural form) meets the symbolic (imaginary societal investment). This is the point at which the flows of power shift a physical form into a cultural structure (Ilmonen 1996).

Urban space

In a post-modern sense, place is a space to which meaning has been ascribed. Both places (micro levels) and spaces (macro levels) constitute the city. Space level relates to the concept city of rational, urbanist discourse and geometric designs. It is the embodiment of social planning and public life, freeways, and housing and commercial projects. In other words, spaces are 'the places where human life takes place' (Day 1990: 77). Place level concerns street level, dreamlike tactics that people use to make sense of the city and survive it. At this level urban myths and sub-cultural legends are created. Environment, according to Heidegger (1958), shows us both the depths of our inner freedom and, at the same time, the bondage of our outer existence. Social realities are created by cultures and by individuals. The social reality of the built environment is a negotiation between the two, through the market.

Markets

A building itself is a single object, but several buildings together could form a market. According to Cao (2000: 2), 'markets can only reflect a prior underlying structure of resource allocation that is shaped by socio-political processes'. When these socio-political processes go through dramatic change (for example, the credit crunch or impacts of climate change), the means of production and the allocation of resources may need to be transformed. This may also lead to a change in the nature of the market. But, whilst this may appear, on the surface, to be dramatic (possibly defined by one event), the seeds of that change will possibly have been germinating in the soul of the society for some years. For example, the credit crunch had one of its origins in the greater use of securitised debt through the 1990s and the impacts of climate change can be traced back centuries.

Market changes over time

What is perhaps important to note here is that, one of the problems with sustainability and real estate markets is the different timeframes within which they operate. Excluding the nanosecond and astronomical time, it is generally agreed that there are three main time zones (Burkitt 1999). The time of longest duration moves at the pace of biological, geo-physical and climate changes. Next is the intermediate level, which includes the pace of change in social structures, economies, political institutions and cultures. Finally, there is the shortest timeframe that relates to changes in everyday life.

The significance of these for any discussion about sustainability and the environment is that there is a mismatch between the context of everyday life and the geophysical. Timeframes are like closed systems, communication across them makes limited sense. The human agent cannot conceive of geophysical time and, consequently, the significance of the impact of actions today over that timescale is unimportant. Even at the intermediary stage, institutional structures neither have the power nor the inclination to push too hard on these issues. This is because, not only is this a problem for tomorrow but also it is a problem outside of each individual's jurisdiction. This is an issue that concerns indeterminate cultural space, it cannot be defined and, as yet, there is no single body that has power to impose any necessary controls.

So it is at this time of longest duration that environmental sustainability matters. It is where the true impact of climate change, resource depletion and conventional energy crises exist. Interestingly, it is also the point where today's monetary values in the market are discounted to zero.

The institutional framework of the property market

The market place is probably the most effective socio-cultural institution for the efficient allocation of resources. In principle, therefore, it could be an effective conduit for sustainability. Taking real estate as an example, such a *sustainable* market would have to be dominated by real estate advisers who are willing to promote sustainable objectives to clients as part of their house views (i.e. the way in which a client organisation wishes to see itself presented). This can be achieved by appropriately equipped advisers through a process of presentations, 'placing financial bets' (i.e. demonstrating the potential financial benefits of sustainable features) and promoting 'rumours' (i.e. using theoretical models and hearsay from market demand). In this way, sustainable 'market opportunities' are produced (Pryke *et al.* 1995).

The property market, specifically, operates as part of a broader institutional environment, which includes political, economic, social and legal elements (Keogh *et al.* 1999). Property markets are influenced by these elements, through urban policy, economic and financial market structures, landlord and tenant law, and government policy. The status and the range of institutional factors influencing property assets indicate the level of complexity involved in transacting and managing such assets. 'Conventional economic approaches to the analysis of property markets lack institutional or behavioural content and tend to ignore many of the defining characteristics of property, such as high transaction costs, illiquidity and information problems' (D'Arcy *et al.* 1998: 1220). Nevertheless getting to understand the institutional framework can provide an insight into the general workings of markets. Keogh *et al.* (1999) thus suggests a three-level institutional hierarchy to analyse the property market (Figure 3.4).

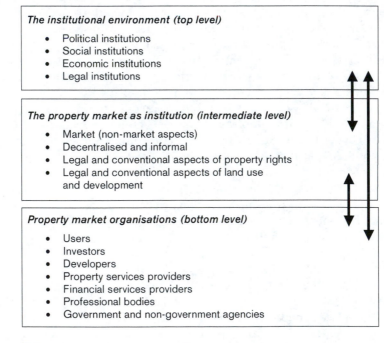

Figure 3.4

The institutional hierarchy of property markets (Keogh *et al.* 1999: 2407)

Property markets as complex adaptive systems

Property markets are complex and can be seen as complex adaptive systems. They have the potential to be unpredictable and self-organising, because of the imprecise and complex nature of real estate assets themselves. This creates a diversity of opinion that itself creates capacity and volume. Property markets are also dynamic (containing simultaneous stability and instability) and uncertain (offering no guarantees for survival). Local deals produce emergent coherence and they have the capacity to be transformative rather than merely formative. Finally, it is almost always the case that 'the spontaneous self-organising activity, with its emergent order, is vital for the continuing evolution of the system and its ability to produce novelty' (Stacey 2003: 253). This therefore suggests not a superficial change, but a more fundamental structural development.

The state of the market as a system changes continually. The pattern of behaviour of participants and their advisers will depend on how well information and actions are 'tuned' to each other and the way in which consequences (i.e. the impact of change) arise in the particular system. Importantly, in the context of the property market, it has been argued that for economic and social systems, it is communication of meaning that is important rather than communication of information (Elliott 1997: 2). Information on its own is unlikely to lead to change. So, supplying more and more evidence of climate change or energy efficiency might actually achieve very little. The real benefits come when a meaning is attached to that information. However, energy efficiency information, for example, will have different meanings for different players. In the case of property appraisals for investment or occupation (and their subsequent management), it is the responsibility of real estate advisers to understand, interpret and communicate the meaning that is significant to their specific clients.

Property markets as cultural entities

Meaning is very often expressed as a symbolic or cultural icon. For example, 'green' buildings send out a message that is less to do with energy efficiency or carbon emission and more to do with the responsible nature of the owner or, more likely, the occupier in pursuing economic activity. This activity is, according to Pryke et al. (1995: 330), both a social and cultural process. It is 'not merely *shaped* and *directed* by distinctive sets of social relations but *constituted* through social and cultural practices (work) that cannot be reduced to inert stimulus-response models of economic persons or to the asocial operation of economic forces'.

Accordingly, this suggests that to understand the workings of the market and the behaviour of the players within it, as part of overall economic activity within a society, it is important to appreciate the cultural and institutional framework within which that market operates and, in fact, to see the market itself as an institution. MacKenzie (2004) suggests that through limitation (of information processing) and imitation ('baboon' sociology), economics might be performative. In other words, how far does economic theory help to bring about the world that it postulates rather than simply describing it?

There is no simple answer to this question. To appreciate the factors that influence the longer term trends in cultural and commercial property, it requires an understanding of 'the changing market dynamic as more than a mere mechanical lever' or press of a button on a spreadsheet that has been programmed to act on yields and rental levels (Guy *et al.* 1997).

> Property supply-demand dynamics do not comprise of a set of linear relationships. Rather, the property market is a complex system in which immediate characteristics of particular markets are contingent upon a broad range of exogenous social, economic, technological and political factors. Numerous interdependent factors are constantly adjusting themselves to changing market conditions. Commitment to property research which is rooted simply in a set of determining absolutes, the iron law of economic indices, encourages an elevation of short-term market conditions to universalised, fixed co-ordinates. This conceals the dynamism and specificity of property markets. In contrast, it is important to see constantly changing market conditions as a reflection of differing social and commercial forces acting on property. In this way, property markets are recognised as cultural entities, shaped as much by tradition, taste, technological and social innovation as by immediate levels of availability and demand. What is required is a new approach to property research which takes these broader analyses of demand seriously.
>
> (Guy *et al.* 1997: 126)

Summary

The market that is set in place as part of the institutional framework often defines the nature of the response. This is likely to be informally founded on conventions, values and social norms (the unconscious state of the nation). But, in time, built on these foundations, it will take a formal character of codified rules in the form of constitutions, laws, regulations and contracts. Culture is passed from one generation to another and, whilst something of its essence can be learned from outside, at the national level each has a *secret language of world feeling*.

According to Spengler (1980) that secret language of a culture, is only fully known to those who have been nurtured in that culture. This is particularly significant when, through globalisation of capital flows, cultural exchange is so prevalent. In fact, there is a danger that the cultural collapses into the economic, becoming controlled by these capital flows, and the economic into the cultural such that culture is simply an expression of financial wealth (Jameson 2000). So, whilst it may be possible to gain knowledge of different cultures and traditions, it is much harder to learn the 'secret language'.

The complex nature of the real estate market mechanism is considered in the next chapter, followed by the financial foundations of real estate assets in Chapter 5. In the complex structures described they are, in a sense, an example more of *the communication of information* rather than the *secret language* that provides meaning. The meaning that we are searching for here in this book is the link between the technological information on sustainability and its interpretation within the complex structure of the market place.

Background to Real Estate and Financial Markets

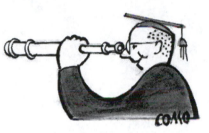

4 Real estate market mechanisms

· ·

Introduction

Real property, the land and buildings that make up the built environment we see around us, accounts for the overwhelming majority of the wealth of the UK. According to ONS (2011), i.e. *The Blue Book*, the total net worth of the UK at the end of 2010 was almost £6.9 trillion. Residential and commercial property accounted for almost three-quarters (£5.1 trillion) of this (Table 4.1).

Table 4.1   Assets total (ONS 2011: 249)

	2010 £ billion
Residential buildings	4,260
Agricultural assets	51
Commercial, industrial and other buildings	807
Civil engineering works	790
Plant and machinery	497
Vehicles (including ships and aircraft)	193
Stocks and work in progress	244
Mobile phone spectrum	22
TOTAL	6,864

Real estate is a very complex asset to manage and it is also a complex matter to implement the technical change both to perform more sustainably and for investors to commit more sustainably. Also in functional terms, this complexity may hamper users' ability to change towards more sustainable behaviours and mindsets. This then raises important challenges for those that manage such assets either for investment or for occupation.

In order to understand both investor and occupier behaviour in relation to real estate, it is first important to have some appreciation of the nature of real estate assets. This chapter therefore provides some context for the rest of the book in terms of the importance of real estate in economic activity, the specific characteristics of real estate and the different legal interests available for real estate ownership and occupation.

Characteristics of property

Given the scale of property within the national balance sheet, as shown in Table 4.1, it is worth reviewing its particular characteristics, which distinguish it from other investable assets. This section explores these main characteristics.

Complex

The financing, construction and operation of property are complex and require a wide range of different skills at each stage of the property lifecycle. Different degrees of risk are also associated with each stage. This contrasts with the acquisition and ownership of assets such as listed securities. The complexity of property means that owners often need to have or to hire people with specialist skills to manage it. For example, property development is complex and risky. It involves coordinating a wide range of activities over an extended time period to deliver a completed product. That product has to meet the needs of both the occupational (tenants) and investment (owners) markets. The overlap between these three activities (i.e. development, investment and occupation) forms the basis of the dynamics of the property market.

Keogh (1994) shows these three activities as elements of a simple structure of a property market, linked by the flow of information between them. In the user market, firms need to occupy a stock of buildings, the required amount of space being determined by output levels, profitability and asking rents. In the investment market, a property owner's return is the rent that they receive. The relationship between rent and return determines the price or capital value of the property. Furthermore, that capital value would affect property companies and construction firms in the development market. When capital values are higher than the cost of provision, new construction projects are undertaken, and the supply in the user and investment markets will change accordingly.

The needs of the three sectors of the market will not necessarily coincide. Occupiers will have very immediate requirements as to the suitability of the space for their business today and the near future. Investors will want a product that is lettable today (so meeting current occupational needs) but that, in their judgement, will remain lettable and also saleable (so meeting future investment market needs) into the more distant future. This often requires some difficult decisions based on a wide range of information and data. Even with professional advice, a decision maker will often concentrate on what is considered the most important information. This bounded rationality recognises human limitations in understanding complex assets and uncertain circumstances (Woffold 1985).

Heterogeneous

All properties are different. Strictly speaking, in English law, it means that all interests in property are different. It is possible for two or more parties to hold different interests (e.g. freehold and leasehold) in the same physical property. This has a number of implications for the asset class including, as already noted, greater complexity.

High transaction and operating costs

Complexity and heterogeneity also lead to higher transaction and operating costs than for listed securities. When considering the acquisition of an interest in property it is necessary to perform extensive checks of its legal and physical characteristics. This 'due diligence' is part of the risk management process that any prudent owner or investor will undertake. It reduces the likelihood of any negative surprises occurring after acquisition. Due diligence itself can be costly as it involves technical specialists such as lawyers and surveyors. To some extent the cost can be regarded as an insurance premium against future expenses. Whilst these costs are significant, by far the greatest cost of acquisition, in the UK but also in many other countries, is the transfer tax. In the UK this is called Stamp Duty Land Tax (SDLT) and is levied at the rate of 4 per cent on all purchases of non-residential property over £500,000. Considerable effort has been expended over the years by investors in trying to devise acquisition structures that minimise or eliminate this cost.

Transaction costs for a vendor are much lower as they do not (in the UK) pay any transfer tax and the professional fees are less as no due diligence is involved. Nevertheless, the round trip (to sell one property and reinvest in another) transaction cost is about 7 per cent.

The extent to which operating costs are an issue for the owner of a legal interest in property depend on the nature of the interest and its relationship with any other interests. As a physical structure, a building requires regular maintenance to ensure its suitable condition. In the UK, it has historically been common practice for the owner of a freehold interest to pass all of these costs onto the tenant(s). This is through the terms of the full repairing and insuring (FRI) lease. There are also operating taxes (called business rates in the UK), which are usually also the responsibility of the tenant(s).

With limited exemptions (fewer now than in the past), business rates are payable whether or not a property is occupied. In the case of a vacant property, they remain the liability of the freeholder. Under the terms of an FRI lease in the UK, the freeholder can generally expect to receive a net income (before tax) that is close to 100 per cent of the rent paid by any tenant. In other jurisdictions the position is not as favourable for the freeholder. For example in the United States it is common for a landlord to be able to recover operating costs and taxes from the tenant, but subject to caps on the annual increase. This can lead to a decline in the recovered overheads over the life of a lease. Both market practice and statute may limit the extent to which a freeholder can recover taxes and other operating costs from a tenant.

Large lot sizes

Property assets acquired as an investment are generally only available in lot sizes in excess of £100,000 and frequently very much more. This compares again with listed securities that can be bought for a few pounds. Held directly, property is therefore limited to investors with substantial finance available and, those who do not have a problem with having capital tied up in illiquid assets because 'the accumulation process experiences uncomfortable friction when capital (i.e. "value in motion") is trapped in steel beams and concrete' (Weber 2002: 519).

Depreciation

Although not factored explicitly into the decision-making process of many investors or occupiers, depreciation is a very real cost that needs to be faced through the period of ownership of a property. In a rising market, it tends to be masked by the general upward movement in prices. It may suppress the income stream and the exchange price but not necessarily a building's use value (Weber 2002). Depreciation comes in a number of forms, namely: physical, functional, legal and aesthetic.

- *Physical depreciation*, the wearing out of a building, is the most obvious form of depreciation. It manifests itself in the periodic expenditure required to repoint brickwork or replace lifts, for example.
- *Functional depreciation* (also known as obsolescence) arises from the changing needs of occupiers that can no longer be met. For example, many older buildings lacked the floor-to-ceiling height needed to install air conditioning when it first became a common requirement. This made them less attractive to occupiers than either brand new buildings or even other older ones that could be retro-fitted with the equipment. This represented a permanent loss of value that could not be recovered, even with additional expenditure.

- *Legal depreciation* arises when the legal requirements of buildings change. In the UK, these are often reflected in changes to the statutory building codes known as the Building Regulations (see later for details). Standards are changing all the time and usually it is only new construction work that has to meet current standards. Existing buildings are not normally in a constant state of modification to meet changing standards. However this is not always the case. Disabled access regulations, for example, have become tighter in recent years and many buildings have had to be retrofitted to enable wheelchair access.
- *Aesthetic considerations* also play a part. Tastes change over time and building features that were once popular fall out of fashion, again leading to depreciation. Aesthetic trends towards open plan offices and a preference for better natural lighting, for example, have also left many older buildings behind. New legal requirements, such as wheelchair accessibility, can also leave older buildings at a disadvantage.

For an investor, the cost of depreciation is not always apparent until it involves cash expenditure, so it tends to be hidden. But it is a very real cost. The effect becomes clear when comparing the value of an older building with a relatively modern one with a current specification. The decision is more difficult in the case of complex office buildings and shopping centres involving high capital investment. For industrial units, which are cheaper to build and generally have a shorter life anyway, it may be easy to accept earlier replacement. The removal of relief from business rates on empty non-domestic buildings in the UK in 2008 (Rating [Empty Properties] Act 2007) provides some guidance. This led to several much publicised cases of vacant (and presumably older and harder to let) industrial buildings being demolished. A change in the law shifted the financial viability from retain to demolish. It was also claimed that the change hindered speculative development of new buildings.

This was an example of accelerated depreciation. The lifespan of these buildings was suddenly and dramatically shortened, such that they were no longer economically viable. Similar concerns exist about how legislation such as the Green Deal will affect the value of other properties. Those that can no longer be let will decline in value. What happens to them will depend on the financial viability of redevelopment. If it is not cost effective to refurbish them back up to a lettable standard, they will remain vacant or be demolished. They will only be replaced with a new building if there is occupier demand and it appears financially viable.

Baum *et al.* (2004) suggest that depreciation rates are also influenced by leasing structures. In the UK with its tradition of FRI leases, responsibility for meeting repair and maintenance costs lies with the tenant. The income for the landlord is therefore what is termed 'triple net'. There is full distribution of income, with no retention to fund improvements to the property. They found some evidence to suggest that in other markets, where landlords retained responsibility for maintenance, this led to lower distribution rates as landlords spent money to maintain the rental value (i.e. offset depreciation). A possible implication is that UK practice tends to exaggerate short-term income returns at the expense of longer term capital growth (which would arise from reinvestment to maintain rental value growth). It was also suggested that multi-let properties, with shorter leases (which provide the landlord with more regular opportunities to spend money on improvements) experienced stronger rental value growth, than single tenant buildings on long leases.

It is an issue that is obscured by the fog of inflation. When people talk about rental value growth they usually mean nominal rather than real growth. Growth in rental values in many property markets has not kept pace with inflation over several decades.

With growing requirements for energy efficient properties in the UK, sustainability is increasingly a driver of depreciation. The pressure for sustainability leads to legal depreciation (e.g. requirement to retrofit a building to improve energy efficiency), functional depreciation and influences aesthetic considerations.

Lack of transparency

Most of what is known about a listed security is in the public domain. This is the intention of securities' regulations in many countries designed to ensure that all investors have equal access to information about publicly traded securities. It is the foundation of open and orderly market operations. Listed companies have to meet statutory reporting requirements as a condition of being listed and are generally also well researched by independent analysts. This is intended to prevent one investor from gaining advantage over others through possession of superior information. People who, because of their role, have access to such information (for example a firm's auditors) are precluded from trading in the shares of the company in question. Insider trading, as it is known, is a criminal offence in the UK and in many other jurisdictions. One of the reasons for the success of the City of London as an international financial centre is the openness and transparency of its markets. The knowledge that it operates in a fair way attracts investors from around the world.

In contrast, very little of what could be known about individual property assets is in the public domain. There is no legal requirement for it and the heterogeneous nature of property makes it very difficult to research properties to the same degree as analysts are able to cover the much smaller universe of listed securities. This makes for a market that, in general, operates on less common knowledge. The selective availability of information is part of normal market practice. Participants actively seek opportunities where they have an information advantage over others. This lack of transparency contributes to both the high cost and long timescales involved in property transactions.

The degree of transparency varies between and within property markets. The UK is ranked as the third most transparent property market in the world

(JLL 2010). This is one factor that attracts international investors to it, particularly to London. Also some sectors of the market are better researched than others. Assets of a type (e.g. City of London offices, where £5 billion of property was traded in 2010) that are generally of interest to institutional investors are better researched, on the whole, than those that are not. The scale of activity in such sectors of the market generates sufficient fees to incentivise a wide range of intermediaries and advisers to prepare and disseminate research. This, however, still does not obviate the need for research and due diligence at the individual asset level.

Illiquid

The effect of many of the above characteristics is to make the trading of property very illiquid. Unlike listed securities, it is difficult to secure transactions within a few seconds (such as over the internet) in the property market. Overcoming this lack of liquidity has been a key driver, over many years, behind efforts to design different ways of holding property assets. Property has a lot of attractive characteristics and investors are keen to find ways of retaining these whilst at the same time improving liquidity. IPF (2004) argues that the liquidity level of different property sectors and regions vary. For example, their report identifies that properties with higher values normally trade less frequently than those with lower values. Although the UK commercial property market trades twice as frequently as the markets in France and the Netherlands, the central London office market trades less frequently than other segments. In the indirect property market, IPF (2004) finds that the liquidity level in UK property companies is greater than that in US REITs or Australian Listed Property Trusts.

Opportunity to add value

Unlike investors in securities, owners of property have the opportunity to enhance their investment throughout the period of ownership. This may be through restructuring leases, changing the planning status for one with higher value and/or redeveloping or refurbishing the property. Generally, investors in securities (unless they acquire a controlling stake) take a passive role and have no opportunity to change the nature of their investment.

Long-term stable income

The quality of the income stream from property depends on a number of factors. These include the tenant covenant, lease structure and legal framework. It is generally good advice for investors in any asset to consider the source of income, which supports the value of the asset. In the case of real property, the income comes from the rent paid by occupiers. If a property is not occupied or the tenants stop paying rent then no amount of financial structuring can ultimately protect investors.

The nature of the income is determined by the terms of the lease under which the tenant occupies a property. An understanding of the rights and responsibilities conferred by these agreements is crucial in assessing the value of a property (or, strictly, the interest in land). In the UK in the 1970s, the typical lease from an institutional landlord was for 25 years, with upward-only rent reviews. This was seen as a cornerstone of the long-term security of the income from property. Since then, although upward-only rent reviews have remained a feature of the market, average lease lengths have shortened to nearer ten years or less. Ultimately, of course, it is the ability of tenants to continue paying the rent that underlies the income security. Across well-diversified portfolios, the risk of loss of income is quite low. The ability to re-let a property means that default risk is lower than that for financial assets. The payment of rent by a company has priority over the payment of dividends. In the generally 'creditor friendly' environment of the UK, obligations under a lease have priority over those to other creditors.

Over time other changes have moved the law in the tenant's favour. Until 1995, landlords were able to rely on the concept of privity of estate as further security for their income. In the event of default by the current tenant, the landlord or owner could follow the chain of any lease assignments back to the original tenant and demand payment from them. This led to a number of well-publicised cases of former tenants who thought they had long lost any responsibility for a property being forced to pay the rent. New legislation in 1995 removed this power for new leases.

More recently landlords have been challenged by the use of so-called 'pre-pack' administrations and company voluntary agreements (CVAs). These use the insolvency system to help companies in financial trouble shed many of their liabilities (including obligations under a lease) and resume trading immediately as a new company. They have arisen as a result of development of insolvency practice, rather than a change in the law. In many cases the results have not been good for unsecured creditors, including landlords.

A good asset for securing debt

Real property has long been an asset against which owners like to borrow and banks like to lend. Undoubtedly, the quality of property income plays a part in this. But property also provides lenders with a tangible asset as security if a borrower defaults. Property investors also borrow against property to enhance the return on their equity. This of course only works if the investor judges both the cost and timing of the debt accurately. Get it wrong and the equity

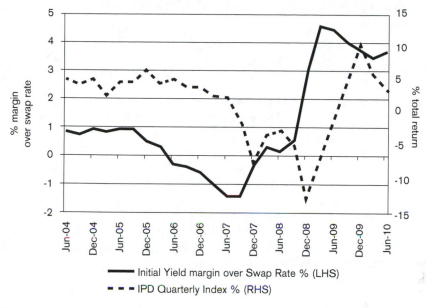

Figure 4.1

All UK commercial property initial yield versus swap rate (IPD data)

can be wiped out. The credit crunch of 2008 and the property boom that preceded it provide a timely reminder of the link between the market value of property and the cost and availability of debt finance.

As initial yields fell below the swap rate, around June 2006, gearing was no longer effective. Property returns started to decline, becoming negative in June 2007. Initial yields remained below the swap rate for two years, until mid 2008, with property values not recovering until mid 2009 (Figure 4.1).

Regulatory framework of the property market

The nature of property as an investment is shaped not only by its inherent characteristics discussed above, but also by the regulatory environment within which it operates. This regulatory environment includes planning and building regulations and taxation. Its inherent characteristics are also influenced by the general legal framework, which, for example, codifies the rights and responsibilities of different interests in land.

This overall regulatory environment is rarely static. As it changes so do the opportunities associated with property. These are reflected in its market value. Decisions about property often involve long-term commitments, but the regulatory environment can change many times over the lifetime of an investment. This section thus discusses the regulatory framework that is operating in the UK.

Planning

The planning system is designed to achieve a wide range of social, economic and political objectives. It forces a different trade-off between the rights and responsibilities of individual landowners and a wider society than would be achieved via an unfettered system of supply and demand. As such, planning regulations involve elements of control over the use, location, design and taxation of property. Many property owners instinctively dislike them. They see them as a restriction on their ability to operate their property as they wish. At the individual property level this is often their effect.

At an overall land-use level, the influence of planning controls on value is very complex. Even though the UK is a densely populated country, only 10 per cent to 15 per cent of the available land is urbanised. To a great extent this has been achieved through the long-term application of a planning regime, the general principles of which were set out soon after the Second World War. The distribution and extent of urban land use is different from that which would have occurred without such a system. The degree to which this has contributed to the achievement of wider social, economic and political goals, such as the spread of economic prosperity around the country, rather than the concentration of growth in limited areas, is the subject of continuing debate.

Planning is but one of many factors influencing the scale and location of urban development. Although sometimes characterised, as noted earlier, as a restriction on use, it is not necessarily the limiting factor.

Rents for office space in the City of London are the second highest after the West End in the country. The amount of office space in the City (including Canary Wharf) has grown dramatically since the liberalisation of financial services (the Big Bang) in the 1980s. It is a highly cyclical market and rents go up and down with economic and development cycles. There are both periodic shortages and periodic surpluses of space. This is not due to changes in the availability of planning consents for office development. In the City of London, there is planning approval for far more square metres of new office space than is ever likely to be constructed over the development cycle. This is supported by the observation that although nominal rents have generally been on an upward trend over the years, real rents after inflation are lower today than in 1980 (Figure 4.2).

Planning affects value not only through influencing the type and scale of land use but also through building design and taxation. Everyone has an opinion on the aesthetics of the built environment. Views on the appearance of a proposed development will often vary widely and can lead to heated debate. For the developer the appearance will be influenced by many factors including personal taste, cost and marketability (to both potential owners and

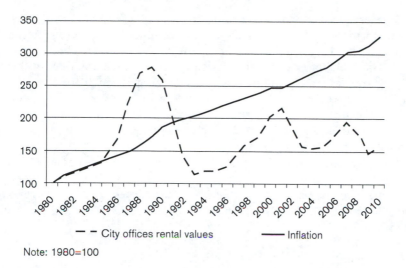

Figure 4.2

City of London office rental index 1980–2010 (IPD 2010)

occupiers) of the finished product. To a varying degree the planning system attempts to arbitrate between a number of different parties, including the owner, adjoining owners, other affected individuals and interested lobby groups.

The planning system is not primarily one of taxation but it is used to tax new development. In the UK this is achieved through what are known as Section 106 Agreements. These allow a local planning authority to enter into a legally binding agreement or planning obligation with a landowner linked to the granting of planning consent. They often require the developer to provide some public or other facilities that they would not otherwise have provided. The cost involved in doing this is essentially a tax. Such agreements are used to support the provision of services and infrastructure, such as highways, recreational facilities, education, health and affordable housing.

Building regulations

The building regulations set standards for the design and construction of new buildings and for many alterations performed to existing ones. The purpose of these is to ensure that buildings meet minimum standards for a range of requirements including: fire resistance, ease of access and egress, thermal efficiency and many more. These regulations are constantly updated to reflect improved understanding of the performance of buildings and the materials and components used in their construction.

In recent years they have increasingly been influenced by the sustainability agenda. This has led to tougher standards aimed at reducing the energy requirements of buildings (including of the materials used to construct them). So, for example, heating boilers have to run more efficiently than in the past and heat losses from buildings have to be lower, through the use of better glazing systems. Following these standards, which are obligatory, generally raises the capital cost of construction work. Increased construction costs feed through into decisions about development, repair and refurbishment and ultimately have a bearing on value.

Rating systems are also becoming a common way of differentiating between buildings. These distinguish the 'greenness' of buildings. The underlying principles and criteria of different ratings agencies, such as LEED in the US and BREEAM in the UK, tend to be along similar lines and cover the following elements:

- sustainable site;
- water efficiency;
- energy and atmosphere;
- materials and resources;
- indoor environmental quality;
- innovation and design process.

'These elements have many prerequisites that are part of the rating system and are required to meet minimal goals at each level of certification. Professionals should be aware of specific requirements for each certification level and how the costs and benefits of each requirement affect the value of a "green" building' (Shalley 2008: 3).

Taxation

Taxation has an important influence on property. Taxes have to be raised to finance the operations of the state, but they can also be used by government to influence resource allocation decisions and achieve wider policy objectives. Real property is an ideal subject for taxing as it is an asset that cannot be moved. As a result, property is subject to a wide range of capital and income taxes on both transactions and continuing ownership. The most common property taxes are those on rental income, on capital gains arising from sales and transaction taxes on purchase.

In recent years the sustainability agenda has led, in parallel with changes to the planning regime and building regulations, to taxation also being used to encourage sustainable behaviour. Gas and electricity is priced to include a tax (Climate Change Levy), which is used to help finance the development of alternative energy supplies such as wind farms.

Another recent initiative, the CRC Energy Efficiency Scheme, is a good example of how quickly tax policy in the area is changing. The scheme is designed to encourage the largest energy users (who are generally also large property owners) to reduce their CO_2 emissions through the raising of a levy. The original arrangement of the scheme included the publishing of a performance league table of the participants. The better performers would receive a payment funded out of the levy raised on the worst performers. Following the UK government spending review in autumn 2010, it was announced that the levy would now be retained rather than recycled back to participants. It is a good example of how one policy objective (to change behaviour) can come into conflict with another (to maximise tax revenue). Although properties are not yet explicitly taxed on the basis of their energy efficiency (in the way that motor vehicles now are), it is possible to conceive of this happening in the future. Energy Performance Certificates (EPCs) for individual buildings are becoming more widespread (they are required before buildings can be sold) and could at some point be used as the basis for a new property tax.

The complexity, scale and ever-changing nature of taxes affecting property means that large property owners devote considerable resources to managing their tax affairs. Property investment decisions should be made for good investment reasons, rather than be tax driven. Nevertheless it is impossible to ignore the effect of taxation in making decisions concerning the development, operation and transfer of property.

Externalities

Planning, building regulations and taxation are used to achieve a wide range of policy objectives in relation to property. One theme that runs through all of these is the issue of externalities.

Externalities arise when a purchase or use decision by one party affects others who were not involved in the decision and whose interests were not taken into account. They can be negative or positive. On a day-to-day basis, many instances are trivial and can be ignored. However others are not and they can lead to a less than optimal allocation of resources. For example one justification for public subsidy of the railway network is that railways produce society-wide benefits that are not reflected in the cost of tickets sold to those who travel on them. The London Underground, built from the end of the nineteenth century, was popular with travellers from the earliest days but the private investors who originally financed it mostly lost their money. The network ended up in public ownership. Conversely the congestion and pollution caused by private motor vehicles is a negative externality that justifies the imposition of taxes to ensure that the users of vehicles incur the full cost of their activity.

Property development and ownership frequently result in both positive and negative externalities. It is in this context that a justification can be found for much of the regulatory environment around it, including the planning system, building regulations and taxation. They constitute a set of rules that is constantly evolving to reflect improvements in knowledge and changing priorities within society. One of the challenges for policy makers, seeking to make significant immediate changes in direction, is that collectively, real property is like a super-tanker.

In the UK, the development of new property amounts to about 1 per cent per annum of the existing stock of buildings (SDC 2005). From year to year the incremental change in the overall built environment is therefore quite small. Most of the buildings that will exist in 30 years' time have already been constructed. The Climate Change Act 2008 mandates a cut in greenhouse gas emissions of 34 per cent by 2020 and 80 per cent by 2050, both from a 1990 baseline. For real estate to make its contribution, policymakers cannot rely on new developments to achieve this goal. They need to see improvements in the performance of existing buildings as well.

This regulatory framework has been in place for decades, but the growing concern in recent years with the wider environmental, social and economic impact of human activities has given the concept of externalities much greater prominence. Much of the movement towards what is referred to as sustainable development is aimed at reducing or eliminating some externalities or, at the very least, ensuring that those responsible bear the cost. RICS (2010: 2) notes one estimate of the scale of real estate's contribution to these externalities as:

> The built environment in its widest sense (including construction) is responsible overall for about 40% of CO_2 emissions, 30% solid waste generation and 20% of water effluents, as well as 40% of all energy used. Commercial property is a major contributor within this overall context. In the UK for example, the Carbon Trust has calculated that energy use in non-domestic buildings accounts for about 18% of total carbon emissions.

This wider public policy agenda has already resulted in changes to planning, building regulation and tax systems as they adapt to achieve the new objectives. In parallel with this, there has been a raised public consciousness about the issues. A growing number of organisations are keen to promote their credentials as being socially responsible over and above any statutory responsibilities. These organisations include those who own or control large property portfolios. Many property companies and property fund managers now have public statements about their policies on sustainability and what is termed socially responsible property investment. Fuller consideration of this aspect will form part of Chapter 9. However, it is clear that sustainability and responsible investment are becoming important variables in the measurement of market performance.

Planning legislation, building regulations and taxation are used in a number of ways to achieve policy goals. Changes to rules are generally not retrospective. New developments have to meet the planning and building regulations in force at the time of construction. Building regulations, in particular, change over time with the result that most existing buildings do not meet current standards in some way or other. But buildings do not have to be constantly upgraded to meet changing standards, except to the extent that new works or repairs comply with the standards then in force. It is the same with planning. Taxation is slightly different. The tax environment affecting property is also in a state of change. If tax rules change they affect all properties, not just newly completed ones.

To some extent this convention is under pressure. The targets of sustainability and socially responsible investment represent, in some way, merely a widening of the understanding of what constitutes an externality. So should they be susceptible, as in the past, to further rule changes designed to internalise their costs? To a degree this has happened. Building regulations, for example, set higher thermal insulation and efficiency standards than only a few years ago.

Summary

This chapter has introduced some of the characteristics of real estate and the context within which it is traded. It is intended as an overview of the real estate market and many of the issues raised that relate to sustainability and sustainable behaviour will be returned to in other chapters in the book. However, it is also important to understand more about the manner in which real estate is held, i.e. its legal ownership rights. Later chapters in this book, therefore, will address these both as direct and indirect investment activities. In many instances, sustainability is seen as an externality. As part of the process to encourage changes in the provision of space, the UK government have used a range of measures including aspects of the planning system, the building regulations mechanism and taxation.

5   Methods of
ownership in the
property market

Introduction

The previous chapter reviewed the main characteristics of property. In order to gain further understanding of how property can be managed more sustainably, it is also important to appreciate the manner in which assets are owned and traded. This chapter, therefore, considers these issues. It is essential to have some understanding of the complex nature of ownership of interests in property in order to appreciate the sustainability prospects for the production, occupation and management of both individual buildings and portfolios.

Overview of property ownership

In everyday conversation the ownership of real property is generally thought of as actual ownership of a building or land. Technically, in English law, the ownership is not of the physical asset itself, but of a legal interest in the asset. This may seem a fine distinction but it is an important one. It immediately opens up the possibility of different interests existing in the same physical asset at the same time. The most common of these are the freehold interest and the leasehold interest.

Within this legal construct, ownership of the physical asset lies with the state or the Crown, as it is referred to in English law. A freehold interest is the least encumbered interest but it may nevertheless be subject to a wide range of restrictions. One needs to look no further than the title documents to see that a freehold interest may be subject to a number of covenants (obligations to do or not do certain things) that circumscribe it. Beyond these there is also the general legal framework, which includes the planning and building regulations discussed earlier. Neither the legal environment nor covenants in a title affect all freehold interests equally so each can come with a different package of rights and responsibilities. The situation is even more complex with leasehold interests.

So it is that freeholds are the preferred interests of most investors in property. They get the closest to owning the building. But, although even a freehold is already one step removed from actual ownership, it has long been common practice for many investors to put at least one more layer between them and the asset. Ownership of the interest in land is often put into a limited company or some other form of collective undertaking. The investors then hold shares in these schemes. There are many reasons for doing this, which will be explored.

Ownership and control

On the face of it, direct and indirect investment can be distinguished by the absence or presence of some form of vehicle or structure to hold an investor's interest in the underlying real estate. If the investor has their name on the title deeds that is a direct investment. If the title is held by a vehicle whose equity is, in turn, owned by an investor, it is indirect. In reality it is more useful to think of the distinction in terms of whether or not management and control are separate from ownership. Although some commercial real estate investors undoubtedly acquire assets in their own name many, for tax reasons or just for administrative convenience, hold assets via some sort of intermediate vehicle. Ownership and control remain together and it can still be considered as a direct investment. The number of individuals wealthy enough to do this is limited. Consequently much investment-grade commercial real estate is held by collectively owned vehicles that separate ownership from control and are therefore indirect investments. Once investors take the indirect route it is also important to consider the motivations and incentives of their advisers as this has a bearing on how the assets are managed.

The institutional framework that has developed to meet the needs of indirect investment is complex and involves many advisers and intermediaries, serving a wide range of different investors. Many investors do not even know that they have a stake in property, as it may be through an insurance policy or pension scheme that has made the asset allocation decision. The network of advisers also influences the behaviour of the market, not least because they earn a living from it and are largely paid for out of the investment returns of the investors.

Types of owners in the market

A central role of the financial markets is to match those with capital to those who need it. Indirect investment provides a convenient way of achieving this for real estate. For small investors, it is often done through insurance funds and pension schemes, which aggregate the savings of many people. The market also includes:

- wealthy individuals (high net worth);
- listed and unlisted property companies;
- overseas investors (e.g. foreign insurance companies and sovereign wealth funds); and
- investment banks.

Individual investors

Small investors are the most removed from day-to-day involvement in the market. Their equity is combined with that of hundreds if not thousands of other investors. The limit of their involvement is to have made a decision to invest. Individually they have little influence on the market, but the way their equity is channelled into it can have profound consequences for the flow of capital. Much of the investment into commercial real estate by small investors is via open-ended funds. These funds issue new units or shares as capital comes in, and cancel units when investors want their money back. This is a very common but, nevertheless, risky financing structure for an illiquid asset – short-term finance for long-term assets. Investment goods are not like consumer goods. When the price of a consumer good rises, demand usually falls; when the price of an investment good rises, demand generally increases. Seeing people making money out of rising share or property prices is a great incentive for others to buy into the market as well. Conversely when prices are falling everyone wants to sell, but liquidity in the market disappears.

Listed and unlisted property companies

There are also plenty of closed-ended vehicles, including the largest listed property companies operating in the market. Closed-ended vehicles have a fixed capital base. Investors wanting to buy into the business have to buy in the secondary market from existing investors who want to sell. If it is a listed company then supply and demand is balanced by changes in the share price, but these transactions do not change the overall capital available. If the vehicle is an unlisted fund there may still be a secondary market for shares/units but it is likely to be far less liquid than for a listed business.

Listed property companies and other closed-ended structures do not have the liquidity problem of open-ended funds. But they are far from immune from the ups and downs of the market. Funds that borrow (and many do) have to maintain certain covenants with their lenders such as a loan to value (LTV) and debt service (DSCR) ratios. When asset prices are increasing it is easier to borrow more money and leverage the return on equity. When prices fall a borrower can quickly find that they are breaching loan covenants.

This happened to many property companies when values collapsed in the wake of the credit crunch. Not only were LTV limits breached but debt became harder to source and more expensive. Interest costs rose above the return on capital and debt made the return on equity even worse. A typical response of lenders to a default would be to force a sale of assets to repay the loan. However this becomes counter-productive when many borrowers are in default. Forced sales risk driving prices down further and causing more distress for the lenders.

Property, like other financial assets, is prone to cyclical price bubbles, followed by market collapses. Investors in property face this risk, whether they invest directly or indirectly, through open-ended, closed-ended, listed or unlisted vehicles.

Types of indirect ownership of property

There are many reasons why investors may prefer to obtain their exposure to the risks and returns of property indirectly, rather than acquiring interests in property itself. These can be understood by reviewing the list of characteristics of property described earlier. Many different methods of indirect ownership have been created over time, often targeted at particular investor groups, but generally with the aim of overcoming the same disadvantages of direct investment.

The biggest drawback of direct investment is the lack of liquidity. Property aspires to be treated as an equal with other asset classes, but in comparison it remains slow and expensive to transact. There are other reasons, too, for investing indirectly. Tax nearly always plays a part and for many investors, it is administratively more convenient to invest indirectly. None of the methods of indirect investment are unique to property and may be used by equity and bond investors too.

There are many different property investment vehicles but they can largely be categorised as being:

- listed or unlisted; or
- open-ended or closed-ended.

The selection of one vehicle structure over another is strongly influenced by tax considerations. In turn this is dependent on the type of investor, their objectives, their location (tax residence) and the location(s) of the assets being acquired. Although tax is always important, investors should remember that they are investing in the risk/return features of the underlying assets. The vehicle itself is just a wrapper, not an investment.

Property companies

Property companies can be listed or unlisted. Listing on an established stock exchange can provide the liquidity sought by property investors, whereas unlisted companies offer no help in this direction. That would be the end of the story except that using a listed property company introduces other problems.

Property companies tend to be valued for their assets rather than their projected profits. With the share price and property valuation to some extent moving independently from each other, it can be expected that the market value of the company will not always equal the value of the underlying assets (net of liabilities). In practice this difference is usually a discount. Property share prices rarely move to a premium over the net asset value (NAV). A persistent and large discount to NAV can make it difficult to raise new equity and make a business vulnerable to a takeover. New equity, raised to acquire further assets, will increase the market capitalisation of the company by less than the amount of the new equity. There is an instant 'loss' of value. To overcome this, new shares can be issued at a discount to the market price, but this dilutes the value of existing shareholders' interests. Equally, if shares are trading at a discount, it could in theory be possible to acquire all the shares more cheaply than acquiring all of the properties.

Property rich companies (i.e. companies that are primarily in some other business, but which incidentally own a lot of property) have, in the past, been taken over for this reason. So-called 'asset strippers' buy the company and sell off all the assets for a profit. In practice it would be difficult to achieve this with a listed property company as the slightest hint that someone was trying to take a controlling interest in the business would cause the share price to rise – probably to a bid premium.

Many attempts have been made over the years to explain the persistence of the discount to NAV. One of these is taxation, which highlights another disadvantage of property companies. In the UK, property companies are not a tax efficient way of holding property assets. Profits are taxed at the company level and in the hands of shareholders. This compares with only a single level of tax when investing directly. Part of the explanation for the discount to NAV was due to the treatment of potential capital gains tax (CGT) liabilities. The sale of assets that had been held for a long time could result in the payment of CGT, possibly many millions of pounds. To avoid this, the assets continued to be held. However, the contingent CGT liability was included in the accounts as a reduction in the value of the company. The UK property industry lobbied successive governments over many years to solve the double tax problem by introducing real estate investment trusts (REITs) into the UK.

REITs

The characteristics of property investment (principally the fact that it requires large amounts of capital), have meant that small investors and individuals have tended to be excluded from entering the sector. The introduction of indirect property investment vehicles has now opened up wider opportunities for investment. The real estate investment trust (REIT) is one such vehicle. The US developed its REIT market in 1961 (Baum 2009).

This means that 'a real estate company or trust that has elected to qualify under certain tax provisions to become a pass-through entity that distributes to its shareholders almost all of its earnings and capital gains generated from the disposition of its properties' (Hoesli *et al*. 2000: 233). The UK REIT was launched on 1 January 2007, after the enactment of the Finance Act 2006.

REITs, or at least vehicles with a similar purpose, exist in many countries. The precise rules and even the name varies from one country to another, but the broad objective is the same: to provide a listed vehicle that puts the property investor in no worse a tax position than if they held the underlying assets directly. The three key conditions that have to be met to become a UK REIT are:

- The vehicle must be a UK tax resident, widely held and listed on a recognised stock exchange, with a simple share and loan capital structure.
- The vehicle must be substantially a property investor with 75 per cent balance of business tests (income and capital); at least three investment properties must be held although the definition of property includes separate real units. Owner-occupied property does not qualify. Development for investment is permitted (subject to a tax charge in certain cases if a sale takes place within three years of practical completion).
- 90 per cent of the otherwise taxable income (but not capital) profits of the property investment business must be distributed within 12 months of the end of the relevant accounting period.

(Clark *et al*. 2010: 41)

The REITS rules were crafted only to be of benefit to companies whose business was predominantly property investment. The UK government did not want profits from property development to be provided with a tax shelter. Therefore a number of companies that were primarily developers retained their existing status.

It was also hoped that REITs' high income distribution would mean their returns (despite being listed companies) would more closely mirror those of the underlying property assets. Evidence at the time, from the US and Australia, was that REITs traded at a much narrower discount to NAV than other property investment vehicles.

That REITs in the UK have not been as successful as many hoped does not mean that they have been a failure. With the benefit of hindsight, it can be seen that their launch coincided very closely with the cyclical peak of the last property boom. Within 18 months of their launch, a number of these businesses were fighting for survival as property values plummeted and banking covenants were breached. Discounts to NAV widened to record levels.

Although the property sector as a whole still faced many challenges arising from the credit crunch of 2008, it appeared by 2010, to be through the worst as values had staged something of a recovery and discounts to NAV again narrowed. Despite these setbacks, both the government and the property industry in the UK see potential for REITs to contribute to the refinancing of property assets (both public and private) that is still required. This may involve further development of the legislative framework governing REITs.

Unit trusts

Unit trusts have long been popular in the UK as an investment structure for collective investment in all the main asset classes. They make use of trust law whereby legal title to the assets may be held by one person for the benefit of another. They are found in a number of common law countries.

Unit trusts can be used to create either closed-ended or open-ended investment funds. In closed-ended form, their capital base is fixed, like a listed company. In this form changes in the ownership of the units in issue do not affect the capitalisation of the fund. Used as an open-ended structure they have a variable capital base. New units are issued as investors buy into the trust and are cancelled when they take their money out. The amount of capital the trust has available for investment changes as investors buy or sell units. An open-ended structure works well when the underlying assets (e.g. listed equities) are quite liquid. If the trust faces large inflows or outflows of money it can easily acquire additional equities with the new cash, or sell them to meet redemptions from investors.

Property is not particularly liquid. An open-ended property fund may have trouble investing incoming cash fast enough and find that it is building up excess liquidity. Conversely, if there is a run on the fund, it may face difficulties selling assets fast enough to meet the demands for cash from exiting investors. This would mean investors facing delays in being able to leave the fund. For this reason, open-ended property unit trusts were restricted for many years in the UK to professional investors. It was not felt that individual investors would understand the risk of this potential lack of liquidity. This only changed in 2006 when legislation, enabling what were called Authorised Property Unit Trusts, was passed. The timing of this change, as with the introduction of REITs 12 months later, unfortunately coincided with an unprecedented bull market in property. When the market crashed a couple of years later some of these funds faced the old problem.

They had to suspend or delay redemptions because they could not realise cash quickly enough to pay out investors.

Prior to this, property unit trusts, in both open and closed-ended form had generally served the property investment industry well for many years. A big advantage of them, for investors, is that the price of the units in the funds is based on valuations of the underlying property assets. This means that, unlike listed property companies (including REITs), they suffer no discount to NAV. Their investment returns, after allowing for the running costs of the fund and the effect of any gearing, track those of the property market. In fairly stable market conditions they also appear to offer good liquidity. Managers of the funds maintain some cash in them so are able to meet redemptions on normal (usually at least one month's notice) terms. Also, professional investors, such as pension funds, are usually not as volatile as individual investors when it comes to reacting to changing market conditions.

Closed-ended unit trusts are often used by small groups of investors who wish to invest on a pooled basis for a fixed period. In this case liquidity is not a problem – the investors know there is none (unless they can find a buyer for their units in a secondary market) at least until (or even beyond) the planned end of the fund. However, during the life of the fund, their units are still priced on the basis of the valuation of the underlying assets. So, again there is no discount to NAV, and performance matches that of the property market.

To an extent the unit trust structure appears to solve the old conundrum and provide property market returns with liquidity. But this is something of an illusion. Liquidity soon disappears if everyone wants to sell. Also, in a rapidly changing property market, the valuations on which the unit price is based may be a poor reflection of the prices at which the underlying assets could be traded. As unlisted vehicles they lack the pressure valve of a market price to match supply with demand.

In looking at listed companies and unit trusts, the principal features of the universe of property investment vehicles have been discussed. That universe is constantly changing but it is worth reviewing a number of other vehicles to underline that the differences are often ones of degree rather than substance. Different structures exist in different countries to suit the tax status of particular investor groups. For international investors, the picture is even more complex as the benefits of different structures also depend on the tax treaties between countries. For example an international investor into Russia might consider a Cyprus registered holding company, whereas an international investor into India would look at a Mauritius holding company. An overseas investor into China on the other hand would use a Barbados holding company to take advantage of the Barbados–Peoples Republic of China double tax treaty. It can be seen that it is important to obtain very specific legal and tax advice in each situation.

Open-ended investment company

Open-ended investment companies (OEICs), as their name implies, have a corporate structure but are open-ended. They were made possible in the UK in 1997, but are also a familiar structure in other European countries. They are popular with fund managers in the UK as they are more flexible than unit trusts and simpler and cheaper to operate. Also, the European Union (EU), as part of its efforts to establish a single market in financial services, allows OEICs that satisfy certain additional criteria (Undertakings for Collective Investment in Transferable Securities [UCITS]) to be marketed across the EU.

Property funds operating within an OEIC have similar characteristics to those using an open-ended unit trust. Pricing of the shares is based on independent valuations of the underlying assets and they provide a similar degree of liquidity. One particular use of the OEIC for property investment is worth noting.

REITs, launched in 2007, provided the UK with a tax transparent, listed property investment vehicle. Still missing at the time was a tax-transparent, unlisted open-ended fund structure. The Authorised Property Unit Trust (APUT), introduced only in 2006, still suffered the same double taxation problem of traditional property companies. There were some complicated accounting issues involved in addressing this, but eventually the property investment industry and the government agreed on a workable structure. This was called the Property Authorised Investment Fund (PAIF) and it was introduced in 2008. PAIFs, with a tax regime that broadly parallels that of REITs, have to be set up as an OEIC.

This completed the picture as far as providing UK based, tax efficient structures for listed and non-listed property investment vehicles was concerned. Somewhat surprisingly they have yet to prove a commercial success. It was 2010 before the first such fund (through conversion of an existing unit trust) was launched.

Limited partnerships

A popular vehicle for indirect property investment, often among small groups of like-minded institutional investors, is the limited partnership (LP). These are set up (in England and Wales) under the Limited Partnership Act 1907. Similar arrangements exist in other jurisdictions, including Scotland whose LPs differ from English ones.

An LP is a partnership between at least one general partner, who has unlimited liability for the debts and obligations of the LP, and one or more limited partners who contribute capital to the LP (either by contributing cash or property). The limited partners are not allowed to participate in the management of the LP, which is the responsibility of the general partner. LPs do not provide liquidity in the way that a listed company or even a unit trust may. They are, however, broadly tax transparent. Investors are taxed directly and only on their share of the income and gains. In terms of the generic categories identified earlier they are unlisted and closed-ended.

A typical use of an LP would be for a group of investors wishing to share in the financing of a very large asset on a long-term basis. Historically, there was no SDLT charge on any transfers of shares in an LP, which also made it relatively inexpensive to restructure the ownership shares of LPs when the need arose. This changed at the end of 2004 when the then government introduced new rules making SDLT payable on such transfers. This somewhat reduced the popularity of LPs. Also, in the brief period between the new rules being announced and implemented, many institutional investors restructured their LPs and transferred several billion pounds of assets to offshore unit trusts to escape the SDLT liability. This episode is a good illustration of the sensitivity of indirect property investment structures to tax legislation.

Exchange traded funds (ETFs)

An ETF is a listed security that tracks the performance of an index or other basket of assets. The first ETF-like security appeared in the US in 1989. They are not a property-specific instrument but are used for tracking returns on a wide range of assets, including property shares.

An investor who, for example, wants to track the performance of the FTSE property share sub-sector could buy all the property shares comprising the sub-sector, in the right proportions, themselves. Alternatively they could buy units in a fund (possibly a unit trust operated by a fund manager) that holds all the underlying shares. In the first case, the investor has to do a lot of administration themselves, keeping the portfolio in line with the index. With a fund, the administration is done for them and the manager computes a daily price for the fund based on the market values of the underlying securities. The investor can buy into or sell out on a daily basis.

An ETF also holds all the underlying shares and is administered by a manager. But, because it is itself a listed security, the ETF can be traded at its market price, at any time on the stock exchange. The unique feature of the ETF structure is that it is a hybrid between open- and closed-ended vehicles. Large institutional investors buy or sell shares in the ETF directly with the manager (as with an open-ended unit trust). New shares in the ETF are created for them, usually in exchange for a contribution of the underlying securities comprising the index tracked by the ETF. These investors tend to be long-term ones.

For the majority of other investors the ETF is closed-ended, like any other listed company, and they buy their ETF shares in the secondary market. This mechanism provides liquidity and ensures that the NAV of the ETF tracks very closely the value of the underlying securities. The ETF combines the valuation features of a unit trust (pricing to NAV) with the liquidity of a listed closed-ended fund. Another benefit for investors is that the management fees charged to an ETF are much lower than those charged by a fund manager of an index tracking unit trust. Over a long period of ownership, this can make a significant difference to the investors' net of fees returns.

ETFs exist for tracking the performance of the property share sub-sectors in a number of markets. It should be remembered that although the NAV of the ETF will match that of the underlying property shares, those shares themselves may still be trading at a discount to the NAV of the properties they own. ETFs offer nothing as a holding vehicle for direct property assets, but they may be a more convenient way of investing in an entire listed property share sector.

Derivatives

Derivatives are not an investment vehicle in the usual sense. They provide another means of obtaining exposure to the risks and returns of an asset class, including property, without owning the underlying asset. They do offer the prospect of liquid access to the performance of the property market, as measured by an index such as the IPD Annual All Property Total Return Index.

The early use of derivative contracts for agricultural commodities was to reduce risk. These remain very important but in the modern era derivatives have come to be seen as associated more with financial products and speculation. The 1970s saw the development of currency and interest rate derivatives. Interest rate derivatives (of all types) are now the world's most widely traded derivative contracts. They remain a risk management tool but the presence of speculators (who want to increase, rather than reduce, their risk exposure), which has become increasingly controversial since the credit crunch of 2008, is essential to providing the liquidity that can be found in these markets.

Property derivatives have the potential to offer many of the features sought by investors:

- buy or sell property market risk, without trading the underlying assets;
- lower transaction costs than direct property;
- faster transactions;
- better liquidity;
- ability to go short as well as long.

Traditionally, working in the property industry involves dealing with the physical asset itself. But for those who work with property as one asset within a multi-asset portfolio, property risk can be regarded as just another risk to be traded in the markets like any other financial asset. Property derivatives are a logical response to this need. Attempts to introduce them in the UK go back to the 1980s. It was not until 2005 that the UK government lifted most of the regulatory restrictions on the development of a property derivatives market. Subsequently, the annual trading volume increased from £850 million in 2005 to £7.7 billion in 2008 (Figure 5.1). The period between 2005 and 2008 can therefore be considered as the first phrase of a new market in the UK (Baum 2009). Despite the effect of the current credit crunch (the trading volume dropped to £2.7 billion), the derivatives market in the UK is the largest and most liquid one in the world (IPF 2010).

Albeit the advantages of the derivatives market in the UK, many of the big direct property owners, who need to participate to provide liquidity, have been slow to sign off on the internal and regulatory approvals needed for their funds to use derivatives. Unlike their equity counterparts, the main commercial property indices are valuation based, rather than transaction price based and this too presents barriers to acceptance by some potential participants in the market. Pricing of property derivatives has involved much wider spreads than are found with interest rate and currency derivatives. The reasons for this are complex and largely related to the valuation-based nature of the IPD index. One attempt to address this problem is the FTSE UK Commercial Property Index (not to be confused with the FTSE EPRA/NAREIT Index, which tracks the UK listed property share sector). This index is a commercial venture between FTSE and a company that runs a portfolio of UK property assets (mostly holdings in a spread of professional investor-only indirect property

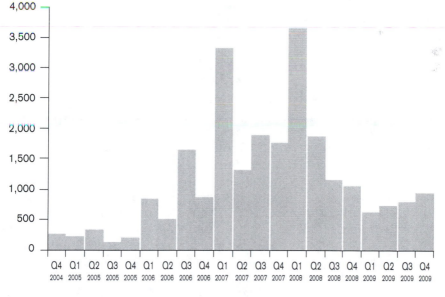

Figure 5.1

IPD quarterly property derivatives trading volumes (IPD 2010: 2)

vehicles, giving it exposure to a share of about £50 billion of assets). Because this is an investable portfolio (which the IPD index is not) and the holdings in it have daily prices (albeit derived from valuations of the underlying assets), swap contracts written against it have much narrower spreads than IPD index swaps.

Although the market has been slow to grow, it does offer the ability to trade property investment risk on a limited scale. There remains a high level of interest in the market by the sort of participants (institutional property investors, investment banks and brokers) that are essential to its long-term development. It is still a market with potential and many of the players have stuck with it despite it not developing as quickly as many would like.

Securitised loans

No discussion about indirect property ownership would be complete without contrasting equity and debt. As explained earlier, indirect property ownership usually refers to investing in some sort of structure that gives exposure to the equity risk of property. The investor buys into a fund and participates in the ups and downs of both the income and the capital value. But debt is a very important feature of the financing of the commercial property market.

There are many investors who want to invest in the debt risk of property. In other words, in normal language they want to lend money against the asset. As debt investors, they do not expect to participate in the profits and losses, as would an equity investor, but to receive interest and at some point get back their original capital. It could be argued that this is not a property investment, but just a loan. However, debt providers in the property market (typically banks) perform much of the same due diligence on the assets they are lending against as do equity investors. In normal market conditions, providing debt capital is a lower risk proposition. There is no share in the profits but the equity capital gives the debt some protection from loss.

To diversify their risks many investors would like to invest in not just one property loan but in a spread of loans made against a diversified portfolio of properties. A popular way of doing this, before the credit crunch, was the commercial mortgage backed security (CMBS). CMBS is the product of securitisation whereby a portfolio of property loans is turned into bonds that can be traded as listed securities. More specifically, in the early 2000s, the use of securitised debt, as an alternative to a bank loan, became popular with some investors. Rather than borrowing from a bank, a securitised loan (CMBS) involves packaging the debt as tradable bonds to be sold to investors. It gives the borrower direct access to the public capital markets, rather than relying solely on a banking relationship.

The banks themselves, whilst still lending conventionally, also used securitisation. They packaged many individual real estate loans they had made into a bond issue and sold it to investors. The proceeds from the sale could be used to make further loans. This was profitable because they could finance a securitisation issue at a lower cost than the loans made to their own customers. Typically securitised loans may be invested in by different classes of bondholders with different rights and objectives, thereby widening the sources of funding for borrowers.

It was no coincidence, in the run up to the credit crunch, that commercial property values enjoyed a sustained period of growth at the same time as the CMBS markets were also booming. The growth in the availability of debt revealed that the value of property cannot be looked at in isolation from what is happening in the debt markets. Property values are driven by the cost and availability of debt as much as by the cost and availability of equity.

What is more, in the light of the subsequent fall in property values, it can be seen that once a loan is 'under water', in the parlance of the market, it looks a lot more like equity than debt. With the protection of a layer of equity capital, debt investors can reasonably expect their low-risk investment to deliver a fixed income return. Once the equity has been wiped out and asset values have declined, to below the level of the debt, the only hope for the debt investor to get their capital back is for prices to rise again.

By 2011, property financing was entering a new place. Many owners found it impossible to refinance maturing loans taken out prior to the credit crunch. Following declines in values and loan write-downs, there remained a gap between what banks were prepared to lend out and what equity investors needed to borrow. This prompted the emergence of many new funds, set up to fill the gap, by providing senior and mezzanine debt to property owners.

However, securitisation also means that the role of place/location is undercut:

> Financial deregulation and increasing securitization of real estate removes owners from actual structures and moves locally determined value away from underlying property. Determining a property's true value requires detailed knowledge of the local real estate market. Distant capitalists will only invest if the property is recognisable beyond its unique character embedded in space and if it can provide short-term returns. When these conditions are met, the particularity of a building is transformed into the uniformity of a financial 'instrument' and place becomes subordinated to 'a higher realm of ordering beyond territorialism: speed'.
>
> (Douglas 1999: 146)

This has potential serious consequences not only for financial sustainability but also for social disruption as a result. Added to this, the 'distance' will also impact on the levels of responsibility felt towards efficiencies within the building itself.

Summary

There are a wide variety of indirect property investment vehicles for equity and debt investors. The diversity of the market can be quite bewildering, the detail of individual structures very complex. Looked at in general terms, these structures have one or more of the following characteristics:

- simplified administration of a portfolio of assets;
- better diversification than holding individual assets;
- better liquidity than individual assets;
- returns (for equity investors) in line with direct property;
- tax features (may be positive or negative).

None provide investors with all the features they would like. In fact it can be a complex process to decide which structure is best, to meet the objectives of a particular investor. The decision has to take into account (1) who the investor is, (2) where they are investing from (i.e. their own tax residence), (3) where they are investing into and (4) what their investment goals are. Chapter 7 considers how investors actually make these decisions.

It is in this context that consideration of sustainability and sustainable practices by owners of property (both direct and indirect) is to be viewed. It is not a simple matter of an owner (freeholder) fitting a building's features and facilities into its sustainable vision and encouraging the occupier (leaseholder) to use the building in a sustainable manner. Because ownership is, in many cases, separated from management and control, the decision to find sustainable solutions is not a unilateral one. It may involve many different parties with various agendas.

6 Sustainability

··

Introduction

With the pressure from findings on climate change, and the fact that 40 per cent of total CO_2 emissions are contributed from the built environment (RICS 2010), sustainability is another element that needs to be taken into the decision-making process. During the course of the last two chapters, emphasis has been placed on the complexities involved in the nature of the real estate market and the manner in which real estate is held (either directly or indirectly). The chapters have highlighted the significance of externalities to the impact on decision making. This chapter starts to look at how sustainability is being integrated into that decision making, moving from a position as an externality (a regulatory imposition) itself to finding ways in which it can contribute to the business case for real estate activities (a net contributor to profitability).

Changing patterns

Sustainability has enjoyed a growing media profile in recent years. Studies concerning sustainability have been conducted over a number of years through a series of national and international reports including, notably:

- report of the World Commission on Environment and Development in 1987 (The Brundtland Report);
- reports of the Intergovernmental Panel on Climate Change (IPCC) from 1990 onwards;
- the Stern Review on the Economics of Climate Change 2006.

In the UK, a number of organisations have responded to these studies positively by making public commitments to sustainability. A survey of corporate real estate (CRE) leaders in 2010 by JLL and CoreNet found that respondents were in favour of sustainable buildings. For example:

- 64 per cent of the respondents considered sustainability as a critical business issue;
- 92 per cent considered sustainability criteria in their location decisions;
- the number of respondents willing to pay more for green leased space jumped from 37 per cent in 2009 to 50 per cent in 2010;
- 87 per cent look at energy labels in administering their portfolios;
- 48 per cent were willing to pay a premium of up to 10 per cent for sustainable space;
- 49 per cent are implementing a sustainability related workplace strategy project, and 48 per cent are collecting sustainability data;
- CRE executives are highly involved in providing sustainability performance data and funding sustainability oriented investment to reduce cost and increase employee satisfaction (JLL 2011).

As stated in the earlier chapter, the regulatory framework is undergoing rapid change to provide a mix of compulsory and persuasive reasons for property developers and owners to change their behaviour. These legislative changes do not single out the property industry. They are part of a broad sweep of legislation aimed at achieving sustainability goals across the whole economy. Property plays a very big part in this, because it makes such a large contribution to the use of energy in the economy, CO_2 emissions and the production of pollutants. There is a constant stream of new legislation addressing sustainability. Some is aimed at implementing specific initiatives (e.g. the CRC Energy Efficiency Scheme). But legislation is also being used to encourage wholesale change in the way organisations think about resource allocation decisions. For example legislative changes in recent years have included:

- Planning and Compulsory Purchase Act 2004 s39(2). This requires planning authorities to exercise their power with the objective of contributing to the achievement of sustainable development.
- Companies Act 2006 s172. This requires directors to have regard (amongst other matters) to the impact of the company's operations on the community and the environment.

These are general directives but they emphasise the need to take sustainability into account in decision-making processes. In the case of companies, this is a specific requirement to have regard to externalities in making decisions, which might otherwise have been considered on the basis of the impact on profit alone. The planning system, on the other hand, has long had a role in ensuring that the interests of a wider society are taken into account in land use decisions. This change broadens that remit.

What is different about the sustainability agenda is the magnitude and timescale of the changes it requires. If the goals are to be met, then owners of existing buildings need to be persuaded (through a mixture of incentives or coercion) to retrospectively upgrade their properties. The Energy Act 2011 provides a legislative framework whereby, through secondary regulations, it may be possible in future for the government to compel property owners to install energy saving measures in existing buildings.

The Energy Act 2011 has three principal objectives: (1) to tackle barriers to investment in energy efficiency, (2) to enhance energy security and (3) to enable investment in low carbon energy supplies. The act affects all real estate although it includes the Green Deal, which is particularly aimed at achieving efficiency improvements in domestic buildings that account for the majority of the building stock in the UK. From 2018 onwards, it will require a minimum level of energy efficiency before any property (including commercial) can be let.

Legislative changes can only achieve so much. Changing attitudes can achieve a great deal more. Property owners and occupiers who have accepted the case for sustainability can make a difference through their actions. This is particularly so for organisations with a large presence in the market. They have the opportunity to both change their own behaviour and use their position to influence that of their suppliers and customers.

Sustainable development

Measures such as the planning system and building regulations represent part of the coercion end of the policy mix. All developers and owners of real property have to comply with them. Even where they increase the cost of building and operating property, without a commensurate increase in the private financial return, there is no competitive disadvantage relative to other property owners. They too, have to incur the costs involved in meeting the standards.

At the other end of the scale, the best *incentive* for a property owner to change the way they develop or operate property is one that makes change more profitable than the status quo. This highlights one of the problems faced, in the early years of the second decade of the twenty-first century, of getting property developers and owners to provide a product that, from a sustainability perspective, exceeds the minimum requirements of the planning system and building regulations. Therefore, this chapter examines the sustainability development issues from both the demand and supply sides.

From the demand side

Property developers and owners that seek to earn a financial return on their investment are in similar positions. They need to construct and maintain buildings to meet the needs of the prospective tenants who will pay them rent. They are also looking to preserve and enhance the capital value of the asset by ensuring that it remains attractive to prospective purchasers, possibly years after the original construction date. The distinction between occupiers and owners is important. They do not necessarily have the same objectives.

Occupiers are more likely to be focused on their own occupational requirements yet less likely to have a specialist understanding of property and not always be skilled at specifying exactly what they want. Owners, particularly the investment driven financial institutions, will understand property very well and have an eye on more than just the needs of the current tenant. If they are involved in the development process, as many institutional owners are, this may lead them to seek a higher specification building to meet a wide range of needs. They have to achieve a careful balance between marketability, current cost and long-term value.

In a market economy, successful providers of products and services (whether these are consumables or assets such as buildings) are those that achieve a profitable alignment of the resources of their business with the needs of their customers. They make money out of delivering what their customers want. Unfortunately, determining what customers want is rarely as simple as just asking and hoping for a straightforward answer. Good marketing involves identifying needs (which may not be obvious, even to the customer) and coming up with ways of meeting them. For the real estate adviser, this could be a proactive and directive role based on an understanding of the structure of a client's business aligned with future prospective changes to that business and the regulatory framework within which it operates.

The result may be an improvement on an existing product or service, or something entirely new that no one had thought of providing before. It can be a long, difficult and expensive process and will not always produce the right answer. Among the spectacularly successful products of which we are all aware, it is easy to forget that thousands of ideas also fail every year.

Even a cursory look around a dynamic urban environment, such as the City of London, reveals that the quality and specification of buildings change substantially over time. These reflect developments in technology, changing owner and occupier requirements and development of the planning and building regulations. The City contains many buildings that are hundreds of years old and still in use in some form. But one does not have to look back that far to see major changes. A mostly low-rise environment throughout history, it began to change with the advent of the first high-rise office building in the 1950s. Since then the skyline has changed dramatically as the number and height of tall buildings has continued to increase.

Taller buildings arose to meet the growing demands for office space in the City, as the UK economy finally recovered from the austerity of the post-war years. Their specification was poor by today's standards. Yet they were built because there was identifiable occupier demand for them. Remarkably they became functionally obsolete far more quickly than many of the much older low-rise buildings.

By the end of the twentieth century, many of the earliest office towers had been demolished or at least substantially redeveloped. They had had a lifespan of less than 50 years. They became obsolete because they no longer met or could be adapted to meet changing tenant requirements. Some had mid-life refurbishments to install facilities such as air-conditioning and double glazing, but these still left them as a second best option compared with newer buildings. The section of London Wall running from Aldersgate Street in the west to Moorgate in the east, for example, was the site of a number of high-rise office developments in the 1950s. Some remain as substantially refurbished buildings, others have been demolished and redeveloped.

From the supply side

As a market changes, owners of individual buildings are faced, from time to time, with decision points. In the light of the competitive position of their building and their assessment of its future prospects, they have to make decisions such as sell or retain, refurbish or redevelop. At some point in the process, particularly if a decision involves capital expenditure, there will be a financial appraisal of the options. Using estimated projections of future cash flows this will seek to show the best course of action.

From a purely financial perspective this will be the option that produces the highest risk-adjusted financial rate of return. The analysis will be based on the private costs to the investor. The dilemma for the investor is that it is impossible to predict the long-term path of many influences on an investment, yet the decision may involve the commitment of long-term capital, with returns being earned over many years.

This is no more so than in the case of a decision to develop or redevelop a property. A property development is profitable if the value of the completed project exceeds the cost of developing it. The end value and the development cost are both large numbers with a high degree of uncertainty, affected by many variables. As the difference between these numbers, the profit can be extremely sensitive to relatively small changes in either. An over-run on development costs or a move in market yields or rents for the completed project can make the difference between losing and making a great deal of money.

With risks like this, developers do not want to spend on features for which there is no evidence of market demand. In the City once air-conditioning became popular with tenants and a feature for which they were prepared to pay a higher rent, developers included it within new schemes. Buildings that meet the highest current standards are also easier to finance and/or sell on to the ultimate investor/owner who is looking for an asset that will produce a secure revenue stream over many years. The provision of air-conditioning may not have been necessary to meet building regulations (even if some form of mechanical ventilation was), but it was a case of the market demanding a higher standard than the minimum set by them.

It is this issue that highlights a problem faced by legislators and regulators in trying to encourage the adoption of sustainable practices in the development and operation of property. A supplier is likely to say no if asked to supply a product that provides, at extra cost, features that exceed any legal requirement, yet offers no additional benefit for which customers are prepared to pay.

This problem has led to initiatives such as the efforts by IPD to create an index of sustainable property performance. The intention is to show up any differences in the private financial rate of return between conventional buildings and sustainable ones (IPF 2009). Until occupiers show sufficient preference for sustainable buildings over non-sustainable ones, to lead to a measurable difference in rents, it is unlikely that sustainability will show up positively in investment performance statistics (see Chapter 7 for more details).

Nevertheless, there are strong arguments to suggest that, even though the current occupier market is unwilling to fully reflect the long-term benefits of sustainable features in buildings, this may be set to change. With the legislative framework changing, general sentiment in the institutional investment market changing and the perceptions of many multinationals changing, developing the minimum may end up providing the minimum return.

This is not a new problem for developers; after all the market is constantly renewing itself and standards and expectations change over time. However, ultimately their response will be shaped by the nature of their business and their relationship to the landowner. Some operate as developers/traders. They identify a requirement, build and let it and then sell it on. Others are developer/ investors. They retain completed developments as investments in their own portfolio. The developer/trader may have less incentive to look beyond the immediate marketability of the product. Once it is sold (although customers for the completed development may be motivated by longer term issues) it is no longer their concern.

Development requires both specialist skills and access to the risk capital needed to finance a project through to completion and sale. Pure developers may have less ready access to capital than landowners, whereas landowners may lack the specialist skills. So whilst there are substantial pure developers with the ability to take on major projects, it is often the case that they will work with landowners.

Wilkinson *et al.* (2008) identify three categories of landowner:

- *Traditional landowners* – These include the Church and the Crown Estate who have interests in ownership that extend beyond the purely financial.
- *Industrial landowners* – These own land because it is ancillary to their main purpose. It includes, for example, manufacturers who own property because it houses the manufacturing facilities for the products they produce. Their main focus is the product. The property is a means to an end.
- *Financial landowners* – These own land as an investment and expect to earn a financial return from it. Major property companies and financial institutions such as insurance companies and pension funds fall into this category. These are also known as institutional investors.

Landowners in any of the above categories may also develop from time to time, with their motives shaped by the nature of their ownership. But few, especially outside the financial sector, maintain significant in-house development expertise.

In relation to sustainable development, it is the financial landowners who possibly have the greatest incentive to look beyond merely meeting current regulations. They are in the business of creating a financial asset that will maintain its value for years into the future. But, even without sustainability as a factor, the involvement of institutional investors or financial landowners in development highlights the sometimes conflicting needs of occupiers and investors. Investors want buildings that appeal to as wide a range of occupiers as possible. This can lead to overspecification (and a less sustainable solution) and occupiers having to compromise on their requirements. The differences are possibly more apparent in the case of office developments, where the needs of occupiers vary greatly. In the City of London, for example, it is difficult to reconcile the requirements of a bank for a large open-plan dealing floor with those of a law firm requiring a lot of private spaces.

Further thoughts

Does sustainability just add to this problem by driving financial investors to yet further increasing specifications, to protect future value, or can it be part of an approach that reduces costs? It is possible that it could go either way. Taking the example of air conditioning again. It could be argued that the growth in provision of air conditioning in City offices was both a response to increased tenant demand and also a response to demand from investors for features that would preserve the long-term value of buildings.

From the early 1980s onwards, the cost of computing power began to fall to the point at which it was economic to provide a computer for everyone in an office. This led to many changes in work patterns including the spread of email and the end of the typing pool. It also led to a lot more heat being generated, and it was not just the banks with large trading floors full of computer screens that faced this problem. Increasing numbers of tenants wanted to keep cool in a way that was more effective than just opening the window. Air conditioning was usually the solution.

It added to construction costs and was more costly to operate, and it was less environmentally sustainable. But plenty of tenants were prepared to pay the extra rent that air-conditioned buildings commanded. For technology intensive ones, which included many of the biggest space users in the City, there was probably no alternative. Investors who financed City office developments wanted to be sure that the buildings they owned remained attractive to as wide a range of users as possible. Many older buildings were refurbished and retrofitted with air conditioning to preserve their operational life.

Where does this leave developers? To what extent should they try to anticipate future requirements, rather than just meeting current ones, when fixing the specification for a new building? The answer to this question depends on the extent to which investors influence the design of the end product. In the City of London, office development is very much influenced by relationships with investors. In fact large developments anywhere, in any sector, are likely to involve investors at an early stage. It is investor/developers who often carry out the largest projects. As well as being the end buyer for a scheme they want to participate in the substantial, but higher risk, development profits that are possible. Some institutional investors may run their own development teams. Others partner with specialist developers from the start.

In these circumstances the investors are closely involved in deciding the specification from the start. In dealing with sustainability issues the problem is essentially the same as it has always been. The lowest standard to build to is the greater of the minimum statutory requirement, and the specification that the occupational and investment markets are prepared to pay for. Any provision above this level (involving additional costs) requires a judgement about what both statutory and market demands may be in the future. Past experience indicates that statutory requirements will continue to become more onerous. Occupiers' needs will also change, but in each case is it realistic to make assumptions today about what those may be in 10, let alone 20, years? Perhaps it is not about providing presumed future requirements today, but trying to build in some flexibility such that a building may be more easily refurbished and recycled at some point.

As noted earlier, it has generally been the case that, once constructed, a building does not have to be kept up to date with changing building regulations. It is only when new works are contemplated for an existing building that those have to meet current standards. However this is beginning to change. The Green Deal is clearly aimed at older buildings, not the ones being constructed now, but it does show how the regulatory landscape is shifting. Further similar changes are possible. As standards continue to improve, for how long will today's sustainable buildings continue to be regarded as such into the future?

Whatever the answer, it is likely that the growing need for sustainability will shift the decision points in the building lifecycle, about whether or when to refurbish or redevelop. The effect on different property types will vary.

Large, complex structures such as City office buildings and shopping centres involve huge capital investment. Typically they would be expected to be among the longest lived structures. The lifespan of many City office buildings, constructed since the 1950s, however, has been less than 50 years:

- *Bucklersbury House, Queen Victoria Street* – Completed in 1958, with the addition of Temple Court in 1962. Vacated in 2007 with a view to demolition and redevelopment with an increase in floor space.

- *Citypoint, Ropemaker Street* – Completed in 1967 as Britannic House and the headquarters of BP. Substantially refurbished from 1998 to 2000, with a small increase in height and the addition of floor space at the lower levels.
- *Stock Exchange Tower, Old Broad Street* – Completed in 1970. Substantially refurbished from 2004 to 2007. Re-clad and floor plates extended. Additional floor space added in a new, low-rise extension.
- *Broadgate Estate, Liverpool Street* – Completed in 1985. 2004–06 further development. 2011 new, larger replacement for some existing buildings gains planning approval.

Even though illustrated above is only a small sample of City offices, it does indicate something of the dynamic nature of that market. Two points stand out. First, all the subsequent refurbishments or redevelopments involved providing additional floor space over the original building. This would have been a key part of their financial viability. Second, the time period between construction and a later refurbishment or redevelopment has shortened. Bucklersbury House was scheduled for demolition after 50 years. Citypoint and the Stock Exchange Tower both underwent major refurbishment at around 30 years of age. At Broadgate demolition is planned of some original buildings after only 25 years (to be replaced by larger new buildings).

Sustainable development case study

Background

Central St Giles in London is a 500,000 square foot mixed-use commercial and residential development on the edge of Covent Garden, completed in 2010. It is an example of current ideas on sustainable development in action (see Illustration 6.1 for photos of the development). The building itself has been assessed as Excellent by the Building Research Establishment Environmental Assessment Method (BREEAM). This places its sustainability performance in the top 10 per cent of new non-domestic buildings in the UK, representing current best practice. Features that have contributed to this include:

- 80 per cent of heating generated from renewable sources;
- 60 per cent of rainwater is collected and reused;
- 100 per cent of cooling tower water discharged is reused;
- 90 per cent of demolition materials were recycled;
- 15 per cent of recycled materials were used in construction;
- over 200 bicycle spaces with lockers.

Legal and General (L&G) who, with their joint venture partner Mitsubishi Estate Company, commissioned Central St Giles, have stated a belief that a sustainable approach to their business will deliver enhanced return to their investors.

Illustration 6.1

Photos of Central St Giles in London

Reflection on the case study

As indicated by the BREEAM Excellent rating, the development achieved a high standard for sustainable building design, construction and operation. The commitment to a long-term involvement in supporting a local school met social objectives. This support included material and practical help in refitting some of the spaces in the school, such as the main hall. But it also involved staff of the joint venture partners providing their time and expertise on a continuing basis to support the school's activities. The community involvement was of immediate value to the school. It also helped the project to be seen by children, parents and teachers as something positive for and part of the local community, rather than just a development that occupied space in the community without belonging to it.

A building that sits comfortably within its surroundings, rather than being in conflict with them, is more likely to maintain its economic value over a longer period of time. It achieves the goal of making both a wider social contribution and providing a better financial return to the owners. Experience with the scheme also provides the owners with an important example for future projects designed to meet their wider sustainability goals, rather than purely financial ones. These include how they were able to use the project to provide opportunities for staff community involvement and as a learning exercise in how a sustainable approach can produce a winning solution for more than just the investors.

L&G sees that 'investing in an environmentally and socially sustainable portfolio of property is a core element of business success' (L&G 2011: 3). This case study demonstrates how a major institutional investor in a joint venture can acknowledge the role of each of the three elements of sustainability (i.e. economic, social and environmental) in a high-profile scheme in the centre of one of London's premier commercial districts.

Summary

Property development is a high risk activity that has always involved making careful assessments about the value of what the market (both occupiers and potential investors) wants compared to the cost of providing it. The requirements of sustainability look set to influence the points in a building's life when decisions are made to refurbish or redevelop. Investors are concerned about the higher cost of developing sustainable buildings and the effect on the value of existing properties that are not sustainable.

They are worried about the 'accelerated depreciation' of older buildings and whether they will be worth refurbishing at all or will have to be redeveloped sooner than previously expected. In the absence, so far, of conclusive evidence that sustainable buildings deliver better investment performance than non-sustainable ones, there is still some way to go in getting the attitudinal changes needed to create a fully sustainable built environment. It is clear that legislative changes can only achieve so much and that inherent behaviour also needs to change. This is beginning to happen as many of the largest investors/developers and tenants are not only making a commitment to sustainability but are also using their position to influence their own suppliers and customers.

7 Property investment decisions

∙∙

Introduction

Growth in the use of financing techniques from the securities markets and the integration of real estate within the global capital markets means that interests in property can be financed with a mixture of debt and equity from a wider variety of sources than was once possible.

This enables the returns from property to be sliced up into many different pieces, each with its own risk/return characteristic (dependent upon but not necessarily the same as the return on the underlying asset). This is far removed from the conventional idea of a single investor making a direct investment in a freehold interest with no borrowing. Now, the equity might be provided by a fund with several investors, while the debt (sourced through a bank) is securitised and sold in different tranches to many bond holders (see Chapter 5 for more details).

The positive outcome of this process is that it widens the sources of capital available for property investment and enables many different participants in the market. A disadvantage is that it is easier to lose sight of what is driving the performance when investment is in a piece of financing or a fund that is several layers removed from the underlying assets. Therefore, this chapter explores how investors make decisions and the criteria or benchmarks that they use in their decision-making process.

Risk and return

One of the key issues in the financial field concerns the influence of the risk of an investment on its expected returns (Perold 2004). Before the 1950s, risk was either assumed away or treated qualitatively. It was not until 1952 when Harry Markowitz introduced portfolio theory that efforts were made to quantify the impact of risks. Over the past few decades, researchers in capital markets have developed capital market theory to demonstrate how investors should organise assets in a portfolio to meet their investment objectives.

On the basis of portfolio theory, researchers also argued that all specific and unsystematic risks associated with individual assets should be diversified away in a completely diversified portfolio. However, every individual risky asset will also be affected by some general factors like macroeconomic issues, which cannot be diversified away and remain in the portfolio. These are known as systematic risks. If an investor wants to add a risky asset to a fully diversified portfolio, it is only the systematic risk of the asset that should be considered rather than the total risk (i.e. both systematic and unsystematic risks) of that individual asset. Subsequently, the Capital Asset Pricing Model (CAPM) was introduced by Sharpe (1964) to price risky assets and enable investors to determine returns on any risky assets.

He recommends using the Beta (ß) coefficient of an asset to measure the systematic risk of any individual asset that is to be added to a portfolio. This calculates the responsiveness of an asset to the movements in the market portfolio, and can be expressed as follows:

$$\text{ß}_i = \frac{\text{Cov}(R_i, R_m)}{\sigma^2(R_m)} \qquad \text{(Equation 1)}$$

where: $\sigma^2(R_m)$ = variance of the market portfolio on
$Cov(R_i, R_m)$ = covariance between return on the security i & on the market portfolio

Since the systematic risk of each individual asset can be calculated by its Beta coefficient, it is possible to determine the expected rate of return from that asset. CAPM describes the relationship between the Beta coefficient and the expected return as follows:

$$\bar{R}_i = R_F + \text{ß}^* (\bar{R}_m - R_F) \qquad \text{(Equation 2)}$$

where: $\bar{R}_i$ = Expected return on security i
R_F = Risk free rate; $ß$ = Beta of the security
$\bar{R}_m - R_F$ = Difference between expected return on market and risk free rate

As far as property investment is concerned, although property has some specific features, such as heterogeneity and fixed location, illiquidity, etc., which distinguishes it from other assets, it is an investment asset class alongside shares and bonds, and should not be treated in isolation from other assets (Hoesli et al. 2000). Understanding property investment in a capital market framework is therefore an important feature of investment advice (Hoesli et al. 2000 and Coleman et al. 1994). Brown et al. (2000) further specify that the systematic and specific risk of a property investment can be explained as follows (Table 7.1).

Table 7.1   Decomposition of property risk into systematic and specific risk (adapted from Brown *et al.* 2000: 268)

Systematic risk	Specific risk
General economic condition Taxation	Tenant Location Constructional aspects Building quality Legal constraints Depreciation

Efficient market hypothesis

Both portfolio theory and CAPM have been developed on the assumption that prices reflect all knowable information (Reilly *et al.* 1999). 'An economy is efficient when it provides its consumers with the most desired set of goods and services, given the resources and technology of the economy. Researchers are centrally concerned with the concept of allocative efficiency or efficiency (sometime called Pareto efficiency or Pareto optimality)' (Samuelson *et al.* 2001: 157).

However, unlike the economic term, an efficient capital market normally refers to informationally efficient. Fama (1970: 383) suggests that 'a market in which prices always fully reflect available information is called efficient'. In testing the notion that the price of a security at any point in time fully reflects all available information, Fama (1970) allocates empirical findings into three classifications of efficiency, i.e. weak form, semi-strong form and strong form EMH.

The weak form EMH assumes the information set reflects historical prices, the semi-strong form EMH concerns information that is publicly available, while the strong form EMH considers any information that relates to prices. In considering the efficiency of capital markets, Fama (1970: 383) further concludes that 'there is no important evidence against the hypothesis in the weak and semi-strong form tests ... and only limited evidence against the hypothesis in the strong form test'. That is, evidence from different capital markets supports both weak form and semi-strong form EMH, but not strong form EMH (Ross *et al.* 1999).

In the property market, investors have claimed that imperfect features of property markets, such as illiquidity, indivisibility and high transaction costs, have enabled them to consistently earn abnormal returns. Property markets are thus commonly recognised as being informationally inefficient by researchers and professionals (Gau 1987, Gatzlaff *et al.* 1995, Brown *et al.* 2000 and Ball *et al.* 1998). Property market imperfections might be a source of market inefficiency. However, it is important to distinguish between efficient markets and perfect markets. As long as the imperfect features of property markets can be fully reflected in the market price, a property market could still be efficient (Gatzlaff *et al*. 1995, Brown 1985 and Brown *et al*. 2000). Empirical tests of return behaviour could thus be the way to answer the question of property market efficiency (Gau 1987).

Because of the importance of market efficiency to investors, a large number of studies have been carried out in capital markets. As far as income-producing property is concerned, previous studies have acknowledged that such investments are less efficient than other capital markets, such as stock markets (Gau 1984, 1985, Brown 1985, McIntosh *et al*. 1989 and Gatzlaff *et al*. 1995). Brown *et al*. (2000) and Brown (1991) further point out that the serial dependence between successive periods in the UK property market weakens when the observation intervals increase. In other words, the UK property market is efficient once annual data is adopted.

Price, value and worth

As discussed earlier, real estate has some special characteristics, such as heterogeneity, lack of transparency, limited numbers of transactions and illiquidity. These characteristics make direct comparison with the capital market more difficult. Because of the nature of property and its relative illiquidity it is important to distinguish between three related concepts, namely price, market value and worth (Ball *et al*. 1998 and Baum *et al*. 2008).

- 'Market price is simply the observed exchange price for a property' (Ball *et al*. 1998: 283).
- However, market value is specifically defined in the RICS Valuation Standards – Global and UK (the 'Red Book') as 'the estimated amount for which an asset or liability should exchange on the valuation date between a willing buyer and a willing seller in an arm's-length transaction after proper marketing and where the parties had each acted knowledgeably, prudently and without compulsion' (RICS 2012: 30).
- As far as worth (also known as investment value) is concerned, this is defined as 'the value of an asset to a particular owner or a prospective owner, for individual investment or operational objectives' (RICS 2012: 32).

So to clarify: 'Market price is the recorded consideration paid for a property. *Valuation* [or value] is the estimate of the most likely selling price, the assessment of which is the most common objective of the valuer. *Worth* is the underlying investment value. ... individual worth is the maximum bid price of an individual purchaser who takes account of all available information in an efficient manner'(Baum *et al*. 1996: 37).

This suggests that, when making any investment decision, investors will examine the worth from such a project (to either compare with internal targets or to compare with an asking price in the market place). The problem here is that unlike the stock market, there is no central trading market for property investment, and trades occur much less frequently than share trading. Property portfolio decisions are usually, therefore, made on the basis of valuations rather than prices.

Accordingly, it is important to clarify whether valuation can be used as a proxy for price (Hoesli *et al.* 2000, Ball *et al.* 1998, Brown *et al.* 2000 and Brown 1991). To answer this question, existing studies do suggest that in general, market valuation can proxy prices in the UK (Brown *et al.* 2000), and especially between 1975 and 1980, prices were able to explain approximately 99 per cent of their valuations (Brown 1991). RICS (2009a) comments that in 2008, approximately 60 per cent of the sold properties were within +/– 10 per cent of their preceding market adjusted valuation. This reflects a 9.6 per cent average weighted absolute difference between sale price and market adjusted valuation.

Property indices and performance benchmarks

In a competitive market, it is necessary to have a benchmark to evaluate performance of either an investor or a fund manager. Existing financial models, such as CAPM, make this possible, because it relates to the overall market and provides guidance towards the level of return that should be achieved. CAPM has also been instrumental in shaping the way of thinking about the relationship between risk and return amongst financial economists. 'Objectives are set relative to a benchmark either of competitors or of the market. This approach ... has come to dominate property investment in the UK since the late 1980s' (Hoesli *et al.* 2000: 143). Nowadays, 'the IPD index is generally regarded as the target to beat' (Brown *et al.* 2000: 578).

Property fund managers tend to use this as a benchmark to monitor their performance either out- or underperforming against the market (Isaac *et al.* 2011). In general, there is no strong evidence suggesting that property fund managers in the UK can systematically outperform, and only a small number of them can sustain such a good performance over a certain period of time (IPF 2008). Xu *et al.* (2007) also report that the performance of the Shanghai prime office market between 1995 and 2004 was not consistent with the level of return that would be expected using CAPM.

Modelling and indexing performance in the capital markets over the last 50 years has tended to accelerate the maths process in decision making, perhaps at the expense of other dimensions to investment advice and management. Latterly, however, individual and market behaviours have received some attention in attempting to explain anomalies, which do not seem to fit into 'rationality'. These will be considered more fully in the next chapter. However, what is also forming part of this 'rational' debate in property markets (as part of the overall financial market) is to what extent sustainable features of property assets are influencing values.

Sustainability tools

In terms of impact on market value, there is currently evidence to support the notion that sustainability credentials add value. The RICS states that 'for now, the value and sustainability link is argued strongly in theory and in opinion, but in terms of hard evidence, it is very limited and restricted to rental differentiation within a tight geographical area and within one sub-sector of the market' (RICS 2010: 8). This suggests that whilst most commentators believe that sustainable buildings should have a higher value than standard buildings, there is currently no real evidence to support this. This section therefore reviews some existing studies that consider whether sustainability can add value to property investment.

The sustainable property appraisal project

Ellison *et al.* (2006: 5) set up the Sustainable Property Appraisal Project, with the objectives of 'providing property investors and occupiers with a system for reflecting sustainability within the appraisal of commercial property assets'. For this, tools were developed to incorporate the sustainability element of a building into a calculation of worth. The specific instruments used were a questionnaire, an appraisal tool, and data from which were fed into a framework to create property investment indexation.

The process was premised on identifying relationships between sustainability criteria, functional performance and worth variables. In this case the sustainability criteria were principally building quality and adaptability, accessibility, energy efficiency, pollutants, waste and water management facilities, occupier satisfaction and impact. These criteria were matched with the worth variables of cash flow, rental growth rate, depreciation rates and risk premium.

Investors were asked to rank the sustainability criteria in terms of their significance in calculating the worth of the property investment to them. Occupiers were asked to rank these same criteria in terms of their importance to their real estate decisions. This enabled the relationships between sustainability factors and variables to be analysed and evaluated in order to assess the likely impact on value and worth. These were then weighted. These relationships will, of course, vary over time, location and type of property. However, they do indicate relative weightings of individual factors and are a basis for more extensive and intensive study.

Using a simple example (Illustration 7.1), loosely derived from the Sustainability Property Appraisal Project, it is possible to demonstrate the potential impact that such an approach could have on the investment worth of an asset. The subject property is a ten-year-old standard office building located in the centre of a provincial town, close to a train station and motorway network connections. For the purposes of this example, the following facts are relevant:

- good general accessibility for a variety of modes of transport;
- limited ability to adapt the building;
- no energy efficiency features in place;
- no waste or water management features in place.

The intention of this example is to demonstrate that sustainable impacts can be factored into the valuation process. They are shown here simplistically and for illustration only. For example, a short-cut DCF has been used to derive worth, whereas this would normally be calculated through a long-form DCF. Also more sophisticated models can be developed to enable scenario testing. The point is that valuers can use such models within existing frameworks by treating sustainability alongside any other risks. There is some correlation between these criteria and 'the sustainability aspects that are most likely to impact on investor considerations' (RICS 2009b: 18). The RICS Valuation Information Paper 13 highlights these as follows:

- the impact of increasing operational costs, including energy, on rental growth and net income;
- the ability of the building to retain tenant demand and the likelihood of voids;
- the failure to meet changing environmental and social standards, meaning shorter refurbishment and/or redevelopment cycles and faster obsolescence; and
- for some specialist investors, the ability of the property to provide external benefits.

(RICS 2009b: 18)

However, this Valuation Paper also says that 'if, at the date of valuation, the market does not differentiate, in terms of either occupier or investor demand, between a building that displays strong sustainability credentials and one that does not, there will be no impact on value' (RICS 2009b: 16). The question here is the role of the property adviser. Most of the evidence seems to point to a significant benefit for both investors and occupiers of sustainable buildings. An occupier may enjoy a better image, reduced accommodation running costs, higher calibre staffing in healthier working environments and increased job satisfaction. Equally, the investor can benefit through higher, more sustained property values, better corporate image, lower property costs and lower voids (Schleich *et al.* 2009).

Illustration 7.1

An example showing sustainability impact on calculation of worth

1. Calculation does not take sustainability into account (MV of £1,357,000)

Information		Calculations		
1. Market rent (p.a.)	£88,000.00	Market rent	£88,000.00	
2. Market yield	7%	Capitalisation 5yrs @10.00%	4.10	
3. Void period (yr)	0	Void adjustment	1.00	**£360,817**
4. Rental growth	5%	Future market rent	£112,312.78	
5. Uncertainty factor	0.00%	YP perpetuity @ 7.00%	14.29	
6. Next rent review (yr)	5	Discount 5yrs @ 10.00%	0.621	**£996,249**
7. Target rate	10.00%	**Investment worth**	**£1,357,066**	

2. Calculation takes sustainability into account (MV of £1,285,000)

Sustainability criteria				
	Weighting (Sayce et al., 2004)	Impact area (i.e. the 4 principal worth variables identified in the information column in the table above)	Property assumptions*	Impact effect**
Accessibility	1.00	2, 4	1.25	1.25
Adaptability	0.80	1, 2, 4, 7	0.60	0.48
Occupier satisfaction	0.70	1, 2, 4	0.90	0.63
Pollutants	0.60	1, 2, 4, 7	1.00	0.60
Energy efficiency	0.40	1, 2, 4, 7	0.70	0.28
Waste	0.30	1, 2, 4	0.50	0.15
Water	0.30	1, 2, 4	0.50	0.15

* These assumptions illustrate the possible consequences of the sustainability criteria for this particular property. The actual values are speculative and will be determined through individual investor sentiment, market conditions and valuer judgement.
**Impact effect is derived from weighting time case study assumptions

Sustainability adjustment factors				
	Weighting[1]	Mean impact[2]	% Net impact[3]	Adjusted variables[4]
1 Market rent	3.10	0.38	−1.18%	£86,958.81
2 Market yield	4.10	0.51	2.07%	7.15%
4 Rental growth	4.10	0.51	−2.07%	4.90%
7 Target rate	1.80	0.45	0.82%	10.08%

[1] derived from weighting times impact area in Sustainability Criteria table
[2] the mean of the relevant impact effects in Sustainability Criteria table
[3] derived from weighting times mean impact in this table
[4] derived from % net impact times original valuation

Illustration 7.1 (continued)

Sustainability factor		Suggested calculation of worth taking account of sustainable features		
5. Adjusted market rent	£86,958.81	Present market rent	£86,958.81	
6. Adjusted target rate	10.08%	Capitalisation 5yrs @10.08%	3.78	
7. Adjusted rental growth	4.90%	Void adjustment	1.00	**£328,956**
		Future market rent	£110,437.11	
8. Adjusted market yield	7.15%	YP perpetuity @ 7.15%	14.00	
9. Next rent review (yr)	5	Discount 5yrs @ 10.08%	0.619	**£956,160**
10. Target rate	10.00%	**Investment worth**	**£1,285,116**	

These issues are being examined further through initiatives such as Sustainable Investment in Real Estate (SIRE), which is undertaking research to explore the measurable impact of sustainability characteristics on the financial performance of retail and office properties in Europe.

Yet, in most cases 'the transactional market still does not explicitly recognise the impact of sustainability factors within its pricing structure' (Sayce *et al.* 2007: 641). There is limited evidence of higher rents and values or lower voids. This might suggest a miscommunication between principal and agent regarding the specific benefits to be derived from sustainable criteria, advice which is too property specific (and thus has limited meaning for the client) or, perhaps more seriously, a lack of knowledge and understanding of both real estate sustainability and corporate sustainability from the real estate adviser. In order to develop a greater understanding of the impact of sustainable features on the financial performance of a building (and maybe its potential impact on values and marketability), the Corporative Research Centre for Construction Innovation (CRC) has attempted to develop some environmental and social benchmarks for real estate (CRC 2004).

Evaluation of financial performance in commercial buildings

In the context of investment decision making, the CRC (2004) is useful in highlighting the critical environmental and social benchmarks that may influence real estate investment decisions. The objective of the research was 'to develop a forward-looking property performance evaluation model that was both structurally accurate and easy to use' (CRC 2004: 3). As such, they are also useful for real estate management generally.

Amongst its features it includes environmental and social factors 'that form part of the evaluation process and the establishment of the triple bottom line evaluation format' (CRC 2004: 3). Table 7.2 (environmental) and Table 7.3 (social) highlight a group of the most important benchmarks.

Table 7.2 Recommended environmental benchmarks: existing buildings (CRC 2004: 33)

	Fields/Topics	Measures
Resource consumption	Energy	• net fossil fuel energy use (assessed on an intra-building and market comparison basis) • effective action to reduce greenhouse gas emissions (particularly from energy use) • office lighting power density and peak energy demand reduction strategies • evidence of alternative energy supplies from renewable sources or from cogeneration
	Air conditioning	• condition of air-conditioning plant • use of ODP or GWP refrigerants
	Water	• water consumption (potable, hygiene and cooling towers) • recycling and water capture measures • wastewater reduction • hazardous and non-hazardous waste and effluents recycling or removal strategies
Design and use	Transport	• public transport availability and standard of service • strategies to discourage single occupancy vehicle journeys, including cyclist facilities
	Building fabric	• age of building (obsolescence or depreciation of materials) • reuse or upgrade history or potential • suitability of original materials for refurbishment and façade retention • ecological impacts of materials used
	Interior	• indoor quality measured by ventilation, natural lighting, individual thermal control, noise abatement • absence of indoor air pollutants
	Environment	• quality of overall built environment and site use in relation to aesthetics, visual blending and connection contribution of its street frontage and wider precinct
Govern-ance	Awareness	• maximisation by management of the potential of the environmental design features through awareness programmes
	Disclosure	• disclosure and transparency of environmental data, regulation compliance, awards, and environmental expenditure of any type

Table 7.3 Proposed social benchmarks: existing buildings (CRC 2004: 89)

Topic	Measures
Health and safety	• compliance with H & S regulations and appropriate signage • adequate public liability and service provider insurance • awareness and training of emergency evacuation and accident first aid procedures for all floor wardens • a first aid station accessible to all building users
Stakeholder relations	• monitoring of stakeholder concerns, views and provisions • transparency and disclosure of landlord/tenant contracts and marketing agreements • supportive use and occupation guidelines for tenants • appropriate training for security and public relations personnel
Community engagement	• encouragement of employment of local residents within the building • provision of accessible public facilities • promotion of and linkage to local service providers • accessible communication channels with building stakeholders
Accessibility	• connections to designated green spaces • proximity to urban spaces (town centres, malls, etc.) • wheelchair access • proximity to childminding facilities
Occupier satisfaction and productivity	• quality of communal service areas • complementary usage of building (compatible tenants) • occupant productivity in terms of satisfaction and physical well-being
Cultural issues	• recognition of indigenous people through cultural space and communication of site history • consideration of gender equity and minority group requirements • preservation of heritage values • value of artwork as percentage of the fit out
Local impacts	• aesthetic implications (compliance with precinct theme, building scale, etc.) • practical implications (traffic generation, off-street emergency parking and pedestrian management) • nature of tenant businesses and naming rights • community linkages and sponsorship of local neighbourhood activities

A cash flow based assessment is used to arrive at either a value or a rate of return. However, again, Boyd (2006: 270) identifies 'very little evidence of market rent differentials', but believes that this situation will change over time. Muldavin (2010) identifies seven clear reasons why this will happen. These are:

- development costs will even out;
- regulator demand will increase;
- user demand for sustainable space will go up;
- investor demand will increase;
- operating expenses will decrease;
- capital expenses will also decrease;
- 'net' risks of sustainable space will appear positive compared to standard space.

The real estate adviser has an important role to play here, both in developing the theoretical basis for change of perception and more so in the disseminating and promotion of the potential benefit.

Further thoughts and summary

To summarise therefore, there is a weight of evidence to suggest that buildings with 'green' credentials should have a higher, more secure income stream; higher value with greater capital appreciation and liquidity. The actual evidence for this is limited. But it seems clear that many are now looking critically at existing valuation and appraisal tools with a view to adaptation or replacement. Bearing in mind the important part that real estate can play in the three dimensions of sustainability (economic, environmental and social), there is an opportunity for advisers, managers, owners and occupiers to benefit their business and to enhance their varying real estate objectives.

For example it may be that to understand the impact of sustainable criteria on value (capital and rental), it is necessary to approach the problem from a different angle. Artificial neural networks (ANN) and auto-regressive integrated moving average (ARIMA) using time series data to predict future trends have been suggested by Lützkendorf et al. (2007).

In the case of valuations, this would move the process on from a linear, logical approach to a more random, behavioural approach. This could significantly change the market within which real estate is assessed and transacted. Equally this approach does not just apply to the way in which valuation is considered. It can also apply to general management of operational real estate. The introduction of green leases and landlord–tenant partnerships are tangible ways in which real estate advisers are becoming involved in the business place as well as the business space. This may give those who own and those who occupy real estate assets a greater sense of their value in its broadest sense (i.e. the triple bottom line of environmental and social as well as economic).

This is not to say that these models should be used in real estate valuation or appraisal, if only for the paucity of data in the real estate field compared to the general business environment. However, this does draw attention to the fact that perhaps real estate advisers need to be aware of alternative approaches based on knowledge rather than information. Risk based models need to be supplemented by resilience tools. In a wider business context, this is already happening, and in parts of the real estate industry it is also happening but it tends to be undertaken by actuaries, asset managers and business consultants rather than traditional real estate advisers who typically rely solely on traditional methodologies. Also the moves in the capital markets towards the inclusion of behavioural aspects of decision making are opening up a wider debate about qualitative as well as quantitative assessments in the decision-making process. The next chapter examines these developments and how they may influence thinking on environmental behaviours and sustainable real estate.

8   Decision making and sustainability

· ·

Introduction

The previous chapter looked at property investment decisions and suggested models or tools that investors could adopt to enhance their decision making. This chapter investigates some of the issues behind these tools. More specifically, this chapter looks at existing studies about people's decision making first, it then moves on to investigate people's behaviours under different circumstances, such as sustainability.

The basics of decision making

One of the basic assumptions underlying classical economic theory and traditional finance is the notion that all investors act rationally. Olsen (2010: 102) points out that traditional finance paradigms are built on the basis of six themes, namely:

- Reductionist science can conquer uncertainty. That is all cause and effect can be known, at least in theory, if not in practice.
- Negative feedback dominates over time, leading to market equilibrium.
- The human mind is a general problem-solving device, much like a computer. Therefore, it can be trained (programmed) to make formally logical axiomatic decisions focused on optimisation.
- Complete objectivity is possible because the observer can stand outside the observed system.
- Emotion has a negative influence on decision making.
- Humans are naturally predisposed to make decisions in their personal best interest.

Furthermore, empirical studies in the 1990s started to challenge the basis of finance traditional (Fama *et al.* 2004). This was partly because of the limits to the degree of complexity and uncertainty that humans can handle at any one time (Woffold 1985). Rationality is thus often bounded through cognitive filtering processes sometimes called the adaptive toolbox (Gigerenzer 2001). This section therefore examines various aspects of decision theory.

The definition of decision theory

The growth of research in the whole area of financial market performance has led to the development of decision theory. Generally speaking, decision theory includes 'the study of individual decision-making, the theory of games, social choice theory and certain philosophical approaches to the study of rational action' (Bacharach *et al.* 1991: 1).

This theory can be divided into three interrelated branches. These are (see Fischhoff 1992 and Kahneman *et al.* 1998 for details):

1. *Normative theory* – This usually looks at the logical behaviour for making decisions. As far as traditional finance or economics is concerned, it falls into the normative theory, since it is concerned with the way in which people should behave in a rational manner when making investment decisions. In other words, when developing financial models, researchers would assume that all investors are rational and would try to find the best combination between risks and returns, so as to maximise their utilities.

2. *Descriptive theory* – It has been long argued that instead of formal statistical judgement in decision making, investors often adopt intuitive approaches (Slovic 1972). Another branch of decision theory, descriptive theory, has thus emerged to evaluate how people actually make decisions. On the basis of descriptive theory, the prospect theory introduced by Kahneman *et al.* (1979) can be regarded as one of the useful tools in financial applications (Barberis *et al.* 2003 and Plous 1993), as 'the behavioural assumptions of prospect theory may offer a richer and more appropriate picture of the determinants of risk choice' (Olsen 1997: 227). The newly developed behavioural finance thus falls into this branch of decision theory (see later in the chapter for more discussion).

3. *Prescriptive theory* – This theory tries to link the normative and descriptive theories so as to improve people's decision making. It aims to use both quantitative and qualitative data to help to understand decisions and seek to describe market activities. In a way, the starting point should be that people act irrationally according to background, sentiment, prior learning, heuristics chosen, etc. In that sense, their rationality is framed and as such it is a personal rationality (i.e. it can be justified by the individual based on their own logical analysis of the situation). 'The thinking appears to be that if people do not behave according to the prescriptions of theory, then something is wrong with people and not with the theory' (Frankfurter *et al.* 2004: 450). This may falsely ascribe an irrationality to the decisions without really questioning the theory itself.

Decision making under uncertainty

Investment normally involves trading off something today in the expectation of future benefit. Since the future is unknown, this means that any investment decision will have a level of risk attaching to it. It therefore becomes important to investigate investors' risk preferences or how investors make decisions under conditions of uncertainty. In this way, it helps an understanding of asset prices or trading behaviour in the financial context.

Risk is defined as 'the extent to which there is uncertainty about whether potentially significant and/or disappointing outcomes of decisions will be realized' (Sitkin *et al*. 1992: 10). This definition captures the three key dimensions of outcome uncertainty, outcome expectations and outcome potential.

From an individual decision maker's perspective, the key factors to understand are the individual's risk preferences, risk perceptions and risk propensities. Taking this further, once an individual is placed within a group decision-making situation, the concept of risk is broadened out to areas such as group composition, cultural risk values, leader risk orientation and organisational control systems. However, regardless as to whether it is an individual or a group facing the risks, both have to be conscious of their own familiarity of the problem and the way in which the problem is framed and structured.

For example, Mulligan *et al*. (2005) carried out studies into the impact of information and the ordering of information on investment decisions. They found that 'much of the qualitative information in the financial investment arena is mentally organized in a story structure ... [helping to] predict the decision outcome and determine the relative impact of items of information on the decision' (Mulligan *et al*. 2005: 146). From their experiments the researchers found that 'the implications of the information were better comprehended when the information was read in a causally-connected, narrative order' (Mulligan *et al*. 2005: 147). They also found that the most important part of any 'story' of information was the conclusion. The results 'show that not only is investor behaviour influenced by the information that is available ... but that decisions also depend on how that information is presented' (Mulligan *et al*. 2005: 154). In a sense this is almost as important as the information itself.

A similar point was made about the meaning of information in earlier chapters. Here again, it is important to realise that progress towards sustainable real estate requires a meaningful narrative that not only clearly maps the route but also is a route that can be identified by its audience.

In a more financial context, studies on people's attitudes towards risk can be traced back to Von Neumann *et al*. (1947), who through the development of the expected utility theory, set out to test rational behaviour in decision making. This later became one of the foundations of traditional finance. Models such as CAPM were developed from this to evaluate the relationship between risk and return of investments in financial markets.

However, since the early 1990s, researchers have begun to notice that the average return of an investment could also be influenced by size, book-to-market ratios and other factors rather than simply the Beta coefficient in CAPM (Fama *et al.* 2004). Similar findings were also detected by Xu *et al.* (2007) when analysing Shanghai prime office market datasets between 1995 and 2004 from three different property consultancies.

Many of the debates about decision making under uncertainty are concerned with the general notion of the rationality of these decisions. However, after studying the internal ('past reinforcing experiences') and external mediation (external environment) of rationality, Smith (2005) argues that there are two distinct kinds of rationality. These are constructivist and ecological rationality.

- Constructivist rationality suggests that 'all worthwhile social institutions were and should be created by conscious deductive processes of human reason. [But] ... human activity is diffused and dominated by unconscious, autonomic, neuropsychological systems that enable people to function effectively without always calling upon the brain's scarcest resource – attention and reasoning circuitry' (Smith 2005: 141). He goes on to argue that external context plays its part by stimulating 'autobiographic experiential memory' (Smith 2005: 141).
- Ecological rationality 'emerges out of cultural and biological evolutionary processes: home grown principles of action, norms, traditions and "morality"' (Smith 2005: 142). As such, Smith argues that, in a market setting, there is always a move towards ecological rationality through volume albeit unintentional on the part of the individual. Left alone, individuals would be more likely to rely on reasoned argument and their own experience.

Smith (2005) further questions the notion put forward by economists that rationality is identified as expected utility maximisation. This is only really understandable in a context. So, isolated survey responses outside of that context (for example, asset markets) fail to capture the information contained within the value structure of any particular environment. Any such survey will have value but it needs to be seen in the context of its limitations. He concludes: ' ... to understand what is ... requires understanding of a great deal *more* that is *not*' (Smith 2005: 144).

Decision-making process

According to Parker *et al.* (2005), decision-making processes require four fundamental skills. These are assessing beliefs, assessing values, combining beliefs and values in order to identify choices and having a meta-cognitive understanding of one's abilities. In their view 'for each skill, performance can be defined in terms of *accuracy*, relative to an external criterion ... or internal *consistency*' (Parker *et al*. 2005: 3). In the last half century, as markets have become more and more complex, heavy reliance has been placed on mathematical models to inform these decisions. Furthermore, the reliability of these models has been delegated to electronics with less and less input from human judgement. Psychologists or researchers in the descriptive branch of decision theory have suggested that there are actually two subsequent phases in a decision-making process, namely editing and evaluation (Kahneman *et al*. 1979).

The editing stage. This initial phase is where acts, outcomes and contingencies are framed (i.e. Simon's notion of 'bounded rationality', Simon 1955): 'People find things out for themselves, usually by trial and error. Trial and error often leads people to develop rules of thumb, but this process often leads to other errors. ... in turn, these rules of thumb have themselves come to be called heuristics' (Shefrin 2002: 13). In general, heuristics are useful tools in judgement. However, it has been shown that sometimes they lead to systematic errors (Shefrin 2002, Barberis *et al*. 2003, Tversky *et al*. 1974 and Montier 2002). For example, when making judgement under uncertainty (as in investment forecasting), people tend to use three heuristics, namely 'representativeness', 'availability of instances' and 'adjustment from an anchor' (Tversky *et al*. 1974).

Kahneman *et al*. (1979) further documented that when making decisions under uncertainty, individuals tend to respond more to the loss of a sum of money than the pleasure of gaining the same amount. This is known as the value function. In addition, people normally ignore seemingly impossible events, but overweight those with low probabilities, so as to simplify the prospects. This is labelled as the weight function.

The evaluation stage. Research studies suggest (as mentioned earlier) that risk preferences, the inertia of the decision maker and the outcomes of prior risky decisions all affect risk behaviour indirectly through the impact on the decision maker's risk propensity. This is how evaluation takes place. March (1978) describes this as 'calculated rationality'. Sitkin *et al*. (1992: 15) identify 'that the general desire to pursue or avoid risks (i.e. risk preferences) does not determine specific risk behaviours, but rather it affects the general likelihood of a person's behaving in more or less risky ways (i.e. risk propensity)'.

Furthermore, emotion, such as *overconfidence* (Camerer 1995 and Hoffrage 2004), also plays an important role in people's decision making process (Elster 1998). This is often caused by inertia, the psychological resistance to change. Wall (1993, cited in Shefrin 2002) further combines issues like frame dependence, heuristic-driven bias and emotional time line, and suggests a layered pyramid model (Figure 8.1) to describe people's needs associated with security, potential and aspiration. For example, at the bottom of the pyramid, individuals prefer things like savings accounts, which would provide them with security. Once this level of security is achieved, individuals will move one level up to bonds and then more risky investment such as real estate and stocks.

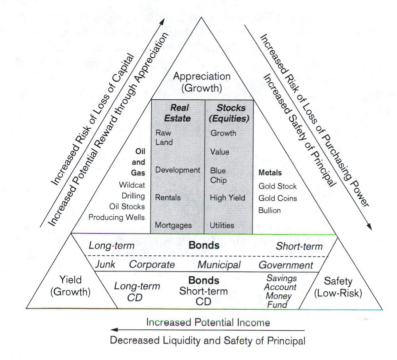

Figure 8.1

A portfolio as a layered pyramid (Shefrin 2002: 122)

Human behaviour patterns

In the psychological field, studies of rationality or irrationality of choices have become of significant interest to cognitive psychology (Arrow 1982), which 'has a profound influence on judgement research' (Kahneman *et al.* 1982: xii). Cognitive psychology refers to 'all processes by which the sensory input is transformed, reduced, elaborated, stored, recovered and used' (Tvede 1999: 84). In other words, it is 'the study of the processes involved in cognition in making sense of the environment and interacting appropriately with it' (Eysenck 1993: 10).

Individual risk preferences are influenced by a range of different factors including culture, experience, knowledge, training, biochemical structure and personality trait. Epstein's work on the cognitive–experiential self has identified two modes of information processing that, in some way, mirror Jung's typology (shown in Figure 3.1). One system, the experiential, is rapid and effortless and could be compared with Jung's vertical sensation–intuition axis. Immediate sensation is sought here. The other, the rational system, runs along the horizontal thinking–feeling axis and is a more deliberative mode of processing (Epstein *et al.* 1996). Here a person would be more focused on means to reach a goal.

In reality, these are parallel, interactive systems, where an individual or a group will have a greater propensity to deal with particular bits of information at any one point in time 'experientially' rather than 'rationally', and vice versa, depending on risk preference and risk perception. Zaleskiewicz (2001: 119) uses these ideas as background for his work on risk taking. He suggests that 'risk taking behaviour can be motivated by different needs which stimulate the engagement of different modes of information processing'. He further distinguishes between two kinds of risk-taking behaviour.

- 'Instrumental' risk taking, which tended to be orientated towards a particular economic goal and 'was found to be related to such personality traits as orientation toward the future, rational thinking (need for cognition), functional and, at a lower level, dysfunctional impulsivity, and disinhibition' (Zaleskiewicz 2001: 120).
- On the other hand, 'stimulating risk taking is more orientated towards the search for excitement. It was associated with arousal seeking, dysfunctional and functional impulsivity, thrill and adventure seeking, and disinhibition'. (Zaleskiewicz 2001: 120). This indicates the importance of the consideration of personality types and traits in trying to explain economic behaviour (Brandstatter *et al.* 2001).

In this context, Price (1995) believes that many organisations have a view of accepted behaviour based on constructed paradigms and mental models. As such, a market can be seen as a network model that establishes and redefines rules about behaviour. It is dynamic and its rules are derived from its principal agents. So, for example, it could be argued that those operating in the property investment market have the power to change the rules from modern lease terms to green lease terms, from standard specification to 'green' specification.

It is also suggested by Marsden (1998) that non-rational behaviour can spread in environments ranging from management practices to market activity. This 'contagion' can be linked to memes or pieces of data that have been copied from one person to another (Dawkins 1976). This can act like an 'anchor' that tends to hinder people's rational judgement. This data may have greater 'psychological appeal' than scientific validity particularly when it is based around perceived control.

Therefore, 'it is quite possible for example that theories implying that markets can be outguessed and profitably exploited using past market data may have more psychological appeal than an efficient view of financial markets' (Frank 1999: 6). Soros (1998) believed that the then current state of affairs on this basis is fundamentally unsound and unsustainable. He has, of course, been proved right by the 2006–08 financial crisis. 'Financial markets are inherently unstable and there are social needs that cannot be met by giving market forces free rein. Unfortunately these defects are not recognized. Instead there is a widespread belief that markets are self-correcting and a global economy can flourish without any need for a global society' (Soros 1998: xx). It may be that participants have become too complacent or it may be simply overreliance on the self-correcting ability of markets. But it does seem that, at times, the fundamentals of asset security are overlooked.

Burrell (1951: 211) asserts that 'the behaviour of markets is a reflection of relatively constant human behaviour patterns and that experimental studies designed to reveal how men behave in the market may be of value in understanding how security markets work'. The problem here is that the 'relatively constant human behaviour patterns' can create markets that can usually be contained in a local economy. However, when, as now, there are global markets, then the effects of those same behaviour patterns are magnified. The recent crisis in 2007 seems to have been exaggerated by 'a curious financial alchemy' whereby investors by 'combining these products in clever ways' believed that they were able to securitise away the underlying risk (Akerlof *et al.* 2009: 87).

Behavioural finance techniques

Frantz (2004: 32) suggests that 'most often, individuals are "selectively rational". … a person's effort is a reaction to pressure [both internal and external]'. External pressure tends to be caused by a degree of market competitiveness, whilst internal pressure is a result of a dual personality, the superego and the id. Essentially decisions are a compromise between the two through an individual's level of personal confidence and the confidence the individual has in the nature and availability of information.

Frantz (2004) then goes on to consider Akerloff's contribution. In this case, not only do people tend to deviate from full rationality because of the use of heuristics such as *representativeness, availability* and *anchoring* (Tversky *et al.* 1974), but, also he suggests again, individuals have a tendency for inertia. Taking these together, it is possible to start to get a picture of the behavioural issues involved in decision making in financial markets. In an effort to systematise these aspects of decision making, as mentioned earlier in this chapter, a new area of research, namely behavioural finance, has emerged.

Behavioural finance is still a relatively new field and there is no one authoritative definition (Wood 1995, Statman 1995 and 1999, Olsen 1998 and Fuller 2000). However, in general, behavioural finance can be defined as:

- the integration of classical economics and finance with psychology and the decision-making sciences;
- an attempt to explain what causes some of the anomalies that have been observed and reported in the finance literature;
- the study of how investors systematically make errors in judgement, or mental mistakes.

(Fuller 2000: 1)

Olsen (1998: 11) suggests that behavioural finance 'is focused on the application of psychological and economic principles for the improvement of financial decision making'. Researchers have argued that investors are not as rational as traditional finance assumes and there may be judgement errors in their decisions (Barberis *et al.* 2003). This can have important consequences for the financial sustainability of decisions and their impact on other dimensions of sustainability (i.e. environmental and social).

Leece (2003: 2–4) sees behavioural finance operating as a system of 'complex interactions of economic actors', driven partly by behaviours that have parallels with sustainability literacy. These include:

- *time horizons* – 'tussle between impulsive short-term behaviour and the need for self-control ... or individual discipline';
- *conservatism* – 'a reluctance to modify existing expectations and opinions: giving too much weight to the most recent events';
- *rule-based behaviour* – 'rules for dealing with complexity and bounded rationality';
- *mental accounting* – 'fragmented attitudes to risk to incorporate direct investments which have an environmental impact' such that risk and return are not necessarily linked for each investment or performance measure;
- *issues in regret* – 'choices that minimise the regret of the investor if the outturn of the actual choice is adverse' both as a financial decision and also as a social decision possibly.

Such behaviours do suggest a fruitful examination of psychological motivations behind finance and investment decisions and how players such as market participants, decision makers and asset managers construct their view of the world (see Figure 8.2). This could help differentiate sustainable property investment policies, responsible property investing and socially responsible

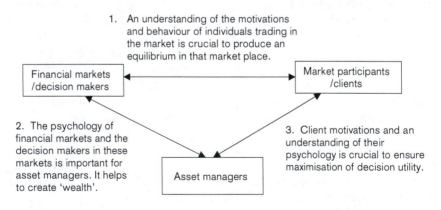

Figure 8.2

Behavioural relationships in financial markets

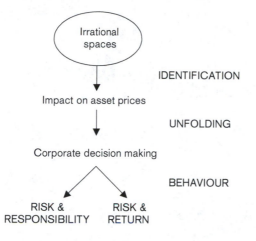

Figure 8.3

Identifying irrational space

investments, which operate at a deeper level in contrast to what might be considered a more superficial marketing mask.

An argument that has been put forward for behavioural finance is 'that rational trades (arbitrage) in financial markets do not necessarily eliminate so-called "noise traders". These are the group of "irrational" buyers and sellers can create their own "space" within which over-reaction and under-reaction to news, sentiment, fad and fashion and so forth have a significant impact upon stock market movements and individual asset prices' (Leece 2003: 3). This can then impact on corporate decision making (see Figure 8.3).

It is suggested that this 'space' is worthy of research not only in the general financial markets but also in specific markets such as property investment. Leece (2003) goes on to argue that issues of sustainability might also be influenced here by this 'space'. Figure 8.4 shows how investment motivation and behaviour can feed back different messages to this negotiated space.

Furthermore, investors do not necessarily act in isolation; so-called 'rational interpretation' is constructed around not only individual understanding and perception, but also social influence. Scherer *et al.* (2003) developed a social network contagion theory to examine the social transmission of sociocultural states (in this case, the perception of risk). This theory 'suggests that it is the relational aspects of individuals and the resulting networks and self-organising systems that should be the units of analysis rather than the individuals and their isolated cognitive structures and processes' (Scherer *et al.* 2003: 262).

This is especially true of financial markets and also property markets as complex adaptive systems (i.e. a system that consists of many components that are interrelated and linked through deep interconnections; the system itself behaves as a unified whole in a dynamic way adjusting to changes in its environment as necessary) (see Chapter 3).

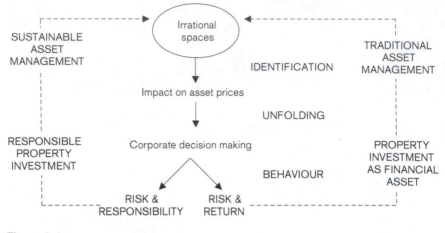

Figure 8.4

Responding to irrational space

Interestingly, Marsden (1998) also observes that whilst market players like to think that their decisions are made consciously and rationally, evidence from his studies of social contagion suggests that this is not always the case. This is true even when information conflicts with the proposed course of action. He goes on to purport that behaviours, emotions and beliefs undermine rational choice. Shiller (2008) also considers this 'contagion of ideas' is a consistent factor in human decision making but it seems 'to be absent from the thinking of many economists and economic commentators' (Shiller 2008: 43).

For property investment this is useful as it helps to determine how far investment decisions are rational opinions and how far they are influenced by some form of social contagion emanating from the property community. This can spread through a range of media including jargon, grandiloquence, professional affect, symbol, market sentiment, etc. It also suggests that these social or professional constructs can play a significant part in incorporating sustainability, beyond pure finance, as part of the decision making.

Behavioural studies in the property discipline

Despite the rich evidence of human imperfection as illustrated, property professionals and academics have been reluctant to accept or partially accept behavioural theory as a paradigm for the study of decision making (Hardin 1999). As far as the decision-making process of property experts is concerned, the majority of studies that have been undertaken in this area have been focused on the behaviour of valuers (Black *et al.* 2000 and Diaz 1999). These can be grouped into the following four categories:

1. *Departures from normative models.* When carrying out a valuation project, valuers are expected to follow normative models prescribed by theory and to begin with general information, such as regional data, and then more specific to the subject property being valued. However, Diaz (1990a) reports that in practice, valuers actually start the task by assessing information on the subject property, then broadening their inquiry to obtain more general information.

2. *Comparable sale selection.* Diaz (1990b) studies the ways in which valuers carry out valuation projects. He identifies that senior valuers, unlike junior / student valuers, normally start with one or two criteria sales and use these cases to screen other comparables, until an acceptable sales price is met. Gallimore (1996) calls this phenomenon 'confirmation bias', as valuers seem to look for confirmation of their opinions rather than objectively setting them to the test. Havard (1999) further reports that student valuers are more likely to adjust a previous valuation upwards rather than downwards.

3. *Valuation biases.* Valuers tend to anchor on list prices, and this anchor effect is influenced by asking prices (Black *et al.* 1996 and Black 1997).

4. *Feedback.* Valuers adjust their valuation figures subject to clients' pressures (Kinnard *et al.* 1997, Levy *et al.* 1999 and Baum *et al.* 2000).

Apart from the study of valuers' behaviour, Gallimore *et al.* (2000) also argue that small- and medium-sized property companies in the UK normally rely on outside finance for investment, and they make decisions on the basis of local demographic and economic data. Because of the limited resources within these companies and the diffuse nature of information in the market, investors in these types of company often overweight or overreact to the private information they gather through market contacts.

In addition, Gallimore *et al.* (2002) identify in their survey that over half of their respondents (i.e. 55 per cent of 213 valid answers from the membership of the UK Investment Property Forum) considered sentiment as an essential element in making their investment decisions. Royston (2003) also suggests that there is a need to conduct studies regarding the framing effect, i.e. individuals' choice preferences under different situations, in real estate investment decision making.

Miljkovic (2005) uses this notion of a framing effect in his research. He observed that 'people may inadvertently be manipulating their own perceptions by causal decisions they make about how to organize their knowledge' (Miljkovic 2005: 622). This being the case, it is important to see if it is possible to mitigate the effects of framing. Simon *et al.* (2004: 91) found, in their study, that 'when participants are more engaged with specific features of the options prior to making a choice, it appears that NC [the need for cognition] moderates the effect of frame on choice'. Here NC is understood to mean 'an individual's propensity to enjoy and engage in thought' in the sense of effortful cognitive tasks not necessarily related to levels of intelligence. The researchers actually found that this was more important than gaining additional technical skills (in this case math skill).

Since 'property forecasting is an important component within a property investment strategy' (Newell *et al*. 2006: 1), existing behavioural studies in the property field have also looked at the accuracy of property forecasting. Gallimore *et al*. (2005) argue that despite the limitations in quantitative models, property market forecasting is also substantially affected by qualitative judgements. This is partly because of the influence of clients, who require forecasters to adjust the output to be acceptable to their users or purchasers. In addition, any extreme forecast from a model would normally lead to 'anchoring'. That is, forecasters often adjust extreme findings or results and make them more closely related to the underlying market (Mitchell *et al*. 1997). Both McAllister *et al*. (2005) and Ling (2005) further point out the existence of errors and biases in the UK Investment Property Forum quarterly survey as well as the quarterly US Research Corporation's investment survey respectively.

From a purely financial point of view this might suggest unsustainable behaviour in markets and, in current mindset, is only understood in hindsight. It appears that the current financial models are inadequate to deal with the nature of world financial and property markets. However, this is not only a financial issue. It cuts across both the social (impact on society and well-being) and environmental (impact on resources and consumption). The next section therefore links people's decision making with sustainability.

Decision making and sustainability

The Turner Review

Leff (2005) suggests that an alternative rationality may be needed to secure environmental and economic sustainability. He believes that '[s]ustainability questions the origins and causes of environmental crisis and its projection towards a possible future, leading to the construction of an alternative rationality, beyond metaphysic thinking, scientific logo-centrism and economic rationality that have produced an *unsustainable modernity'* (Leff 2005: 3). This may suggest that theory should go to another level built around risk and responsibility rather than risk and return that traditional finance suggests. This responsibility needs to exist at governmental, organisational and personal levels. As a direct response to the 2007 financial crisis, Lord Turner was asked in October 2008 to review the causes of this crisis, and 'make recommendations on the changes in regulation and supervisory approach needed to create a more robust banking system for the future' (FSA 2009: 5).

At the core of traditional economic assumptions has been the theory of efficient and rational markets that supported, according to Turner (FSA 2009), five key propositions as follows:

1. Market prices are good indicators of rationally evaluated economic value.
2. The development of securitised credit, since based on the creation of new and more liquid markets, has improved both allocative efficiency and financial stability.
3. The risk characteristics of financial markets can be inferred from mathematical analysis, delivering robust quantitative measures of trading risk.
4. Market discipline can be used as an effective tool in constraining harmful risk taking.
5. Financial innovation can be assumed to be beneficial since market competition would winnow out any innovations that did not deliver value added.

The Forum for the Future (2009: 23) further extends these five propositions to wider sustainability issues as follows:

1. Collective responsibility means that people either feel powerless to take a different path, or hide behind the inaction of others.
2. Securitisation has been used to enable investment in important areas, such as microfinance. It can play an important role so long as the underlying assets are (a) properly valued and (b) valuable to society.
3. Systemic credit and liquidity risks were not properly modelled in the run-up to the financial crisis. Regulation must also take into account the massive systemic risks arising from climate change and other social and environmental externalities.
4. Much financial innovation has been designed simply to serve the interests of a rich elite. However, financial innovation may be needed to enable activities that serve the public good – for example, microfinance investment structures, healthcare, and public–private partnerships around investment in climate change mitigation or adaptation.
5. This clear recognition of the failure of the market shows the need for a fundamental rethink of the way information is generated, analysed and acted upon. A much wider perspective on this will enable new risks to be understood and managed more effectively.

Behavioural barriers towards sustainability

One of the main issues here is not regarding responsibility and sustainability in themselves. In fact, it would be assumed that most investment decisions are based on responsibility towards shareholders, policyholders and stakeholders, and sustainability in terms of sustainable returns, sustaining health and well-being of staff, sustainable use of capital, etc. The real issue is less to do with these terms as variables in the traditional business model (in a sense they already exist for the financial dimension and in some part for the social dimension). However, the point is worth making that when wealth was built around industrial capital, the manufacturing sector sought to secure the future through forecasting trends forward from the present. Now, where mature economies are dominated by financial capital, the financial sector seeks the reverse of this process, i.e. it spends the future in the present on little more than a bet. This can have serious consequences if it is not tempered with the caution of constraint through pro-environmental behaviour including broader aspects of behaviours towards communities. However, this can only happen, realistically, with an appreciation of the long-term consequences that both natural and social capital depletions could have on financial capital.

Pro-environmental behaviour

The assumptions that simply providing and gaining more knowledge will lead to pro-environmental behaviour are flawed. Knowledge of the scientific evidence concerning the impact of CO_2 emissions does not necessarily lead to a change in mode of transport, way of living, ethical or moral decision making. Changes in behaviour are driven within a much more complex schema, which is defined by both internal and external factors. Early behaviour models saw the process of change as a linear progression from the acquisition of knowledge to the unfettered change in behaviour as a natural corollary (Figure 8.5).

However, later models were developed in the knowledge that this was a too simplistic representation of the psychology of response and change. There was, in fact, a 'gap' between knowledge and attitude (values) on the one hand and behaviour (actions) on the other (i.e. despite knowledge of sustainable solutions, attitude limited their impact on commensurate changes in behaviour). A research study undertaken by Blake (1999: 265) suggests that we do not have a fixed, rational and ready-made set of values that will be activated; rather people's values are 'negotiated, transitory and sometimes contradictory'. According to this research, there are both psychological (individual) factors and institutional (social) factors that affect individual action. The barriers identified as reasons why there may not be a clear correlation between values and action fall under three headings (Figure 8.6). These are:

Figure 8.5

Basic model of pro-environmental behaviour (Kollmuss *et al.* 2002: 241)

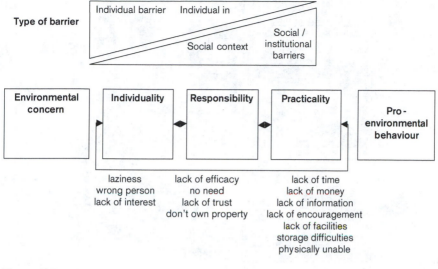

Type of barrier

Individual barrier   Individual in

Social context

Social / institutional barriers

| Environmental concern | Individuality | Responsibility | Practicality | Pro-environmental behaviour |

laziness	lack of efficacy	lack of time
wrong person	no need	lack of money
lack of interest	lack of trust	lack of information
	don't own property	lack of encouragement
		lack of facilities
		storage difficulties
		physically unable

Figure 8.6

Barriers between environmental concern and action (Blake 1999: 267)

- Individuality. This is related to personal attitude, temperament or cognitive structure. Basically, the barrier is strongest when there is no interest, no energy or no concern about the issue.
- Responsibility. This barrier, within the social context, is concerned with the way in which external social factors influence people's assessment of the likely consequences of particular environmental actions. It relates to the perceived level of control that individuals consider they have in influencing actions.
- Practicality. This final barrier identifies the level of social or institutional constraint that people feel exists, potentially preventing them from adopting pro-environmental action regardless of their attitude or intentions.

Whilst this is useful in identifying the barriers that limit behavioural change, it does not go beyond this. It does not link personal values with pro-environmental consciousness. Kollmuss *et al.* (2002) attempt to remedy this with their own diagram, which indicates the significance that old behavioural patterns have on change in mindsets (Figure 8.7). It also indicates (via the smaller arrows from internal and external factors to pro-environmental behaviour) environmental actions that are taken for non-environmental reasons. It could be argued that much of the sustainable actions taken by organisations are in this category (i.e. the primacy of the actions is ethical marketing, USP, financial reward). This does not, in itself, make them bad decisions; it simply suggests that they are financially sustainable but, as long-term pro-environmental actions, they may not succeed.

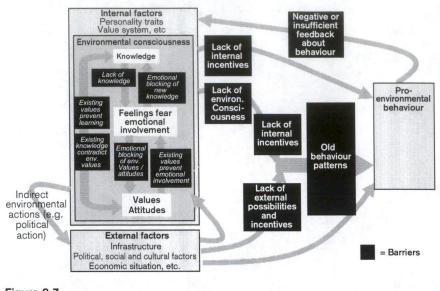

Figure 8.7

Model of pro-environmental behaviour (Kollmuss *et al.* 2002: 257)

To be of real value therefore the motivation should come from an awareness and understanding of sustainability. According to O'Brien *et al.* (2009) synergistic or strategic corporate responsible behaviour (CRB) is seen as the way forward. However, from their research it was clear that the most notable trend that has emerged is the weak connection between corporations' real estate and CRB strategies.

The built environment has a profound effect on the natural environment and for facilities to support the workplace and create long-term value, organisations must understand that human and environmental issues are considered as essential components of business processes rather than the consequences of those processes. There can never be a blueprint for encouraging environmental action: different strategies must be designed to be appropriate to specific relationships between individuals, communities and institutions. The 'value-action gap' cannot be overcome simply by using an 'information deficit' model of individual participation as 'empowerment of individuals to act does not of itself guarantee action without an appropriate institutional location within which action is located' (Smith *et al.* 1997: 282).

Summary

Including behavioural finance in the study of markets is a relatively new approach. As such, the amount of evidence to support the theory is much more limited than rational models. However, Dorner (1996 cited in Olsen 2010) considers four primary reasons for the failure of logic in decision situation. These are:

1. Human thinking is quite slow relative to unconscious information process. Thus, humans are predisposed to resort to mental short cuts, especially when time is short and decisions are complex.
2. Short-term memory is very limited in its information processing ability but long-term memory is quite capable of storing very large amounts of information in a gestalt form wherein framing and felt intuition become significant decision attributes.
3. Evolution has caused thinking to be focused upon concrete evidence required for adaptation. Thus, what is not salient or concrete is not a significant element in the decision process.
4. A positive view of one's competency is an important element for maintaining a healthy sense of 'self'. Thus, information is screened and weighted to suit a psychological need.

(Olsen 2010: 114)

These may equally apply in real estate markets. However, there is an interesting parallel in the general debate about the integration of sustainable behaviours into financial decision making. The complex interactions that are examined to overcome such failures through behavioural studies have some clear links with the criteria for sustainability literacy in real estate decision making.

The chapter has highlighted existing behavioural studies in real estate and identified some of the barriers to pro-environmental behaviour being more widespread within markets. There is also the suggestion that theory should go to another level built around risk and responsibility (including consideration of the impacts on social and natural capital as well as financial return) rather than risk and return. This responsibility needs to exist at governmental, organisational and personal levels.

In the context of financial sustainability of investing institutions and corporate organisations, the influence that psychology can play in decision making if incorporated into traditional financial models, can have a significant effect. But, it may be less easy to see how it can 'arbitrate between wider debates on sustainability and provide methodologies and research questions compatible with both free market and regulatory arguments' (Leece 2003: 8). What it can do, however, is to provide some important insights into the way particular markets work and to distinguish between 'the effects of market failure, incentive and contract design problems' on the one hand, and 'fundamental aspects of human decision making that invite psychological exploration' on the other hand (Leece 2003: 8). In this way, it might help to focus the social and environmental sustainability debate. In the context of the property investment market, for example, the introduction of a behavioural dimension to a psychological oriented study of financial decision making might reveal reasons for such failures. It might also motivate incentives that can inform the change of mindset that could accompany more sustainable actions in markets.

9　Responsible property investment

· ·

Introduction

The increased public awareness of sustainability issues is reflected, informally, in shifting attitudes and formally in legal and regulatory changes. These trends have led to a greater need for many organisations to either address the issues or, at least, to be aware of them. This is very much evident in the world of commercial real estate investment. Large property companies and institutional real estate fund managers have devoted considerable resources to integrating sustainability within their business and investment processes. As part of this, many of them also produce public statements about their policies in this area and provide a degree of transparency as to their sustainability targets and progress made towards them.

This provides an opportunity to evaluate how sustainability is influencing real estate investment in the UK today. Whilst a lot of the public discussion about sustainability is focused on energy efficiency, it is worth noting that this is just one part of the agenda.

There is no single agreed definition of what constitutes corporate social responsibility (CSR). Kimmet (2009), for example, argues that sustainable commercial property investment is not necessarily socially responsible. It may vary in time and place and between different organisations. However, in a general sense, it does refer to the obligation of a business to be accountable to a wider audience than just its shareholders, with a view to achieve wider social, economic and environmental goals. It is often linked with concepts of ethical behaviour. This too has difficulties of definition. A common understanding of ethical behaviour is a behaviour that is consistent with the objectives and values of society, despite the fact that it may differ over time and from place to place.

Wilkinson *et al*. (2008) identify three types of CSR:

- Ethical – mandatory fulfilment of certain responsibilities even if the firm is not seen to benefit itself.
- Altruistic – giving money away because it's a good thing.
- Strategic – doing good works that also benefit the company.

Some might see CSR as being merely philanthropic, running a business in the usual way, but donating some of the profits to good causes. Others see it in more holistic terms, integrating wider goals within core business activities as part of the process of value creation. On this point, Burke *et al.* (1996) highlight the following dimensions:

- centrality – a measure of the closeness of fit between a CSR policy or programme and an organisation's mission and objectives;
- specificity – an organisation's ability to capture or internalise the benefits of a CSR programme, rather than simply creating collective goods that can be shared by others in the industry, community or society at large;
- proactivity – the degree to which CSR activities are planned in anticipation of emerging economic, technological, social or political trends and in the absence of crisis conditions;
- voluntarism – the scope of discretionary decision making by an organisation and the absence of externally imposed compliance requirements;
- visibility – the observability of a business activity and an organisation's ability to gain recognition from internal and external stakeholders.

It is with these thoughts in mind that it is possible to view how real estate organisations have approached sustainability in investment. There is no doubt that many property investors have appreciated the need to be seen to be addressing the issue. They have placed extensive documentation in the public domain, which is freely accessible via their websites.

Sustainability plans

Table 9.1 shows samples of public statements from several larger property companies and real estate fund managers to indicate a widespread commitment to the principles of sustainability. They use a variety of terms to describe what they believe in and what they are doing. Without defining each of these precisely, it is not possible to assert that they are all trying to achieve the same goal. However, there is a sense from all of them that they see a degree of alignment between sustainability commitments and financial returns. This is built around the dual objectives of intellectual rationalism (i.e. profit maximisation) and emotional rationalism (i.e. benevolence) (Amaeshi *et al.* 2006).

Table 9.1 Public statements of selected companies

Company	Public statement on sustainability
PRUPIM	Our vision is to deliver superior investment performance through integrating sustainability into our core business culture, activities and decision making.
Legal & General	We believe that through the integration of sustainable thinking and behaviour, we will deliver enhanced returns to our investors.
Henderson	Sustainability is not a concept whose relevance ebbs and flows with property's cyclical tide, but one that underpins the embedded value of assets and the long-term performance that we deliver.
Schroders	Responsible Property Investment (RPI) is integrated into Schroder's overall property investment process with the overriding objective of optimising financial returns for clients.
Land Securities	Put simply, we don't invest in Corporate Responsibility (CR) to be nice; we do it because it makes us more successful.
British Land	We're committed to doing business the right way; managing, developing and financing buildings in environments where business and local communities can thrive.
SEGRO	We believe that sustainability equals value.
Hammerson	Our vision is to be the best at demonstrating value to us and our communities through sustainable property.
Igloo	We believe that the application of SRI (Socially Responsible Investment) principles in a real estate investment fund requires an ongoing programme of research and innovation in order to make better decisions to maximise investment returns.

A review of the supporting documents behind these statements suggests that they all exceed the definition of ethical CSR. Their commitments extend beyond meeting minimum statutory requirements. They also appear to have moved beyond the merely altruistic. All are spending some money on outright gifts (grants) to charitable or community organisations, but this is a relatively small part of their activities. They have all reached the strategic level, seeing CSR as being beneficial to them and to the wider community.

Also evident from the sustainability policies, in particular those of the listed property companies, is the extent to which these organisations have committed themselves to open disclosure. An individual company's sustainability targets, therefore, need to be clearly stated, and successes and failures against them with supporting data must be reported. This degree of transparency contrasts with the level of detail that one might, in the past, have expected to see in relation to the operations of these businesses. For example, UNPRI (2011) promoting the following principles in investment decision making: client protection, fair treatment, responsible investment, transparency, balanced returns and investor standards.

Sustainability reporting

To what extent does this flurry of openness and reporting reflect a fundamental shift in the approach of real estate investors? Sustainability reports are a medium for reporting a wide range of corporate activities. These include activities that were previously reported elsewhere and those that, although long performed, were hitherto not reported at all, such as health and safety outcomes. Health and safety is a statutory requirement and has always been a key compliance issue for any real estate operating business. Historically it would have been reported less prominently elsewhere. It should be no surprise that it is monitored very closely.

Many businesses have a long tradition of providing support for staff involvement in charitable activities, such as matched giving for fundraising. They might not have disclosed these but now they appear in the sustainability report. More significantly, the reports also include achievements such as operational cost savings. These are not statutory requirements but they are things that investors in these businesses would very much expect the management to be doing anyway. They should be part of the normal responsibilities of a competent management team. If an activity such as installing low energy light bulbs saves the business money, it could be argued that there does not need to be a sustainability policy to make it happen.

Clearly, sustainability reporting exists, partly, to meet the need to be seen that actions have been taken. There is nothing wrong with this but it is important to look through the reported activities and be clear as to which represent something different about the way a business operates.

The layout and emphasis of different organisations' sustainability reports varies but they generally share similar themes:

- philosophy – statement of the beliefs underlying the organisation's approach;
- policies – statement of the overall sustainability goals;
- targets – quantifiable measures of specific initiatives to implement the policies;
- processes – how the business designs its operations to achieve the targets;
- outcomes – report of what happened, compared with the targets.

In the pursuit of social, environmental and economic goals, the principal aspirations of sustainability programmes are:

- achieve efficiency in the use of energy and other resources;
- support biodiversity;
- engage with all groups (often called stakeholders) affected by the business' operations;

- provide leadership on the issues and collaborate with industry initiatives in the field.

Each of these includes a wide range of activities. Although sustainability has three pillars (i.e. economic, social and environmental), it is the environmental one that attracts the majority of real estate investors' attention. It is no coincidence that this aspect is the one subject to the most new legislation. At the very least, environmental factors are a compliance issue. Businesses need to have in place systems and processes to ensure that they do comply. Mere compliance involves the ethical approach to CSR but many businesses have chosen to try and exceed these standards, thereby moving to the strategic level.

The Better Buildings Partnership and the Greenprint Foundation

An example of this move towards strategic solutions is the Better Buildings Partnership (BBP), which brings together a number of the largest commercial and public property owners in London in one collaborative organisation. They are working together to improve the sustainability of London's existing commercial building stock and accelerate the reduction in CO_2 emissions from these buildings. In January 2011 an alliance between BBP and The Greenprint Foundation was announced to advance their common goal to reduce carbon emissions and to improve the sustainability of their members' property portfolios and, by example, the entire property industry.

Greenprint Foundation is a worldwide alliance of leading real estate owners, investors, and financial institutions. It is committed to reducing carbon emissions across the global property industry through education and action. It is 'a catalyst for change taking meaningful, immediate and measurable actions to generate solutions that improve the environment through energy efficiency while demonstrating the correlation with increased property values. Greenprint focuses on reducing the carbon footprint of the built environment, which currently represents one third of all carbon emissions' (Greenprint Foundation 2011: 1).

Together their membership represents approximately £300 billion (US$480 billion, €352 billion) of assets under management. One of the most significant aspects of their alliance is the participation of BBP members in Greenprint's Carbon Index, which ensures that the index, already one of the largest global measurements of real estate's carbon footprint, is positioned to become the worldwide market standard for measuring and benchmarking carbon emissions. In addition, the BBP will make available to all Greenprint members its Toolkits, which include the Green Building Management Toolkit, the Green Lease Toolkit, the Sustainability Benchmarking Toolkit for Commercial Buildings and the Low Carbon Retrofit Toolkit.

Sustainable approach to business

There are a myriad of activities that can contribute to a sustainable approach to business, which largely fall within the categories that are listed in Table 9.2. As a more detailed example of sustainable attitudes and actions, below is a case study of RREEF, a member of Deutsche Bank AG.

Table 9.2   Sustainable activities in business

Energy and resource efficiency	• Reduce overall energy consumption • Use renewable 'green' energy (e.g. solar, wind, biomass, etc.) • Reduce CO_2 production generally • Reducing embedded CO_2 in construction materials
Waste	Develop strategies to reduce waste production and associated costs through: • Waste audits • Recycling
Water	• Managing a sustainable supply of water • Rainwater and grey water capture
Transport	• Effective integrated transport planning • Sustainable transport facilities • Vehicle park management

Biodiversity and land use	Preference for used sites over greenfield ones
	  – Avoid sites providing rare habitats
	  – Remediation of sites
	  – Procure sustainability certified products
	  – Prepare site biodiversity plans

Engagement with key stakeholders proactively	• Staff • Shareholders • Customers (e.g. tenants) • Companies in the supply chain • Local environmental and community organisations • Academia
Leadership and collaboration	• Working to engage professional bodies to develop ideas and common standards for best practice • Participation in collaborative organisations and publication of research, etc. • Provide thought leadership on sustainability issues

Case study

Background

RREEF is a real estate asset management business that operates real estate portfolios around the world. It works mostly for institutional investors, such as pension funds, insurance companies, sovereign wealth funds, endowments and foundations. However, it also manages money for retail and private client investors through alliances with organisations specialising in servicing those client segments. Sustainability is an integral part of their operations. Figure 9.1 shows the tactical dynamic as the inner circles moving clockwise through time. The outer circles are where the strategic positions are negotiated grounded in sustainable principles.

RREEF's view towards sustainability

Across the globe, a significant percentage of primary energy use (US: 39 per cent; EU: 42 per cent) is from commercial buildings, resulting in increasing public concern about the environmental impact and social impact of commercial buildings. RREEF (2009) research suggests that more than two-thirds of corporate real estate (CRE) executives surveyed worldwide identify sustainability as a 'critical business issue' for their real estate departments, while 40 per cent rated sustainability a 'major factor' in their company's

Figure 9.1

Strategic and tactical sustainable principles (RREEF 2011a)

location decisions (RREEF 2009: 10). Governments are raising even higher energy-efficiency standards for their buildings and occupancy.

Astute investors are increasingly aware that focusing on the expanded definition of environmental and social impact of buildings has the potential of enhancing long-term value and returns, resulting in an increasing number of consultant surveys and request for proposals (RFPs) enquiring about details for sustainability programming elements that are well beyond traditional Environmental, Social and Governance (ESG) policy enquiries.

Governmental resolve to address global warming through stricter coercive action is strengthening. Many governments initially provided subsidies and incentives to encourage green building and energy efficiency retrofit. The pendulum is increasingly swinging towards mandates.

RREEF sees sustainability in the context of investment drivers, the business case and challenges.

Drivers of green building and investment

- tenant demand – changing needs, impacts on income streams;
- the role of government – as regulator and enabler;
- investor demand – the balance between the holistic risks and returns;
- globalisation – the shift from local determinants;
- global environmental change agents – understanding cultural shifts.

Business case for green buildings

- new construction – smart design and the procurement chain;
- existing building retrofit and repositioning – creating the symbolic identity;
- operating efficiency – aligning real estate with business operations;
- financial returns – the future determinants of the bottom line.

Sustainability: contextual factors challenges

- split incentive – balance between costs and benefits;
- market value – demonstrating the value added;
- limited awareness, experience, standards – the shock of the new, change management;
- recession and capital preservation – economic resilience.

RREEF guiding principles towards sustainability

RREEF's business is to provide real estate investment management services consistent with client objectives for diversification, preservation of capital and superior long-term, risk adjusted performance. It believes there are economic, environmental and social implications associated with the full range of real estate investment management decisions, and that a commitment to decision making based upon sustainable real estate best practices will add long-term value to the investments managed for clients. To address this issue, RREEF's Sustainability Council provides the framework for a global real estate investment business that seeks to demonstrate the value of sustainability and to position it as a leader in the advancement of sustainability within the industry. They have produced a set of Guiding Principles for Sustainability, through which they strive to:

- Appropriately balance economic, environmental and social considerations within the full range of its real estate investment management decisions.
- Actively monitor government regulatory requirements for energy efficiency in real estate and reporting, within investment business plans and associated activities.
- Play a leadership role in the discussion of energy efficiency, as well as the financial value of sustainable features, in commercial real estate investments.
- Promote awareness and actively communicate the value of performance against key indicators of environmental care to clients, colleagues, tenants and peers in the real estate investment industry.
- Establish methods to monitor the environmental impact of the physical assets that make up the investment management portfolio; implement economically feasible strategies to minimise the impact on the environment; and periodically report performance using available industry standard metrics for sustainability.
- Seek cost-effective improvement in the environmental performance of building operations by conserving resources, reducing waste, lowering harmful emissions and improving energy efficiency, with the goal of providing a more productive working environment.
- Develop, implement and communicate best practices that deploy environmentally conscious technologies, materials and methods.
- Pursue independent certification of energy efficiency and sustainability efforts through industry programmes for existing buildings and new development, where economically feasible and indicative of increased market value.
- Establish strategic alliances with those organisations whose guiding principles for sustainability and environmental well-being are aligned with RREEF's Guiding Principles for Sustainability.

- Protect and enhance the environmental interests of the communities within which RREEF operates, while promoting the general health and welfare of colleagues and partners in achieving long-term value for clients.

RREEF's sustainability initiatives

These case studies (Illustration 9.1) illustrate and highlight some of the sustainability initiatives adopted by RREEF around the world. They are part of a policy of continually seeking economically feasible improvements in sustainability through acquisition, management, leasing, retrofit or development.

Illustration 9.1

Photos of RREFF case studies (RREEF 2011b)

UnileverHaus, Hamburg

Wilshire Courtyard, Los Angeles

Xiwang Tower, Dalian

UnileverHaus, Hamburg

In December 2009, RREEF acquired 'Unilever-Haus', Unilever's state of the art headquarters in Hamburg. The property has an overall floor space of approximately 25,000 square meters and was completed in June 2009. The building received the 'World's Best Office Building' award at the World Architecture Festival Awards (WAF) in 2009. In addition, Unilever-Haus was recognised as an 'Outstanding Contribution to the Built Environment of Hamburg' at the Building Exchange (BEX) Awards in the same year.

Some of the sustainable systems utilised include LED lighting throughout, the use of high-tech water-saving technology and the largest 'vertical film energy saving' façade in Europe, which is designed to reduce the heat and wind load on the building and enables a highly efficient heating and cooling system. In October 2010, Unilever-Haus was awarded a Green GOOD DESIGN award by the European Centre for Architecture Art Design and Urban Studies, and the Chicago Athenaeum Museum of Architecture and Design.

Georg Allendorf, Head of RREEF Germany, commented: 'The acquisition of Unilever-Haus shows that green buildings represent the future'.

Xiwang Tower, Dalian

In 2008, on behalf of its German open-ended fund 'Grundbesitz Global', RREEF acquired Xiwang Tower, one of the two premium grade A office buildings in Dalian, China. In 2009, it was awarded 'National Best Managed Building' by the Chinese Ministry of Construction. This award represents China's highest accolade for building management and property management services. RREEF also successfully achieved ISO 9000 & 14001 certification for the building. These international standards measure the quality of property management of the building and the environmental responsibility of the processes deployed at the building.

Mark Cho, Head of RREEF in China said: 'RREEF started to pursue the ISO certification in June 2010 as part of our initiative to improve service quality and drive efficiencies to our building operations. Global best practices with sustainable features have been introduced to conserve energy, reduce waste and to improve the overall service experience to our building tenants. It is RREEF's strong belief that a commitment to sustainability will add value for our clients and our business'.

Since acquiring Xiwang Tower, RREEF has installed power transducers to intelligently monitor and control the power consumption, achieving utility cost savings of over 15 per cent. In addition, an energy conservation programme was implemented to monitor the building temperature by adjusting the air-conditioning and heating systems floor by floor, which has resulted in a reduction in energy consumption of over 24 per cent. The landscape surrounding Hope Tower was designed by the internationally acclaimed landscape planner Earthasia Ltd. to promote greenery to the city.

Wilshire Courtyard, Los Angeles

Wilshire Courtyard was one of the first commercial office buildings in Los Angeles to receive the prestigious Silver LEED (Leadership in Energy and Environmental Design) certification for Existing Buildings in 2009. RREEF has continuously supported energy-saving improvements at Wilshire Courtyard, which resulted in high ENERGY STAR ratings since the buildings were initially benchmarked in 2006. Some of the recent energy improvements performed include installing variable speed drives on all HVAC equipment to improve operating efficiency and reduce electrical consumption, installing a NeoGuard elastomeric coating to the roof system, which reflects up to 91 per cent, to significantly reduce heat gain and cooling load, and extensive lighting retrofits with occupancy motion sensors.

Other sustainable measures include implementing electronic waste recycling for computers and related equipment, installing higher efficiency water fixtures in bathrooms with faucet aerators, using Green Seal-certified cleaning products and launching a paperless online tenant manual and forms for tenants to submit requests to building management. Since initiating the e-waste recycling programme in February 2009, Wilshire Courtyard has diverted more than 25,000 pounds of electronic waste from landfills. Based on water efficiency measures at the property, consumption is down by more than two million gallons annually, saving approximately $16,000 per year.

RREEF, along with the property managers, continues to explore opportunities to increase the buildings' sustainable and economical use of natural resources while improving the performance of the buildings and the environment of its occupants.

In summary, RREEF is demonstrating a business model that seeks to achieve both social and environmental sustainability as part of its overall property management portfolio whilst at the same time securing financial sustainability.

Investment process

The typical investment process for an institutional real estate investor or their agents involves making buy, sell or hold decisions on the basis of a judgement about the expected risk adjusted return from the investment. This judgement is subjective but it is done within a structured framework and tries to take account of all the factors thought likely to influence the future performance of an asset. As a financial appraisal, taking into account private costs, it attempts to identify whether assets are over- or underpriced by the market.

In the case of RREEF, for example, they have identified their environmental drivers in advising clients as being influenced by tenant and investor demand, the changing institutional framework, cultural shifts and globalisation. These have to work within a sustainable business case that relies on operational efficiencies and financial returns. These are achieved by maintaining active portfolios for clients through transactions, development and asset enhancement. This approach has its challenges and RREEF sees these principally around resilience, balancing costs and values and the agility to respond effectively to change. To take an example, many costs previously regarded as external (e.g. CO_2 production) are becoming internalised through changes in legislation and customer attitudes.

When the expected costs of owning an energy inefficient building increase because of taxation or an increased rate of depreciation, it is possible to build that expectation into the normal financial decision-making process. To that extent environmental considerations are taken into account. For the sustainably aware investor, there remain other factors that are not yet in the price but that, at their own discretion, they can include, however subjectively, in the analysis. This is not sustainability at all costs. The investors reviewed earlier that take account of sustainability risks in acquisition and disposal decisions use terms such as cost effective sustainability measures.

This is a recognition that trade-offs exist. 'Market innovation requires new evidence or new guarantees of real costs and real investment returns[.] ... [S]tandardised practices ... continue to support a gap between market reality and possibility. The challenge in financing energy efficient retrofits of existing buildings lies in generating objective, accessible, peer-reviewed information for the tools, technologies, and full costs associated with the energy savings over specified payback periods' (ULI 2010: 3).

Public commitments

The behaviour of a real estate investor that is fully committed to CSR is about more than just its acquisition and disposal decisions. Those that make a very public statement about their commitment, across a range of activities, increase the reputational risk they face for not meeting the expectations this creates. Such statements have a public relations' value in their own right, but the act of making a public commitment itself provides an incentive for the business to deliver. This is no small motivation. Household name financial institutions and public companies are very sensitive to their reputations and really do not want bad media coverage. This can have a very direct financial effect on their businesses. Public commitment plus transparency in reporting provides a basis for them to be judged on their words.

Looking beyond their investment process, the contribution that real estate operating companies can make to sustainability is shaped by the nature of the business. They typically employ relatively small numbers of staff: in the hundreds rather than thousands. Their contribution to sustainability from employee engagement is therefore likely to be quite modest in absolute terms, whether this comes from support for volunteering, mentoring or other staff activities.

In contrast they do control very substantial capital assets. This provides them with the ability, as both large customers and suppliers in the industry, to influence other organisations. They have the buying power with suppliers to demand that they too fulfil certain CSR commitments. For example, some require ISO 14001 accreditation to qualify for tenders or to achieve preferred supplier status. ISO 14001 does not specify levels of environmental performance but it provides a framework for a holistic, strategic approach to the organisation's environmental policy, plans and actions (ISO 2004).

They can also engage with their tenants (i.e. customers) to achieve, in particular, environmental improvements through initiatives such as green leases (promoted by, among others, the Better Buildings Partnership). These are leases where landlords and tenants attempt to agree mutual obligations to minimise environmental impact arising from energy and water use and waste production. Many tenants are themselves substantial organisations that have also made a commitment to CSR and will be seeking to reduce their environmental impact. Greenprint Foundation (2010) set out some guiding principles to remove barriers to energy efficiency and sustainability in leased office space. These are:

- Landlords and tenants should agree to operate the buildings as sustainably as is commercially feasible.
- The value of energy savings achieved through building efficiency improvements should be available to pay for the improvements.
- To the extent feasible, usage and demand for resources throughout the buildings should be measurable and transparent to both landlords and tenants.

(Greenprint Foundation 2010: 2)

In endorsing these principles, leading organisations agree to:

- Establish green lease principles to influence owner/occupier agreements and act on these principles across the portfolio over time.
- Require leasing agents who work on behalf of participating organisations to complete a basic orientation about sustainability, green lease principles and ways to resolve barriers to sustainability in leases.
- Establish/adopt green site selection criteria for tenants and consider these criteria for new space acquisition.
- Establish a standard for landlords to communicate key energy and environmental ratings to tenants and to prospective tenants and deploy this process at 50 per cent of their properties within three years.

(Greenprint Foundation 2010: 2).

For example in the UK, BBP (2008) published a Green Lease Toolkit. Pinsent Masons (2009: 3) summarises the 'light' green minimum provisions as:

- a general cooperation obligation on energy, waste and water reduction;
- the setting up of a building management committee to review data and agree reduction targets;
- data sharing obligations and rights to install separate metering of demised areas;
- access for landlords to demised areas to carry out works that improve the environmental performance of the building and restrictions on works by either party that adversely affect the environmental performance of the building;
- restrictions on requirements for reinstatement of works that improve the environmental performance of the building.

Engaging with suppliers and customers up and down the supply chain is a very powerful way for real estate operating businesses to drive greater CSR across the entire industry sector. This will help all to avoid focusing solely on 'rather isolated correlation analysis based on mere financial performance data, and neglect to incorporate value assessments of the current and ongoing benefits of sustainable design. This practice has led to both a one-sided understanding of the economic value of property and to an artificial separation of economic, environmental, social and cultural measures and components of value' (RICS 2008b: 10).

Implementation issues

Data collection

Adopting a more CSR led approach to real estate investment is not without its problems. On first going down this route, businesses need to establish a baseline for their performance against selected metrics (e.g. annual CO_2 production). They can then measure progress from this baseline in subsequent years.

Take the example of energy consumption, the apparently simple question, 'How much electricity/gas/oil/other did we use?', is more complex than it appears. The business needs to define what it is measuring, how it wants to report the results and then match it against all the different units of space and utility meters across its portfolio. For property management and service charge purposes, much of the data may already be collected, but not necessarily in the format needed for sustainability reporting.

It may come from several sources including the business itself, its managing agents or joint venture partners. Gross energy use figures are part of the picture. These need to be stated in consumption per unit floor area terms to enable valid comparisons of energy intensity over time. It is a complex exercise and software and other tools are available to help manage it. The output is further management information, which has a cost and should have a value that exceeds that cost.

Measurement standards

In the UK, for property investment performance measurement, there is one organisation, IPD, that not only processes the data but effectively sets and maintains the standards that are used by the vast majority of institutional commercial property investors. This facilitates comparisons between properties and operators and all sorts of very useful cross-industry analysis. An example of their work is the IPD Environment Code (IPD 2010: 6), the objective of which is to measure and compare the environmental impact of buildings through:

- enhancing their widely adopted set of definitions for environmental measurement;
- providing a transparent basis for measurement, comparison and benchmarking;
- supporting the communication of data, information and knowledge;
- improving knowledge of how to use resources and produce waste;
- helping organisations make better decisions in a rapidly changing world.

There is no equivalent organisation for CSR reporting, but there are a lot of different standards in use. Making comparisons between different properties and organisations is more difficult. These standards all have their uses and they may each address slightly different aspects of the CSR spectrum. Some also help to enhance the credibility of the efforts of the business that certifies alignment with them. Among the more widely quoted standards are:

- Global Reporting Initiative (GRI) – A sustainability reporting framework, which is international in scope and has been under development by its participants since 1997.
- United Nations Global Compact – A policy framework for the development, implementation and disclosure of sustainability principles and practices related to: human rights, labour, the environment and anti-corruption.
- International Standard on Assurance Engagements (ISAE 3000) – Originally released in 2000 provides a basic framework for large-scale audits concerned with non-financial data process monitoring. These include environmental, social and sustainability reports.

Independent assessment

In addition to producing reports to one or more standards and possibly having those reports audited (to confirm compliance with the standards), some firms also publish some form of independent assessment of their efforts. These are often written by advisers who have helped the business with its implementation of CSR reporting and provide a degree of reflective or critical appraisal of the progress made by the business. They do not carry any legal weight, but they add credibility to a report and demonstrate a willingness by the business to share its successes and failures with a wider audience.

Summary

This chapter has examined the wide role institutional investors, asset managers and corporate organisations can play in the sustainability agenda. From public statements in CSR principles, sustainability reporting and voluntary undertakings, organisations are showing social and environmental outreach whilst maintaining fiduciary responsibilities. The Better Buildings Partnership and the Greenprint Foundation also highlight the broader industry commitments to responsible property investment.

Section III

Sustainable Real Estate and Business Tools

"SCEPTICS THIS WAY."

10 Real estate and shear zones

....

Introduction

Corporate sustainability has become synonymous with an organisation's ability to operate in a market of rising environmental concerns and stakeholder pressures. The 'triple bottom line' has become the measure of an organisation's performance in terms of corporate social responsibility. This chapter considers this measure along with others in the context of aligning an organisation's real estate with their business operations.

The triple bottom line

The triple bottom line (TBL) was first referred to by John Elkington in 1994 and later developed by him as a tool to examine an organisation's economic, environmental and social value. At its very least, it can be seen as a management as well as a reporting tool. In the context of overall management of organisations, the challenge is 'to create the metrics to gauge corporate sustainability and to find new forms of accounting and accountability' (Adams *et al.* 2004: 20). As a reporting tool, TBL is seen as 'potentially improving the quality of information reported to society' (Adams *et al.* 2004: 23). However, TBL was always intended as a means of thinking about corporate social responsibility, not a method of accounting. These three elements are also the ones to be taken into consideration when including sustainability in property investment decisions.

Shear zones

Whilst it is important to examine the economic, environmental and the social bottom lines to raise awareness of the holistic nature of the decisions to be taken and the performance to be measured, what is perhaps more interesting are 'the shear zones' that Elkington identified as lying between the three

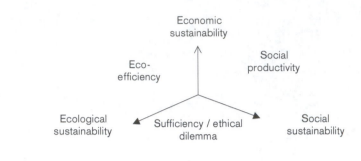

Figure 10.1

The shear zones of corporate sustainability (Hockerts 2001: 5)

pillars. Hockerts (2001) later identified these shear zones as eco-efficiency, sufficiency and ethical dilemma, and social productivity, in order to create a link not only across the three pillars of the triple bottom line but also between production, consumption and efficiency (Figure 10.1). None of these three elements can operate without the other and sustain an organisation.

As such they become seen as totally interconnected with equal weighting. They are useful labels for any discussion about real estate because they can be understood as follows:

- *Eco-efficiency* – this dimension in this context is principally concerned with the ability of 'sustainable' real estate to generate acceptable returns for investors and the ways in which this can be achieved most efficiently. This raises issues both about the 'right' balance between environmental concerns and financial viability and the concept of 'efficiency' (i.e. what does it mean and efficient to whom?). Real estate advisers need to understand the complexity of investment decision making not just from a financial point of view, but also from a symbolic viewpoint (i.e. buildings have the potential to make statements about organisations).

- *Sufficiency/ethical dilemma* – this relates to the occupation and use of buildings. Not only does it concern operational management issues of health and safety in building, energy efficiency, green leases, etc., but it also questions more fundamentally the requirements for space. It raises issues of sustainable consumption by questioning the need for space. This then leads on to questions about organisational structures, transformation and real estate needs. Real estate advisers tend to spend a lot of time with clients on the former (operational management issues) and much less on the latter (the need for space). Again the nature and complexity of organisations and their need for agility should be reflected in their real estate. Solutions are least effective when they involve incremental expansion or contraction without first reviewing the medium-term trajectory and any underlying cultural shift. This requires a model that seeks to align real estate with business operations.

- *Social productivity* – this relates to the development/refurbishment process, the delivery of profitable schemes that satisfy human needs and bring quality of life to both communities and occupiers through energy efficient 'green' credentials. Again this requires more than financial bottom line thinking. Any development scheme is a tangible addition to an environment (both urban and rural). There is therefore a social as well as a financial aspect to all such schemes that needs to be addressed. The real estate adviser can play an important role in this process through anticipatory learning and lateral thinking.

Seeking sustainable solutions

It seems that, in the past, real estate advisers have defined a relatively narrow role for themselves in the market place. Yes, they are good at 'doing the deal', but when that deal is in isolation of wider issues in the organisation, the community, etc., then is it good enough in today's climate? 'The real estate industry was slow to capitalize on the potential of sustainable development, leaving corporate owner-users, government agencies, schools and universities, and non-profit organizations to pioneer the green building revolution' (RREEF 2009: 12).

Quantifying either the three dimensions of TBL or the three shear zones does not necessarily provide sustainable solutions. Sometimes, any one of the three may be in conflict with another and trade-offs are therefore needed. These three elements/zones are independent, but they are not isolated entities to be considered separately. They need to be seen as a whole. It would, however, be fair to say that in most business decisions, the principal driver is the economic or financial dimension. If a course of action is financially viable, its ethical and environmental considerations will then be examined. Equally, if certain specific ethical or environmental objectives are sought as part of vision or within a corporate social responsibility setting, then these will only be implemented providing the financial bottom line is not unduly disturbed. When institutional and individual investors are more focused on wealth preservation, then few 'are likely to be motivated solely by social principles to ramp up their sustainability efforts or pressure real estate advisers to improve their sustainability records' (RREEF 2009: 12). Maybe, that is why it is easier for organisations to work within the first and the third shear zone and there tends to be less comfort with the middle one (i.e. sufficiency/ethical dilemma).

Interestingly, following the publication and circulation of the sustainable development definition from the Brundtland Report in 1987, it was this middle shear zone that first attracted attention from the environmental lobbies. It could therefore account for the long gestation period between the need and the realisation through action by the business community. It is now much clearer that it is possible (and legitimate) for organisations to aim for sustainability without jeopardising their profitability.

Consumption

In any consumption decision that seeks to find a sustainable solution, whether it is a decision to acquire a particular type of car or building, there are three fundamental questions:

- *What is to be consumed?* Here, the decision concerns both 'horizontal substitution' (i.e. standard specification office buildings or zero carbon office solutions, for example) and 'vertical substitution' (i.e. replace significant elements of office requirements through the use of 'third space' facilities).
- *How is it to be consumed?* This relates to the way in which accommodation is used. Efficiencies in energy, water, waste, etc. can all be gained through adopting sustainable practices and developing sustainable mindsets within organisations.
- *How much is to be consumed?* This concerns the amount of space required for organisations to operate efficiently. This aspect relates to the concept of 'sufficiency'.

Real estate advisers have an important part to play in guiding organisations regarding their property solutions. There are certain possibilities and limits to increase what would be perceived as sufficient and efficient for a client. Sufficiency in its strict sense for an individual means decoupling 'quality of life from consumption and income' (Schwegler *et al.* 2008: 12). It relates to wealth per person or wealth per organisation and has two levels: 'economic wealth per quality of life and quality of life per person' (Schwegler *et al.* 2008: 18).

However, in the context of an organisation's accommodation needs, it can be reinterpreted as sufficient space to enable the organisation efficiently to realise its strategic potentials. This then raises questions about the concept of efficiency. To help an organisation to increase efficiency, a real estate adviser will need to connect business efficiency with space sufficiency to provide a sustainable solution. It could be argued that over-consumption of space is in many organisations an unsustainable way to carry on business from both an environmental and a financial point of view. It is thus part of the role of the real estate adviser to advise on more effective use of space. For organisations and their advisers to be able to contribute effectively to sustainability, they, first, need to understand the necessity of sustainability and how it can be introduced throughout the organisation. This requires information and education.

Organisational symbols

Earlier, it was suggested that real estate advisers need to understand buildings as symbols, i.e. representations of an organisation's persona or what the organisation believes itself to be. These symbols are both cultural symbols (i.e. social branches) and natural symbols (i.e. unconscious roots). It is the job of the real estate adviser to unearth both of these types of symbol in order to provide effective solutions. Real estate decisions tend to be taken following discussion of the former (i.e. strategic plans, organisational charts, policies, budgets, etc.) with less attention being paid to the latter (i.e. friendships, power struggles, grapevine, ambition, etc.). The cultural element portrays the form of the building (i.e. its image), whilst the natural element facilitates the structure of the organisation and its working environment (i.e. its productivity).

Having a particular type of building can contribute to an organisation's capacities for doing and being (Belk 1988) and it can also be a part of the ideological structure of the organisation. Buildings help to create, enhance and preserve a sense of identity in a continual cycle of constructing and reconstructing that identity (Jackson 2005). Currently, many organisations are seeking to reconstruct themselves as sustainable entities. The obvious point where this can be most effectively demonstrated is in organisational space and the tangible identity of real estate. Admittedly, for real estate, 'there is a deep and multifaceted set of reasons as to why sustainability is moving forward and will continue to move forward having to do with the investor side, the tenant demand side, the government regulation, and frankly just good business sense' (RREEF 2009: 1).

However, many organisations use it most obviously as a cultural (explicit) symbol to state organisational personality without addressing the natural (hidden) symbol. This is often not really appreciating the role that real estate can play on the productive (as opposed to the cost) side of the business. But it is also often the case that an organisation will repress 'undesirable' contents by inventing ideological structures, so that, within accommodation decisions, there are unconscious (or shadow) symbols. These are implicit but they can expose something of the true nature of the organisation (Bowles 1990).

It is often difficult to dig to the unconscious roots of the organisation through traditional committee structures and formally structured meetings. However, it is possible to manage the process through a series of dialogues.

> In Dialogue a group of people can explore the individual and collective presuppositions, ideas, beliefs and feelings that subtly control their interactions. ... [It] is a way of observing how hidden values and intentions can control our behaviour, and how unnoticed differences in culture or gender can clash without our realizing what is occurring. It can therefore be seen as an arena in which collective learning takes place, and out of which a sense of increased harmony, fellowship and creativity can arise.
>
> (Bohm *et al.* 1991: 2)

Dialogue is discussed again later in this chapter as it relates to the case study example.

Reporting

Many organisations now include environmental and social sustainability within their management and reporting structures. This is partly due to changes in regulatory frameworks but it is also due to a change of perception and external business environment. However, concerns about environmental change generally have had an impact on many organisations' risk assessments. 'Climate change is fundamentally altering the competitive landscape for business. It exposes companies to physical risks such as increased intensity and frequency of weather events, droughts, floods, storms and sea level rise; and regulatory and competitive risk associated with mitigation strategies such as exposure to increasing costs of carbon' (WWF 2007: 29). As such, David Miliband, then UK Secretary of State for Environment, Food and Rural Affairs was quoted as saying in November 2006 'every industry needs to be an environmental industry in one sense or another' (WWF 2007: 34).

Accordingly, this chapter now explores issues that exist for real estate between the three dimensions of sustainability that make up the business triple bottom line (i.e. eco-efficiency, ethical sufficiency and social productivity).

Eco-efficiency

There are two main issues here. First, there is the relationship between 'sustainable' real estate and 'acceptable' returns. Second, there needs to be an understanding of the term 'efficiency'. When considering the criteria to apply to assess eco-efficiency, we need to be aware that these will, of necessity, be 'temporally dependent' (because of rapid change in environmental science and the business world) and also 'culturally and socially dependent' (because different organisational cultures will attribute differing meanings to the symbolism of sustainability).

The notion of eco-efficiency in most organisations tends to concentrate on mitigating perceived risks often through adaptation of buildings and existing technologies. However, when risks are much less understood and conceived, there may be a need for a broader temporal, social and cultural dimension to the response – a transformation. This suggests more resilience than is apparent in the current environment where market values (determined by market perceptions of short- and long-term risks) tend to be used as the criterion for eco-efficiency. Perhaps, it is preferable, therefore, to think in terms of resilient adaptation, transformation and evolution rather than financial, environmental or social risks. (Korhonen *et al.* 2008). These need to be linked into the strategic (developing a shared understanding of sustainability), tactical (overcoming structural barriers like market conditions, for example) and operational (learning and developing about innovation and new technologies) (Loorbach *et al.* 2010).

Sufficiency/ethical dilemma

Within this shear zone, taking account of the objectives of owners and occupiers of buildings, sufficiency will have a different meaning for investors and for users. Investors in real estate are concerned about the relationship between risk and return. Whether they are risk takers or risk avoiders, they will be seeking to achieve a return that at least matches the level of risk involved. On the other hand, occupiers of real estate seek suitable accommodation from which to conduct their business. Their criteria is not only about minimising costs but also maximising productivity through specific space requirements. However, in the ethical dimension of this shear zone one would expect to see broad similarities across both groups.

Discussion on the nature of sustainability as a variable in the determination of financial returns was considered in Chapter 7. This chapter will therefore concentrate on issues that arise for occupiers.

Occupation decision making

An enhanced income stream to an investor is dependent on a tenant who is willing to pay a higher rent. A tenant will be willing to pay a higher rent for 'sustainable' accommodation if the accommodation offers some greater tangible benefit over and above that which could be achieved through 'standard' accommodation. This could relate to running costs, health and safety, productivity, staff quality and retention, corporate image, the legal and regulatory framework, etc. This is very much about the 'what' of space, i.e. traditional vs. 'green', for example. For new build today, sustainable design is not a separate element, it should now be an intrinsic feature of the design. As such, there should be 'no significant difference in average cost for green buildings as compared to non-green buildings' (Matthiessen *et al.* 2007: 3). However, the situation may be different with existing buildings that represent the vast majority of accommodation in the market place.

So when considering the various characteristics of sustainable buildings it is possible to identify some of the ways in which (1) risk can be mitigated and (2) resilience enhanced for occupiers. These are the 'how' of accommodation usage. But they can only be effective if what is provided is used in a sustainable way. This requires some understanding of sustainable behaviour from the occupiers' points of view. Tables 7.2 and 7.3 in Chapter 7 do include some aspects of education and training for both environmental and social aspects, but these need to be instilled in all users and uses of such buildings to be effective. Lorenz *et al.* (2008) attempt to suggest means by which changes could take place through risk reductions. However, again, awareness and appropriate alignments will need to be in place along with these actions.

It is clear that 'tenants need to be educated about the benefits of making their occupied space energy efficient in order to encourage adoption' (Bodnar *et al*. 2010: 21). What form this education or training might take will vary from organisation to organisation. However, it would appear that there is a gap between attitude and behaviour, between intention and action as outlined in Chapter 8. It is a part of the corporate sustainability process to bridge this gap. In doing so, there are implications for the real estate adviser.

Aligning real estate with business operations

Real estate advisers as professionals are employed by organisations to provide solutions to accommodation needs for investment or occupation. As such, they need not only detailed technical, legal and financial knowledge of the property interests under consideration, but they also need to understand the client, the client's business and the underlying environment within which real estate holdings are perceived. Clients are consumers of real estate and as such often seek advice from professionals on their consumption requirements. Quite often, clients do not know what those requirements are, or they think that they know and accordingly articulate these requirements to their real estate adviser. It is argued here that the role of the real estate adviser is not simply to accept those instructions uncritically, but to evaluate them systematically in order to ensure that they do align with the client's business requirements. Real estate advisers are not experts in business, but they are experts in understanding the potential of individual buildings. As such, working with the client, helping them to articulate their real needs, will enable the real estate adviser to match real estate with their client's business operations.

Approaches to change

There are some guidelines specifically around Education for Sustainable Development (ESD). These suggest more than rational intelligence in that 'sustainability is not a smooth, cumulative, or linear process or a single desired end state. Instead, sustainability often requires social transformations that are complex and continuously changing' (Miller *et al*. 2011: 181). What is required is an ability to see the bigger picture, intelligence that 'gives our lives an overarching canopy of meaning and value' (Zohar *et al*. 2004: 64), i.e. wisdom intelligence, or what Zohar *et al*. (2004) call *spiritual capital*. This is 'a transformative intelligence that allows us to break old paradigms and to invent new ones' (Zohar *et al*. 2004: 67). It helps us to re-contextualise issues as they exist and to find new ways of thinking and new ways of action.

For example, the real estate industry and the corporate sector may identify an issue such as change/transformation in differing ways. They both work within their own discipline's bounded rationality. One tends to identify change as a mechanistic process and, accordingly, uses a rationalist approach based on facts, whereas the other tends towards a more critical, realist perspective of multiple complex behaviours (Dent *et al.* 2011). That only becomes a problem when one is the professional adviser of the other. It might therefore be argued that a purely rationalist approach is not good enough in times of rapid organisational and environmental change.

Cultural shifts

When a system that is perceived as stable suddenly appears to be in crisis, 'it can move to the edge of chaos' (Zohar *et al.* 2004: 113) and it becomes radically unstable. It is at times like these that elements of the system (and sometimes the whole system) are scrutinised. This often occurs immediately after financial crises because of their rapidity. But, equally, they could occur during social/political (or less likely, environmental) crises.

From this, it is apparent that '[s]hifting behaviour requires shifting underlying motives, that is shifting a whole paradigm' (Zohar *et al.* 2004: 113). It is further argued that '[t]he dialogue process is the most effective way known to bring about deep motivational shift and the resulting behavioural change in a group or an organizational culture. ... [D]ialogue makes us surface and challenge the assumptions that support our motives. It leads to a change in our existing paradigms or mental models. It is a structure that dissolves previous structures' (Zohar *et al.* 2004: 118). However, there are significant risks involved. The possibility of new understanding means there is no going back. There is no 'money-back guarantee', once the closet door has been opened a new meaning may emerge. It therefore requires a degree of courage for an organisation to start a dialogue process. It is not necessarily a short or an easy process and it also needs to be properly managed as an integral part of the transformation process. Here, dialogue has a very specific meaning, but, equally, focus groups or targeted discussions can achieve similar results if built around the same principles.

Dialogue

As mentioned earlier in this chapter, the process of dialogue can be an effective means of exploring beneath the surface. Often 'participants find that they are involved in an ever changing and developing pool of common meaning' (Bohm *et al.* 1991: 5). This can help management to start to structure change around the roots of the organisation rather than the branches. For example, total rationalisation and relocation of real estate rather than added extra satellite accommodation.

This can lead to a level of creativity that is unlikely to be unearthed through meeting agendas or discussion. Of course it can also cause some level of anxiety due to its unfamiliar approach, but working through these can lead to valuable insights. Zohar *et al.* (2004: 119) shows the distinction between dialogue and debate. The former (dialogue) covers issues such as (1) finding out, discussion; (2) questions; (3) sharing; (4) equal; (5) respect and reverence; and (6) exploring new possibilities and listening. However, 'debate' mainly concerns (1) knowing; (2) answers; (3) winning and losing; (4) unequal; (5) power; and (6) providing a point or defending a position. From this, it is possible to see that the starting point for a dialogue is at a point of equality regardless of rank; it is not based on power or defence of positions. Instead it is a process of finding out through sharing, listening and exploring new configurations and positions.

In order to illustrate what could be achieved by entering into a formal dialogue that might help to remove the boundaries around the set formulas, which any professional discipline such as real estate management may be tempted to proffer as standard solutions to individual problems. The following sections set out a case study example of this approach at Brockwood Park School, Hampshire, UK.

Case study

The Brockwood Park Estate consists of parkland stretching to 19 hectares with the main house and outbuildings (including cloisters accommodation and art barn) now used as a main school; a more modern adult study centre building within the estate; and infant school buildings located within a short distance of the main estate. The trustees were seeking to develop and implement a new estate strategy that could provide additional accommodation, thus increasing the capacity of the school without impacting significantly on the values of the organisation. A balance between the financial, community and environmental was therefore implicitly sought in any solution. However, this meant different things to different people in the organisation and various views were expressed by staff, school pupils and mature students.

Sustainability was to be a part of the process, not apart from the process. But at an early stage it was important for the trustees to understand what that actually meant to the organisation as a whole. All staff and students were therefore invited to focus group sessions that took the form of dialogues. In total, 40 people participated (i.e. 14 staff, 6 heads and 20 students). The participants were given the following guidance regarding the exercise. The general purposes were:

- not to infer but to understand;
- not to generalise but to determine the range;
- not to make statements about the community but to provide insights about how people perceive a particular situation.

These group meetings were to be a part of the research study to inform the estate strategy. They were not intended as decision-making or planning committees. The intention was to gather information from staff, school pupils and mature students and then to share these aggregated perceptions with those who were making decisions (i.e., essentially, the trustees). The groups tended to look for a range of ideas from people and to understand the different perspectives that people had about the overall estate strategy and the options contained therein. Each group was to 'become more than the sum of its parts' to exhibit a synergy that individuals alone did not possess.

The main themes of these focus group meetings were framed around certain set questions. The following are a selection of these:

- What are the benefits of working/studying here?
- What to you is important here and how can this be enhanced?
- Supposing you were asked to designate £1m to improve the infrastructure, how would you allocate the money?
- If a decision was taken by the trustees to commission a new building, what would be your vision?
- What is the major problem with the facilities here?
- What is the greatest challenge facing Brockwood today?

For much of the time the discussion concentrated on the relationship between the vision of education and the nature of space and accommodation. For example, in response to the question, what are the benefits of working/studying here? Figure 10.2 highlights the focus as follows:

| **Freedom**
Space
Thought
Networks | **Diversity**
Cultures
Places
Authority |
| **Sustainability**
Environmental
Community
Buildings | **Reflection**
Dialogue
Building form
Identity |

Figure 10.2

Some of the benefits of working at Brockwood

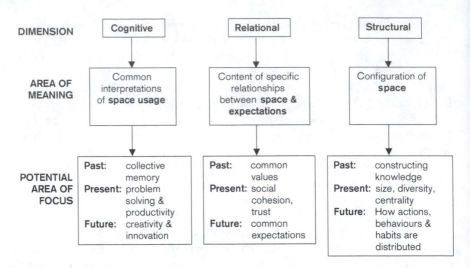

Figure 10.3

Social capital dimensions

Like many senior schools, Brockwood has spaces offering social capital opportunities. These spaces can be structural, relational or cognitive related (Widén-Wulff *et al.* 2004). Whichever dimension the space serves, it is part of a complex map of spaces that give the impression of being unmanaged (Figure 10.3). The intention of this was to give the impression that 'there was considerable freedom to use the space to create social capital' (AERS 2005: 12).

One of the problems that confronted pupils at Brockwood in particular in the focus group discussions was the difficulties they anticipated in 'reading' the signposts to new spaces and the consequent danger of finding no place to go to access social capital (AERS 2005). Their views therefore tended to be more conservative towards any changes to the accommodation proposed.

Many of the views expressed, in response to other questions, related to the social use or physical configuration of space and the quality of that space as motivating activity or emotion. This suggests that the participants considered consciously or subconsciously having the right type of space is important to enable them to maximise the benefit from the educational experience, whether teaching or learning.

Reflection on the case study

Strategy

In this way i.e. dialogue, it was possible for the trustees at Brockwood to learn something about not only the physical form required (i.e. size, location, design, use, etc.) but also to understand the way in which the right solution can reinforce the social structure and the purpose of the organisation. Sometimes the exercise undertaken by organisations is more radical in that it seeks 'to create a whole new field of meaning from which the majority of individuals can draw in attempting to shift their own behaviour' (Zohar *et al.* 2004: 126). That starts by looking at the underlying motives for either maintaining the status quo or for change. From here, it may then be possible to explore the values that support this motivation. 'We don't *begin* by trying to shift the culture' (Zohar *et al.* 2004: 126).

This is an important message for any organisation. This one has been used here for quite deliberate reasons to show that a governing body working very closely with its constituency can still learn much from close communication – listening, sharing and showing respect.

The principles remain the same for larger corporate organisations. The approach followed is likely to be a standard strategic process from conception to inception. Stringer (2009) sets one out for a green project or strategy as follows:

- Mobilisation – establishing a project charter with goals and objectives, roles and responsibilities, expected outcomes and measures for success. This is the stage where some form of dialogue can aid understanding. It is about relationships and empowerment.
- Diagnosis and discovery – the current state, the degree of change needed, building and business strategies that address the four pillars of human behaviour, technology, operations and design. This is the stage where culture, technology and behaviour come together and concerns flexibility.
- Strategy and programme development – prioritise strategies through an environmental impact–ease of implementation matrix. This is the strategic asset management plan. This is about communication and power.
- Implications and recommendations – create a structure for implementation of the green initiative step by step. This is all about trust.
- Implement, measure and adjust – be constantly vigilant and invest in research, education and green partnerships. This final step relies on fairness and truth.

Sufficiency

This might help an organisation to understand something about the 'what' and the 'how' of their accommodation. Now it is important to consider the 'how much'.

This again will depend on individual organisational requirements. It is the role of the real estate adviser to provide professional guidance. Often, a client will specify the need for space incrementally without having a strategic perspective. It is important therefore for the real estate adviser to question the client critically about their needs, how they use space and why they use space.

As with financial resources and good human resources, good real estate resources are scarce and valuable. As individual assets, they are often the most valuable and/or costly asset that an organisation has and it therefore should follow that real estate resources need to be managed efficiently and effectively. The financial resources utilised to fund and maintain real estate carry an opportunity cost and can be looked at in terms of the organisation's overall financial position. Sustainable designs and maintenance efficiencies can therefore have an impact on that position.

The way in which real estate resources are managed, as well as the profile of real estate resources, can have an impact upon an organisation's ability to achieve its business objectives. The size and nature of the existing real estate portfolio, the number of properties and their size, shape and condition, the geographical spread of the portfolio, the cost of maintenance and running costs all have an impact upon the organisation's business activities and, therefore, can contribute to the overall business and the profit margins available.

Social productivity

Social productivity is the final shear zone to be considered. It is the shear zone between the social and the economic dimensions as illustrated in Figure 10.1. Social sustainability occurs when the formal and informal processes, systems, structures and relationships actively support the capacity of current and future generations to create healthy and liveable communities. Socially sustainable communities are equitable, diverse, connected and democratic and provide a good quality of life. However, social sustainability is the idea that future generations should have the same or greater access to social resources as the current generation. This requires 'a radical redefinition of the social contract between business and society' (Elkington 1997: 142). It points to a new way of thinking that needs to be introduced through the value chain in organisations.

In itself social sustainability does not act counter to profitability. However, the two need to be seen in some form of balance, in order to achieve greater productivity without adverse social cost. Each organisation, each region, will have a particular set of circumstances that will require critical analysis bespoke to those circumstances. However, it may be possible to define a route that will structure that analysis. For example, Castells (2000) sees the social dimension of sustainability as (1) acknowledging plural identities and creating bridges, (2) seeking social inclusion, (3) making cooperation and competition compatible, (4) social mobilisation against structural violence and (5) decentralisation of power for greater accountability and greater flexibility.

This structure, or framework, needs to be cognisant of the setting within which decisions are taken. The real estate industry has, up until now, tended to concentrate, in general, 'more on "green buildings", "green travel plans", "smart workplaces", with less focus, for example, on the issues of futurity, or the socio-cultural dimensions of property investment, development and management within the communities where these companies operate' (O'Brien *et al.* 2009: 10). Thus the 'hard' technical side of sustainability is being addressed without the parallel 'softer' aspects of the social or cultural forming part of the thinking. This, for many real estate advisers, therefore, becomes a question of technical knowledge during the development, investment and management process rather than the less tangible aspects of behavioural learning and efficiency evaluation and usage of space.

However, it is not only a question of 'hard' and 'soft' approaches that the real estate adviser should be considering here. There is also the issue of whether there is a role in dealing with the cause (unsustainable behaviour) rather than concentrating on responding to the effect (climate proofing).

On the face of it, social sustainability seems to have much less to do with real estate than either financial sustainability or environmental sustainability. But, in a way it is the one area that both produces and consumes sustainably. Without the social neither of the other two aspects of sustainability would have real meaning outside of themselves.

In order to understand the implications of this, it is first important to define the scope of social sustainability. This has two main strands. It relates first to the social environment of community and second to workplace environments. Social sustainability seeks a process that aims to achieve life-enhancing conditions within communities (MacKenzie 2004). This relates to equity within communities, between communities and across generations. Within the workplace, this relates to the working community and its successors. Here it is necessary to consider not only sustainable urban designs and urban sustainable landscapes but also drivers of sustainable organisational change. This involves an examination of the overlapping concepts of social capital, social cohesion and social exclusion.

Social capital

Social capital relates to the networks that have been formed within communities and within organisations and the value systems that are negotiated and empowered. Social capital relies heavily on networks, norms and trust and requires a 'physical medium' through which it can operate (Davidson *et al.* 2009). Often that medium is real estate but it could also be the wider local environment generally. So, for example, in the Brockwood case study, Figure 10.3 shows the social capital dimensions as they relate to real estate. The main problem with social capital is its measurement.

Widén-Wulff *et al.* (2004) have identified some possible measures for the social capital dimensions. These range from organisation assessment tools looking at, for example, profile, culture and linkage to broader behaviour and social exchange methodologies. These do not necessarily measure in quantitative terms, but nevertheless they can offer a framework within which it might be possible to develop an understanding of an organisation (in this case) but equally a community or a region (as in the case study example in Chapter 11).

In the case of organisations, social capital consists of the bonds between employees within a business, and also of the bridges the business builds with its surrounding communities. Both are necessary for social capital to help create value. They, however, rely on creativity and trust to be most effective. Table 10.1 suggests ways in which real estate can enhance the social capital of an organisation.

Table 10.1   A four-way matrix for social capital aligned with real estate (MacGillivray 2004: 123)

	BONDING	BRIDGING
CREATIVITY	Enhancing real estate value, in multidisciplinary teams, using sweat equity and incentives	Brainwaves in the third space, among random individuals from friends to strangers, as serendipity
TRUST	Building the brand through a combination of shared ethos, mission, morale, storytelling, gossip	Marketing the brand by real estate symbolism and business reputation (expressed often through CSR), rooted in the community

Summary

The Brockwood School case has been discussed earlier in this chapter to demonstrate how to maintain and enhance the bond between people with similar characteristics and/or interests and to reinforce homogeneity and exclusivity. It also shows how the real estate needs can be fitted into the overall ethos and sense of place. Real estate has an 'idea' function (as a passive symbol) and a 'response to place' function (as an active creative force) (Day 1990: 107). Equally bridging between people from diverse contexts through outreach and developing new links with the local community can also be achieved through new development or through existing space, which can be used in a different way. A third form of social capital that is particularly relevant in the case of Brockwood is linking social capital. This concerns the relationships established between people with differential power. Brockwood already follows a strong 'dialogical method' in its teaching and so the focus groups used in the case study were conducted very much on those lines, where first year pupils shared views with heads of department. This allows much greater access to ideas, information and knowledge than would normally be seen in a school or many other organisations. From this, it can be seen that there is value in each type of social capital, and different combinations lead to different outcomes (AERS 2005).

Given the right environment, an emphasis on social capital can help to create social cohesion. This identifies the need for a shared sense of morality and common purpose together with aspects of order, inequalities and interactions. Again, both in communities and in organisations, social cohesion can establish a sense of belonging to place (Forrest *et al.* 2001: 2128).

The significant factors in social sustainability are the provision of social infrastructure, the availability of opportunity, accessibility, design, preservation of valued characteristics and ability to fulfil psychological needs (Chan *et al.* 2008). These are inclusive. Social exclusion, on the other hand, denies many of these factors.

These elements need to work with financial sustainability to be viable both in the public and the private sectors. How this is achieved is often a balancing act between competing resources. However, it is also a fertile ground for collaboration and integration of expertise. In some respects, it is not the specific problem that needs to be addressed, but the way in which it is to be addressed. The arena can therefore be an office, an organisation, a city or a region. Issues will be different but the way of thinking to come up with effective solutions needs to be holistic.

In general the real estate sector has identified three sets of behaviour associated with sustainability: consuming less, producing more, and wasting nothing. This sounds over simplified, but in reality this requires a dramatic change in thinking and behaviour, in terms of, for example, 'transforming urban centres in terms of what purpose they have, re-sourcing material used to construct buildings, and of course we are also looking at fundamental shifts in policy relating every aspect of sustainability. Sustainable real estate is not just about buildings, it relates to land, water, energy, transportation, air, and climate change.

(O'Brien *et al.* 2009: 50)

This not only supports the notion that sustainability is transdisciplinary but it also cuts across space and time. Tschakert *et al.* (2010), for example, set out a framework of anticipatory learning that helps to ensure that transitions in thinking and action are successfully navigated through an in-depth understanding and awareness of the holistic nature of the problem. From this position, it is possible to 'build knowledge, diversify ... ideas, reflect, communicate, develop a shared vision, and act ... to take advantage of windows of opportunity' (Tschakert *et al.* 2010: 16). Their five element framework of memory, analysis, discontinuities, anticipation and design is a useful vehicle to examine how real estate decision making can be sustained as a long-term predictive activity as opposed to simply forecasting. In this way, particularly with regard to area and regional development, the task of the real estate adviser is to offer a sustainable real estate input. To illustrate this, the next chapter sets out in detail a case study in Lincolnshire (UK) using the framework suggested by Tschakert *et al.* (2010).

11 Portrait of place

Introduction

This case study is used to try to demonstrate how a region examines its economic, environmental and social activities to try to find sustainable solutions to growth and well-being. It also demonstrates that '[s]ustainability is not about adding up values in three different columns but about systems analysis, integration and holistic thinking' (Terry 1999: 19). This is achieved through the methodological framework mentioned at the end of Chapter 10 together with the integration of key stakeholders.

Case study background

Central Lincolnshire is in the East Midlands of the UK (Figure 11.1), bordering areas of coastal Lincolnshire to the east, the fens to the south, Nottinghamshire to the west, and the Humber sub-region to the north. The Central Lincolnshire Joint Planning Unit is responsible for preparing joint planning policy for the area, which is comprised of the City of Lincoln, West Lindsey District (to the North of Lincoln) and North Kesteven District (to the south of Lincoln).

To understand how a place can change for the better, it is essential to understand its landscapes, its economies and its people. A deliverable vision for the future depends on a true grasp of local issues and opportunities and importantly an appreciation of the aspiration and capability of communities and systems to make change.

AECOM is a global organisation providing fully integrated professional, technical and management support service for a broad range of markets. In Central Lincolnshire, AECOM Design and Planning have undertaken the 'Portrait of Place' project, and conducted a sustainability audit for the area and its communities in the context of developing the strategic planning direction for the area. The project was undertaken as part of the evidence base for the emerging Central Lincolnshire Core Strategy, and it aimed to test the area's current performance against a range of sustainability aspects and to recommend

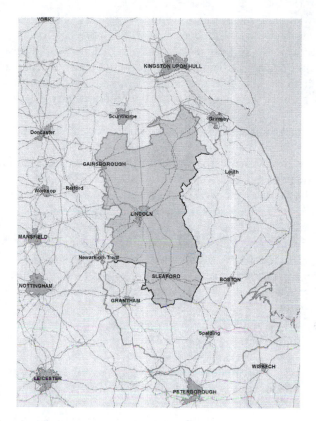

Figure 11.1

Location of Central Lincolnshire (AECOM 2011: 18)

key actions for the future to support the sustainable development of the area. The project considered the potential of the area to support advanced sustainability initiatives and development requirements, and specifically the use of the eco-town standards developed by the UK government. These standards require all buildings to aim to be zero carbon and 40 per cent of land to be designated as green space. The standards cover carbon emissions, employment, transport, local services, green infrastructure, biodiversity, water, flood risk, waste, healthy living and landscapes.

The intention was to develop a portrait of Central Lincolnshire from a sustainability perspective, considering its current social, economic and environmental performance as a whole, as well as considering the differences between the communities in the area. It was an attempt to understand Central Lincolnshire's current level of sustainability, and its potential for improvement in the future. To do this, the project made use of spatial and statistical analysis, as well as stakeholder workshops and community surveys to gain an understanding of both actual and perceived different communities' levels of sustainability.

This 'Portrait of Place' project is presented through Tschakert and Dietrich's five element framework (Tschakert *et al*. 2010) and principally followed aspects of the three shear zones (i.e. eco-efficiency, sufficiency and ethical dilemma, and social productivity) covered in detail in the previous chapter. In other words and broadly speaking, the relationships that communities have with each other can be described under the following headings:

- physical interactivity: the connections between places and their relative isolation;
- economic interactivity: the presence of employment sectors and their economic draw;
- social interactivity: the social networks in an area and the importance of settlements in terms of leisure or cultural support.

This project was central to the understanding of where and why growth was needed to promote a more sustainable future, and how it should be used by the Joint Planning Unit and communities alike as a tool to inform change and action in the area.

Project framework

The framework for facilitating anticipatory learning as an iterative socio-institutional process consists of five elements. These were identified in the previous chapter as memory, analysis, discontinuities, anticipation and design. These form an appropriate framework for an examination of AECOM's work in Central Lincolnshire, although, it has to be borne in mind, their actual tools of analysis did not necessarily follow this typology exactly.

Element 1: lessons learnt from the past (memory)

This element is concerned with understanding at all levels the consequences of past experience and now remaining open in decisions to learning. This is not only to ensure that mistakes are not repeated, but also that future opportunities are identified.

In the case of the individual, this would relate to being conscious not only of the tangible consequences of actions but also the emotional aspects and being open to future choices based on present decisions. In relation to this case study, AECOM have addressed this, as a starting point, through the roles that they assigned to individual communities within Central Lincolnshire.

Their classification was drawn from several pieces of analysis including area visits, local perspectives, bespoke analysis and telephone surveys. The roles of settlements could be understood simply by the degree to which their relationship with other settlements is based on 'attraction' or 'support'. An attractor was a settlement that other settlements were drawn to for its service provision, employment and facilities. A supporter was a settlement that had a primarily residential focus and relied on attractors nearby to provide key services. Clear criteria were defined for the relative nature of attractors and supporters (Table 11.1).

Table 11.1   The seven roles of communities in Central Lincolnshire (AECOM 2011: 10)

Role	Description
Regional attractor	A regional attractor is equivalent to a city or urban settlement that has significant economic and cultural draw on a regional scale. It is a place that is geographically and demographically large, with a complementary level of community facilities, services, and employment opportunities. A regional attractor's urban design is larger in scale, has specific residential and employment areas in addition to one or several central cores offering many retail and entertainment options. A regional attractor attracts residents from surrounding areas for employment, entertainment, shopping and other activities.
Primary attractor	A primary attractor is a town or neighbourhood that may have the potential to grow to be a city of its own. Towns have many of the amenities that a city might offer – employment opportunities, shopping and community facilities – but much fewer of them. People living in primary attractors can meet the vast majority of their needs locally, but are attracted to cities for the occasional shopping requirements, nights out and often for employment. Similarly, primary attractors attract residents from smaller settlements for local employment and basic facilities.
Secondary attractor	Secondary attractors are smaller towns that are predominantly urban in nature, but their urban character is focused in the town core. Outside the town core, the urban character gives way to a more rural nature. There is generally a smaller residential proportion compared with a primary attractor, as its main function is to service surrounding villages. Aside from local retail and services, local service towns generally have few employment opportunities.
Tertiary attractor	Tertiary attractors are predominantly small villages that act as local service centres in rural areas. Tertiary attractors are mainly residential settlements, often with larger single detached housing. They contain very basic amenities such as a small shop, pub, post office or restaurant. They attract residents from nearby villages, but retail and service establishments do not create an urban setting. Any 'urban core' that does exist fits in with the surrounding residential character. Residents tend to travel to other attractors for some of their daily requirements, especially employment.
Primary supporter	Primary supporters are large settlements located on the outskirts of a primary or secondary attractor. They have basic amenities but the settlement is dominated by residential character, with no recognisable service core. Primary supporters are well connected to an attractor and most residents commute to the local attractor for employment and key services. They are often separated from a primary or secondary attractor by a development gap or preserved landscape area. Properties are often large with sizable single detached houses.

Role	Description
Secondary supporter • Accompanied • Solitary	Similar to primary supporters, secondary supporters work as benefactors for attractors. These are often the smallest, more remote settlements, very rural in nature, and lack the vast majority of services needed to sustain themselves. Residents travel to attractors, large and small, for many of their basic needs. However, residents benefit from large swaths of greenspace surrounding these villages, contributing to a highly tranquil atmosphere. An 'accompanied' secondary supporter shows strong connections with local attractors, while a 'solitary' secondary supporter shows less reliance on attractors with predominant local economies.

Element 2: monitoring and analysis of trends to anticipate future events

The past and the present will inform the need for change but any system, whether an organisation, an individual building or a region can still be constrained by a number of factors. These could include the consequences of its past, external variables, the drivers of change, insufficient knowledge, etc.

In the context of the 'Portrait of Place' project, this element represents the point at which actions and trends from the past that have created the present are analysed and interpreted as a series of indicators. Here they are specifically related to sustainable criteria and help to inform a range of sustainability domains, or areas of particular concern or interest and community connections.

So, as part of the 'Portrait of Place', a set of indicators were defined, grouped and analysed. In this way AECOM Design and Planning were able to develop a comprehensive statistical framework for assessing the sustainability of both existing areas and possible new development locations, responding to both national drivers and local needs and possibilities.

The nine sustainability domains that were identified as being significant were (1) managing resources, (2) ecological quality, (3) future resilience, (4) economic performance, (5) cultural vibrancy, (6) connections, (7) efficient living, (8) successful communities and (9) effective places (Table 11.2). Now, of course, each of these had to be qualified in the context of the project. However, they proved useful in providing a comprehensive yet balanced perspective of social, economic and environmental issues. From these, it was then possible to prepare a specific sustainability index to use in articulating the sustainability of existing communities and areas, bringing together a range of indicators.

Table 11.2   The sustainability domains (AECOM 2011: 52)

Sustainability domain	What this domain considers
Environmental and landscape layer	
1 Managing resources	The performance of infrastructure and services regarding the efficient management of resources.
2 Ecological quality	The natural environmental context and current diversity and value of key eco-systems.
3 Future resilience	The resilience of the area with regard to the future effects of climate change.
Economic and cultural layer	
4 Economic performance	The current performance of the economic markets and skill sectors and their viability into the future.
5 Cultural vibrancy	The provision of cultural facilities and the role of tourism and historic assets.
Community and settlement layer	
6 Connections	Accessibility to key services, schools, jobs and community facilities and how much communities are using public transport, cycling or walking.
7 Efficient living	The performance of buildings and their users in managing resources at a local level.
8 Successful communities	The characteristics of local populations in terms of local governance, cohesion and community concern.
9 Effective places	The urban design and sense of place of a community, which determines its performance as a neighbourhood.

By breaking the analysis into domains it provided a more sophisticated picture than a single overall score, as it made clear which aspects perform poorly or well in a certain area. Those aspects could then be targeted for change, whether that was through community initiatives or physical regeneration and growth.

Element 3: planning for surprises, perturbations and discontinuities through scenarios

'Ignorance and surprise', along with calculable risks, are part of our everyday lives. Our ability as individuals or communities to cope with these depends largely on open-mindeness in learning and an agility that accepts change as inevitable. Tschakert *et al.* (2010: 25) 'advocate for the use of participatory scenario planning/building as a methodological tool not only to explore interconnectedness, surprises, and uncertainties but also to offer empowering learning spaces where multiple voices, experiences, and constraints can be heard'. AECOM used interactive sessions and games together with stakeholder and community workshops (Illustration 11.1).

Illustration 11.1

Stakeholder participation (AECOM 2011: 55)

Stakeholder and community workshops – 19 January 2011

Harnessing local knowledge was an essential part of the development of the 'Portrait of Place'. Two workshops were held in Lincoln in early 2011, which gathered together key stakeholders and community representatives. The workshops included presentations of the emerging analysis, and included two important sessions:

1. Defining Sustainability Priorities: Participants discussed the sustainability priorities for the area and tested the appropriateness of the nine sustainability domains identified in the study.

2. Examining Community Types: Participants broke into groups to discuss different case study settlements that varied in terms of type, scale and location. Participants examined what sustainability issues were most pertinent to these communities, and what actions needed to be taken to make positive change. As part of this exercise they discussed if any sustainability domains became particularly important to those communities.

The workshop sessions were important to the development of the study, and highlighted a number of important conclusions, including:

- The nine domains contained within the sustainability index were all validated as important. When asked to rank the domains in terms of importance to Central Lincolnshire, participants found this challenging as each domain is important for different reasons. The corollary is that weighting the index – suggesting some domains are more important than others – was determined to be counterproductive. It is for this reason that the sustainability index remains unweighted.

As a result, it was not possible to create one overall map of sustainability for Central Lincolnshire as this would inherently carry a weighting.

- Workshops designed to establish priorities for each of the 14 case studies identified some common priorities at a local scale. These priorities have helped us to establish sustainability objectives for the different types of communities in Central Lincolnshire. The workshop feedback helped to establish robust case studies for this report.

- The workshops demonstrated how the wealth of information generated in this study can be used for analysis by the councils, key partners and communities. Participants were given maps as resources to judge the relative performance of case study areas. This trial both introduced participants to the information and showed how it can be useful as a neighbourhood planning tool.

Element 4: measures of anticipatory capacity

This element moves the project from a range of possible future scenarios to a point where the semblance of a plan can be formulated that is both flexible and directive. This involved critical reflection to enable the project to move from vision to action. This is similar to preparing for system change in resilience thinking (Tschakert *et al.* 2010).

From the data that AECOM gathered, they were able to develop a sustainability index that brought together a set of statistical indicators under each domain. The indicators were selected to provide coverage of key issues and opportunities for the area. A large selection of indicators had been reviewed in the development of the index, and the index was eventually refined back to *key* indicators. A scoring system (Table 11.3) was then developed to interrogate and compare indicators within the sustainability index. The scoring of performance against the indicators selected was comparative.

Table 11.3   Scoring system (AECOM 2011: 56)

Score Awarded	Criteria for Achievement
3 Points	Performance significantly above the comparison average
2 Points	Performance in line with the comparison average
1 Point	Performance significantly below the comparison average
No points	Area makes no significant contribution to the achievement of this sustainability indicator or performance is very poor (two standard deviations below comparison average)

A relevant comparison average was identified for each indicator to allow AECOM to identify whether an area performed relatively better or relatively worse. The comparison average selected varied according to the nature of the index. In all cases, the most meaningful comparison was sought to allow an understanding of the local idiosyncrasies of the area (Table 11.4).

Element 5: design of dynamic decision-support tools for adaptation planning

According to Tschakert *et al.* (2010: 28) this element is related to the integration of climate change data into anticipatory action learning processes, which 'calls for a skilful blend of a potentially top-down external agenda with local-level awareness and agency building'. AECOM achieved this through radar diagrams and domain performance maps.

To build on the statistical base provided by the index, the project brought together several other pieces of evidence:

- Desk-based research: each domain was researched in detail, drawing on existing studies and non-statistical evidence to build a portrait of place. Whilst the index provided a directly measurable and spatially intelligent means of assessment, it was only intended to utilise key decision indicators that act as a proxy for broad issues. The index was therefore used at this stage in conjunction with results from this wider research to gain a comprehensive overview of Central Lincolnshire's sustainability performance.
- Case study communities: a series of case study communities were selected for closer examination at a settlement scale. The aim of the case studies was to examine sustainability issues and opportunities at a settlement scale, providing interpretation of the index and other research, and setting actions for the future. To complement the case study analysis, community consultation events were undertaken with five rural and five urban communities using the case study results. The consultation process helped to develop a framework for understanding sustainability at a local level, using the sustainability index as a tool for communities to set out the changes they would like to make to their area.
- Telephone surveys: as part of the study, 2,000 phone interviews were conducted with residents across Central Lincolnshire. The case study locations were surveyed specifically and a quarter of the surveys were scattered across Central Lincolnshire. The questions aimed to both cross-check statistical assessments, picking up idiosyncrasies related to individual settlements, but importantly also to understand the aspirations of communities and their desire for change.

This helped to identify strategic opportunities to improve/refine domain performance (Table 11.5).

This, then, helped AECOM to come to some clear conclusions about the sustainability level and requirements for each domain within a local setting to inform the core strategy decision-making process.

Table 11.4 Sustainability domains comparison to SCSs (AECOM 2011: 54)

Bespoke sustainability index for Central Lincolnshire	Sustainable communities strategy for Lincolnshire	Sustainable communities strategy for Lincoln	Sustainable communities strategy for West Lindsey	Sustainable communities strategy for North Kesteven
		Environmental and landscape layer		
Managing resources	Manage natural resources prudently; reuse, recycling; develop renewables	Well-managed natural resources; reduce, reuse, recycle; reduce transport GHG emissions; secure energy supply	Improve recycling; assess derelict land	Minimise waste
Ecological quality	Countryside, coastline, towns much richer in biodiversity; environments cared for; enhance green infrastructure	Well-maintained natural environment	Conserve and fund important landscapes; minimise environmental crimes	Maximise open space; enhance local biodiversity
Future resilience	Embrace CC challenges; flood risk mitigation	Reduce flood risk	Manage flood risk	Flood risk mitigation; tackle sustainability agenda; climate change mitigation
		Economic and cultural layer		
Economic performance	Spending money wisely; clusters of excellence in agriculture, food, engineering, leisure and creative industries; economic diversity	A workforce with skills and opportunities; better incomes; increase inward investment; job creation via urban extensions	Improve housing market opportunities; diversity industries' higher skilled jobs	Increase inward investment; max tourism; skills development; strong and diverse economy
Cultural vibrancy	Balance people, heritage, nature	Enhance sense of place	Community engagement	Youth strategy related to sport, arts and culture

Bespoke sustainability index for Central Lincolnshire	Sustainable communities strategy for Lincolnshire	Sustainable communities strategy for Lincoln	Sustainable communities strategy for West Lindsey	Sustainable communities strategy for North Kesteven
		Community and settlement layer		
Connections	Widespread digital technology; effective public transit; more sustainable modal split	Improve transit infrastructure; improve sustainable access network	Extend public transit infrastructure	Better choice of transport facilities; community transport schemes; walking and cycling
Efficient living	Minimise energy use	Carbon reduction; water efficiency		Water efficiency; maximise energy efficiency; high quality housing
Successful communities	Health and well-being; top 30 UK university; high quality skills training; community feels safe	Good public health service; excellent access to services, affordable housing, recreation; safer communities; new design consider how to minimise crime	Improve healthcare facilities; support parishes; reduce anti-social behaviour and crime and fear of crime	Diversity and cohesion; health inequality; parish partnerships; older persons; volunteering; tenant participation; reduce fear of crime; reduce business crime
Effective places	Good condition homes; affordable	Affordable housing; engaging learning and living environments for children, leisure provision	Increase affordable housing; new housing built sustainably; decrease disused retail	Affordable housing; review housing priorities; reduce homelessness; max use of open space

Table 11.5 Summaries of opportunities to improve sustainability (AECOM 2011: 59–150)

Domain	Strategic opportunities to improve domain performance
1 Managing resources	• Increase wind energy provision in suitable areas • Deliver renewable heat networks • Support further improvement of waste management and recycling • Make land available for growing food in urban areas • Focus on water reduction in supply and end-use efficiency • Brownfield development
2 Ecological quality	• Improving agricultural land as • Ecological habitats • Creating ecological corridors • Improving urban ecology
3 Future resilience	• Improving strategic flood resistance • Reducing flooding impacts locally • Preparing for climate change • Changing our habits
4 Economic performance	• Improving the economic and social mobility of residents • Driving up investment • Diversification • Driving up the knowledge base • Resilience through critical mass and agglomeration economies • Reducing deprivation and providing new employment
5 Cultural vibrancy	• Building on Lincoln's assets • Building on links with the university • Delivering cultural activities in other centres
6 Connections	• Encouraging residents' behaviour change • Improve the provision of services
7 Efficient living	• Community-led behaviour change • Targeted building improvements • Gain focus on water efficiency • Working with industry
8 Successful communities	• Foster urban communities • Health and crime focus • Supporting longevity
9 Effective places	• Open space provision • Creating effective rural clusters • Broadband interventions • Housing provision

Summary

The portrait of place project in central Lincolnshire has been used to demonstrate the process a consultant would go through to evaluate the opportunities for the continual growth of an area. This relates to physical, economic and cultural growth whilst at the same time being mindful of the crucial sustainability issues that will ensure that the communities and the linkages between the communities remain sustainably viable into the future.

Economic sustainability involves the reproduction of the ability to generate financial wealth which it requires increasing connectivity and human resources. Social sustainability, on the other hand, involves recognition of differences within the city or region and active bridging that reproduces the differences but does not use them to exclude. What is sustainable is getting competition to recognise its basis in cooperation. Finally, environmental sustainability concerns natural resource depletion and the impact of human activity on changes to the climate. Sustainability as a whole is not about stagnation nor is it about preservation. It is a proactive engagement with human and natural resources as an 'emergent evolution' to create and recreate long-term well-being for individuals, communities, organisations and nations. At the outset, therefore, it should be understood that, through such a process, no city or region should necessarily be guaranteed survival, as of right, in its current form or status.

As an example, Castells (2000: 121) considers the main problem for urban sustainability may be the 'sustainability of the notion of city in itself'. This notion, or any such similar transformatory hypothesis, is interesting in that, without identifiable centres, there would be a danger that nobody would know where they were in the social, and to a degree psychological, sense. Without re-learning (i.e. a different way of thinking about space and its use), there would just be people in space. People occupy space without having a sense of place. An example might be a lower income family winning £150 million on the lottery. Moving from an estate house to a landed 'estate' is semantically simple but psychologically a whole new mindset is needed to understand the network of meanings and symbols that constitute this cultural shift. That is why, at both the macro and the micro level, it is important to learn about change and uncertainty and, ultimately, 'manage for resilience rather than learning by shock' (Tschakert *et al.* 2010: 14).

In addition, there are similarities here between what might be required at a community level and the process that corporate or investing institutions might undertake when addressing sustainable decision making. The approach introduced by Tschakert *et al.* (2010) is equally applicable to such organisations. So, for example, corporate memory will feed into current status as background to developing a future strategy through a series of scenarios. The detail in each case will be different but the fundamentals are likely to be very similar.

In the context of real estate decision making, such thinking and systematic evaluation needs to be incorporated more profoundly. O'Brien *et al.* (2009: 11) believe that such approaches can lead to 'a new corporate mindset and encourage managers to anticipate what lies ahead for their company, by looking beyond traditional ways of thinking, breaking down political, economic and social norms, and creating a new corporate philosophy based on responsibility'.

Furthermore, future thinking is an iterative process that works to develop scenarios rather than trying to forecast. This helps to develop ways of anticipatory thinking rather than ways of predictive thinking. In turn this opens up a participatory dialogue and creates the space for the whole community to get involved and to stay involved in such strategic planning. This can often lead to new insights and greater resilience.

12 Sustainability balanced scorecard that aligns real estate with business

· ·

Introduction

The previous chapter applied Tschakert and Dietrich's framework of anticipatory learning to the sustainability plans for a region (i.e. Central Lincolnshire) through the 'Portrait of Place' project. This chapter concentrates on how organisations can implement transformational and sustainable change. Just as with the 'Portrait of Place' initiative, the relevant statutory authorities found it difficult to separate themselves from the issues that confronted them. They employed outside consultants to help them to formulate effective solutions in partnership. Similarly, this chapter demonstrates how a consultant was able to identify the issues surrounding their client organisation. The client, AAT (The Association of Accounting Technicians) and the consultant (Corpra) worked very closely in partnership to achieve a long-term solution that addressed deep-rooted organisational issues as well as sustainability criteria. The chapter shows how established organisational and corporate strategy review methodologies can be used to improve sustainability in a business, especially with respect to its use of real estate.

Real estate's five dimensions

Chapter 3 of this book introduced the concept of the building form as a cultural product. As such, the building becomes symbolic of the organisation

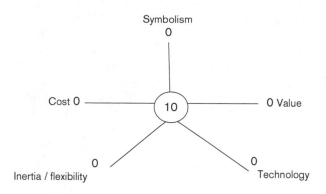

Figure 12.1

Five dimensions of real estate analysis tool (RICS 2009c: 24)

occupying it. The building reflects the organisation's core business and public statements. In helping organisations to understand their relationships with their buildings, Corpra have identified five dimensions of real estate that will go a long way to signifying the fit of the space to the business. These five dimensions are: technology, inertia, cost, value and symbolism (Figure 12.1). The way in which they relate to each other and their relative strength within an organisation will indicate how well aligned real estate holdings are to the organisation's business operations. For example, if an organisation claims high regard for the environment in its business dealings, their real estate holdings should help to symbolise that attitude. If the organisation actually occupies low-quality, highly energy-inefficient buildings then, potentially, this will impair their ability to support their mission as probably stated in their CSR statements. The crucial axis is the central core of the five dimensions model (i.e. the cost–value line). This is then affected by technology and inertia, which is often part of the unconscious and unchangeable aspects of the organisation. On the other hand symbolism is very much the external image that is expressed to the world.

Technology: a property or the portfolio facilitates and does not constrict the business, and enables the organisation to be flexible and agile. Technology is defined by design and explains the whole life experience of the building from initial design and construction elements through lifecycle assessments to ongoing management systems (including decisions about refurbishments and eventual redevelopment).

Inertia: this dimension relates not only to the resistance that can be experienced with the introduction of new working practices, initiatives and office design solutions. It also relates to the concept of inertia where, set on a trajectory, an organisation will find it hard to alter the speed and direction of that rate of travel. The dimension is principally concerned with the energy and motivation found within the organisation to address change.

Cost: an explicit balance will have been decided upon within an organisation between the cost and the value of a property or the portfolio to its business. In this case, management of cost is aligned to sustain that balance. This dimension is less influenced by initial costs and is more concerned with the overall lifecycle and the impact this has on marketing and efficiency.

Value: as with cost, an explicit balance will have been decided upon within an organisation between the value and cost of a property or the portfolio to its business. Here, it is principally the management of value that is considered as needing to be aligned to sustain that balance. To achieve value that achieves sustainability criteria it needs to be the link between the market and eco-efficiency. This should be the central horizontal stream.

Symbolism: bearing in mind that buildings are often one of the most powerful conveyors of a corporate brand (see Chapter 3 for a more detailed discussion about this issue), this dimension helps organisations to understand what their workplace or real estate is saying about their business both internally and externally. This dimension is therefore principally concerned with the vertical flow from eco-design through eco-marketing to eco-niche strategy.

Organisational change

The ability of an organisation to shift any of these dimensions is expressed as its agility and its ability to maintain and enhance its position. It is an indication of its resilience. The terms on which a property or the portfolio is owned and the way it is managed will help to indicate the impact the cost and the illiquid nature of real estate could have on organisational agility. This is an illustration of the flexibility that exists within the overall flow from process to customer engagement and satisfaction.

However, in any organisation, change is difficult. Attempts to quickly understand the world of change in organisations are often thwarted by the fact that there is more than one type of change. For simplicity, we can break these down into three major types: anticipatory, reactive and crisis.

The key feature of *anticipatory* change is that it is by far the least expensive to do but also the hardest to implement. It requires certain conditions of leadership and dynamic capabilities. This is also the domain of world class organisations. Frequently, this is not seen internally as change but simply the constant process of adaptation and anticipation of customers' needs. Business as usual!

Reactive change is easier to do because it is clear to all, the external environment within which an organisation has to react. This is the 'burning deck' that less agile organisations wait for before they change. This type of change is more expensive for an organisation, but it helps that it can be tangibly seen as solving a problem and can become a project. Many organisations live by this routine and it can also become the norm.

Crisis change is theoretically easier to accomplish than the other two types of change (i.e. anticipatory and reactive). However, it is the most expensive to complete and if it becomes routine, it becomes terminal (unless it is an organisation like the NHS, which tends to lurch from single big solutions to crisis). With this change, crisis managers are recruited to lead any changes, as the leadership team that got the organisation into the crisis, are unlikely to get them out of it. Yet if the change agents and leaders do not stay, then the old routines emerge again. Such a change is conditioned by pattern or by tradition and is just a continuity of what has gone on before.

This suggests that different techniques, approaches and capabilities are required in all three types of change. However, it is possible to define a framework for addressing these. In this regard, MacIntosh *et al.* (2001) have developed a broad framework for conditioned emergence, consisting of conditioning, disequilibrium and feedback management, which can be adapted to meet the needs of a particular set of changes that circumstances required.

Conditioning starts by identifying and reframing the deep structure and rules (both content and process) that underpin the organisation's current archetype. *Creating far-from-equilibrium conditions* creates the space for the new deep structure to become established. It opens up the possibility for 'radical, qualitative change [with the capacity] to import energy and export entropy [thus creating] a dissipative structure' (MacIntosh *et al.* 1999: 301). In other words, transformation is destabilising because it has the capacity to shift beyond the boundaries of the structure to open up new opportunities. The inertia is moving from the known, the familiar, the tried and tested into the unknown, new market, new mindset. Finally, *managing the feedback processes* involves acknowledging traces of the old archetype and related negative feedback but, at the same time, promoting the positive feedback from the new deep structure, which will lead to the development of new systems.

A balanced sustainability scorecard

Real estate is part of the business decision-making process. The models discussed in this chapter, therefore, relate to the business as a whole, particularly when significant change is occurring. In 1987, Schneiderman at Analog Devices, developed 'the first balanced scorecard', a business tool that has since become the standard general management model for many organisations. This tool has been modified over the years since its original development and it has been specifically focused on both sustainability (Hockerts 2001) and corporate real estate (Lindholm *et al.* 2006). For the purposes of this book, it has been further modified to help show the process of effectively introducing sustainable practices and processes into an organisation through real estate realignment (Table 12.1).

Table 12.1   Real estate in the business decision-making process

Perspectives	Real estate measures
Financial	Return of real estate assets Value of properties Cash flow Own:lease ratio Maintenance and management
Internal business process	Occupancy rates Real estate alignments (process, people, design) Process constraints Sustainability objectives and EMS Building lifecycles
Learning and growth	Levels of expertise and capability Professional relations and networks In-house training/learning opportunities Atmosphere and ambience
Customer	Customer satisfaction/expectation Cost:value balance Customer retention Market share Real estate capacity and market growth

More specifically, Figure 12.2 demonstrates an iterative process whereby the starting point in a cycle is the strategic position of the organisation. This is not a fixed point on the cycle, it is itself fluid and will change both in the short term and over the long term depending on the four interrelated components. These are commonly called learning/growth, internal business processes, customer and financial.

Figure 12.2

Balanced scorecard (strategic perspectives) (Procurement Executives' Association 1999: x)

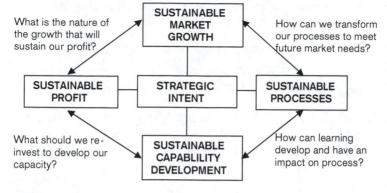

Figure 12.3

Sustainability balanced scorecard (strategic perspectives)

For the purposes of this book and following Hockerts (2001) these four elements can be relabelled as: (1) sustainable capability development, (2) sustainable processes, (3) sustainable market growth and (4) sustainable profit. These four elements can be expanded into a more detailed matrix of relationships built on a strategic intent that aspires towards sustainable business practices as shown in Figure 12.3.

The strategic intent here is to implement sustainability through both the working practices and real estate holdings as part of corporate culture. This can only effectively be achieved within resource capabilities and the structures that are in place. Here resources relate to both internal and external human, institutional and fixed resources. The structures are the processes by which the performance of these resources is monitored. This requires organisational learning focused on developing sustainability literacy. *Capabilities and cooperations* describe the starting point and the development of learning. This involves both a space audit of the accommodation and a skills audit of the human resources.

- *Space audit* – A space audit is prepared to provide an overview of the characteristics and performance of an organisation's existing real estate. In addressing these it should be possible to devise a progressive and proactive strategy. Information for this audit should be obtained from surveys, inspections, existing plans and discussions with management, staff and other relevant stakeholders. The audit will provide information on size, age, building condition, infrastructure, compliance, running costs, functional suitability, occupancy rates, etc.
- *Skills audit* – A skills audit is intended to review existing skills against the skills needed both now and in the future. In this context, skills include both technical and transferable skills. These skills are highlighted in individuals and groups through a five-stage process consisting of:

1. the identification of existing skills and levels of knowledge;
2. an outline of skills needed in the future and anticipated levels of knowledge;
3. an assessment of ability rating;
4. a review of that ability rating; and
5. identification of future development needed.

Through both space and skills audits, it might be possible to determine the level of competency and compatibility of staffing and accommodation for the organisation and its business environment. Such skills need to be cross-referenced with partners, who may be technical, commercial, social or academic, in order to capitalise on the joint skill base but also to identify gaps where additional competence and training might be needed.

In terms of *the processes*, these can be divided up into operational, tactical and strategic processes (Figure 12.4). In relation to sustainable real estate these can be identified as management, life cycle analysis and design. Management here is not only an issue of environmental management but also the impact that managing spaces can have on social aspects such as productivity, health, well-being, etc. These are day-to-day operational issues. They are influenced by longer term evaluations of occupation and use of the building in line with the strategic intent, along with the basic building fabric and design aspects. These processes therefore connect the three 'bottom-line' issues of finance, environment and the social not only across an organisation but also external to that organisation.

In this way, an organisation will move towards effective action in the three shear zones identified in Chapter 10, i.e. eco-efficiency, sufficiency and social productivity. Eco-efficiency is seen through the continual monitoring of the occupation and use of space in the organisation. Sufficiency is also concerned with occupation and use but more specifically it relates to duration (lease terms) and rationalisation of space (right sizing) to ensure agility in real estate solutions that match the rate of change in the business itself. It is the sufficiency element that is important to the real estate adviser as it feeds back into the value or worth calculations on particular properties. Finally, social productivity relates to the broader issue of identity in the market place for an organisation and its products or services.

The image creates the identity and helps to retain, expand or contract the market base. Symbolism will play an important part in the marketing activities of the organisation and real estate again will be significant as a representative icon. This will also be significant in the attraction and retention of key staff. This journey leads hopefully towards sustainable profit, a combination of turnover driven by sustainable principles and reduced costs through efficiency and sufficiency.

Success will be attained through different balances being achieved in different organisations, so it is not possible to be prescriptive. However, getting the mix right for an organisation is important and the real estate adviser

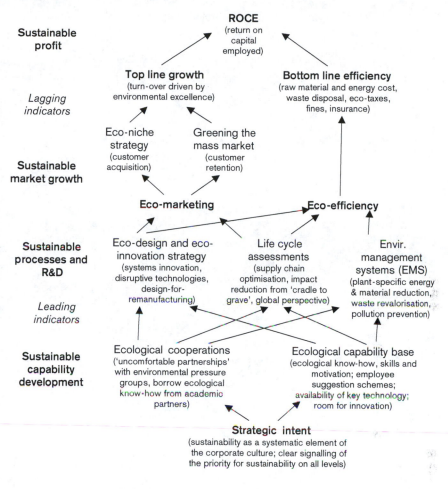

Figure 12.4

Illustrative example for an eco-efficiency balanced scorecard (Hockerts 2001:17)

needs to be aware of the value drivers in any one situation. The crucial information is contained within the middle sections of the balanced scorecard (Figure 12.5). It is in the processes and the markets that business is won or lost and it is these components that will influence the learning and the profit. The next section uses the Association of Accounting Technicians (AAT) project to demonstrate how this balance scorecard can actually be used in practice.

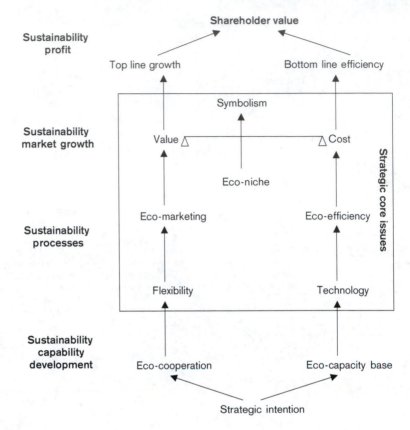

Figure 12.5

Strategic core issues

Case study

Background

AAT wanted to reach out to more people. Traditionally, they have helped students who have not been to university or cannot afford to train for accounting qualifications. Membership was stagnating and thousands of potential candidates were missing out because they did not know about the organisation. Former AAT students were not being encouraged to keep in touch and continue their professional development. By their own admission, they were not working well as a team, and the organisation was being hampered by its own red tape. Managers were preoccupied with pleasing AAT's ruling body or 'council', rather than nurturing their staff; while staff were overburdened with projects that lacked clear timescales and objectives.

Many employees appeared to have lost sight of the organisation's mission and had little sense of how they, as individuals, could contribute to it.

In answer to their growth aspirations, Corpra were engaged as management consultants to advise AAT on their relocation and growth plans. The council members believed more floor space was necessary if they were to expand their services. They planned to buy another freehold property, wanting the security and status that outright ownership of a large asset traditionally provides

Project stages

Corpra saw the move as an opportunity for a significant cultural change within the organisation. What began as a simple 'lift and shift' job – the physical relocation of the AAT – turned into a far bigger project, involving a wholesale review of the way the organisation worked.

Stage 1: sustainable capability development

Corpra spent three months in the discovery process undertaking space and skills audits. They consulted the council, management and staff about how they worked. They conducted over 50 interviews, speaking to every member of the board and a cross-section of staff. They discovered a mismatch between what the client was trying to do, and what they wanted to achieve. In order to help the organisation achieve *agility* the opportunity for transformation was high – AAT had the will, and the resources.

Stage 2: sustainable processes

The next step was to question the physical move. Based on lifecycle *cost/value* assessments, Corpra challenged the assumption that AAT needed to buy a large new freehold property. Due to its age and size, the old building cost around £500,000 a year to maintain. For the same annual sum, AAT could move into more sustainable, smaller leasehold offices, and release substantial amounts of capital by selling their old HQ.

This was at the heart of positioning AAT for the future. Corpra believed that instead of working in two different buildings, spread across eight floors, staff could be in open plan offices on a single floor. This would help them work better as a team. They sought to get to the position where the *technology* was an opportunity and not a barrier to their operation.

Stage 3: sustainable market

In the heart of the financial district, modern office space was more readily available for leasehold. The council members were initially wary – swapping a freehold for leasehold was highly unusual for a membership organisation. The feeling was that significant *symbolism* was invested in the old building and this would be lost with such a move. When the £6 million sale of AAT's old building twice fell through at the eleventh hour, they could have been forgiven for running scared. However, they realised that pressing ahead would release valuable capital for investment. In addition, it would give staff an opportunity to work differently.

In contrast, previously, property consultants had advised AAT that they would need to increase their office space by 5,000 square feet to achieve their aims.

Stage 4: sustainable profit

Corpra helped AAT to realise that their new 'home' could actually be smaller and more productive. By introducing flexible working – a move enthusiastically welcomed by staff – AAT was able to reduce its occupancy needs from 22,000 to 14,000 square feet (i.e. a saving of 8,000 square feet compared to an increase of 5,000 square feet).

This achieved the necessary balance between cost and value, which was supported by the technology. Working practices became more agile and resilient and the new building represented a new symbolism, which was aligned to the reborn organisation.

Stage 5: re-learning sustainably

Corpra then helped AAT to ensure every employee understood what their organisation was all about, and how they fit into it. Many AAT employees had become so embroiled in day-to-day minutiae that they had forgotten the bigger picture. AAT's aims were not clearly spelt out, leaving employees with little idea of their real roles.

Stage 6: re-processing sustainably

With Corpra's help, AAT clarified its raison d'etre, setting out four key aims. These were: (1) acquiring students, (2) deepening student knowledge, (3) retaining members and (4) providing fulfilment through an environment for continuous learning and professional development. For the first time, staff had a common understanding of why they were there and how their performance would be measured.

Case study summary

Jane Scott Paul, CEO of AAT, stated: 'Ambitious growth and innovation is now in our business plan and is at the heart of what we do. We are constantly looking at driving performance. This gives us the permission to be bold and brave. Being brave, helps us to go forward – status quo isn't an option' (Corpra 2008: 6).

Reflection from the case study

The AAT case study demonstrates the importance of real estate in releasing energy in an organisation. In this case, the sustainable solution of downsizing space whilst upscaling productivity has been achieved through a process that digs deep into the organisational structure. Once real estate has been considered separately from the business then there is a danger that, first, there will be a mismatch between the business operation and the space provision. Second, there will be a less than optimal utilisation of that space. In either case there is the prospect of unsustainable activity. Through this AAT project, Corpra demonstrates how a property management consultant can answer the question rather than simply respond to the request.

In the AAT case study, it can be seen that all three types of change (anticipatory, reactive and crisis) are present. The original impetus was the internal view that more space was needed. This led to a deeper understanding of organisational issues that would, in a very short space of time, have emerged as a crisis. However, through a process of exploration and understanding it was possible to implement reactive change. Providing the organisation remains agile and reflexive, the continuing process of change takes on an anticipatory character. This is sometimes called 'conditioned emergence'.

Conditioned emergence is concerned with a fundamental redesign of the deep structure of an organisation rather than the operational systems or procedures. Real estate alignment can have a significant impact in the way that this is actualised through this broad framework. There is a link between changes in an organisation's real estate and its culture. Cultural change is 'embedded in people's bodily experiences of constantly changing physical environments, and their understanding has to involve learning about how these physical environments operate in the absence of human-induced transformations' (Engel-Di Mauro 2008: 94).

Sustainability leadership

How the real estate alignment is achieved depends significantly on the nature of leadership and the change agents in place. These can weave together multiple stakeholder interests in proportion and in balance. This leads to dynamic capabilities, which is a level above competency and capability as it develops the practice of changing routines in indirect response to consumer needs for mutual benefit.

Traditional approaches to change tend to fix what is wrong (particularly reactive and crisis change situations). In doing so, the structural effects within the organisation are addressed, but often the cause is not. Authentic leadership within more proactive, anticipatory approaches can create these dynamic capabilities in resources, assets and structures.

'Authentic leaders genuinely desire to serve others through their leadership. They are more interested in empowering the people they lead to make a difference than they are in power, money, or prestige for themselves. They are as guided by qualities of the heart, by passion and compassion, as they are by qualities of the mind' (George 2004: 1). As such, authentic leadership is a position of ego-death. What is required is a shift in the business paradigm based on a new understanding of how a business system can be managed intelligently. This requires a different type of leadership, one that links values with intelligence and enables meta-strategic thinking (Zohar *et al.* 2004). In this way, organisations can move from top-down, outside-in and deficit-based approaches to change to bottom-up, inside-out and asset-based approaches (Pascale *et al.* 2005). In order to achieve this, there needs to be a close alignment of all assets in the organisation including real estate. It also requires agility in organisational structures and management of assets.

Organisational constraints

Chapter 10 highlights the process of dialogue to try to understand situations at a deeper level, i.e. to get behind the assumptions (conscious or unconscious). This approach can equally be applied here. Through a process of ongoing dialogue, it was possible to unravel the true nature of the problem. Once that was revealed it was possible to move towards a negotiated solution.

Another way to consider the issues raised in the AAT case study is to unearth the barriers that are holding back the organisation. This can be done through what is known as the theory of constraints (TOC). For example, Corpra found blocks in the ability to look beyond existing structures that represented essential symbols of the organisation. Removing these was seen as tantamount to destroying the organisation itself and the ground on which it held its status as a professional body. Without that, it would not be able to serve its members. This theory is particularly appropriate because it is based on the principle that once the weakest link is sorted out then it is most likely that the sustainable solution will be achieved. It uses 'trees' and 'clouds' to explore unexamined assumptions and believes that conflicts, as such, only exist superficially. Once someone can get beneath the surface then consensus is very often found. Just as with the Corpra approach, there are essentially three stages to a TOC analysis. These are:

1. thought processes, consisting of the 'five focusing steps' of current reality, conflict resolution, future reality, prerequisites and transitions;
2. management tools; and
3. innovative solutions.

Birkin *et al.* (2009) further address that the five focusing steps in the first stage can be applied to real estate. More specifically, acknowledging the *current reality* is the first step in the thought process. This is the process to help to identify the main barrier(s) to achieving sustainability. It seeks to get behind the language and hype to try to understand existing relationships, inertia and undesirable behaviour that conspire to provide or maintain unsustainable real estate solutions. This is the auditing process, not only to identify resources but also to seek the assumptions and behaviours that lie behind those resources. For human resources this would be the current mindset established by organisational structures as well as the physical structure of the building. For the real estate resources themselves, this would be the 'fit for purpose' criteria and the alignment between the physical and organisational structures.

Conflict resolution, as the second step, begins the process of breaking down assumption clouds that allow the current reality to persist. This enables a *future reality* to be identified and constructed around the concept of a tree. It seeks to lay out a complete solution or strategy that includes desired effects and aligns with strategic 'bottom line' objectives. However, it goes further to identify ways in which cultural shifts can take place to provide long-term transformation. This process is cyclical and ongoing. Mindsets have a habit of returning to a former 'comfortable' status quo. Cultural shifts help to keep the vision to the fore.

The final two steps (i.e. *prerequisites* and *transitions*) map the overall course for getting from the current reality to the future reality using prerequisite trees (which help to turn obstacles into an implementation plan) and transition trees (which go to a deeper level to identify critical actions).

This is important when considering ways in which fundamental changes towards sustainability thinking can take place in organisational cultures rather than simply dealing with consequences. In all this, it has to be remembered that, from a business perspective, it is the sustainability of the organisation that is uppermost – not the larger social, economic or environmental system. Nevertheless, as the focus of business concern expands from a debate about the specifics of environmental management to the broader concerns of sustainable development, so the basis of the organisation's strategy towards the environment must expand from a risk to a resilience approach.

Real estate advisers tend to find it easiest to respond to the physical form of buildings than the organisational behaviour that those buildings engender. This is not always helpful when trying to address real estate as part of the process of organisational change. The change opportunity is often strategic in nature and connected as much with the symbolism of the workplace as it might be about the cost, the value or the space itself.

However, technically sophisticated building forms rarely provide effective solutions if their potentials are not fully understood or if new ways of behaving in the use of those buildings are not learnt or taught. The sustainability credentials of 'green' buildings can remain redundant if not used in a sympathetic way. This is a learning process towards sustainability literacy. If this is understood by real estate advisers then their advice can be at the interface of mechanical systems thinking and human systems reality.

If real estate advisers were able to master 'the blend of pure science (proof and causality) and social science (causal relations) through knowledge, personality and common sense (undefined)' (Dent *et al.* 2011: 277), they could potentially release the energy of the workplace for the benefits of all stakeholders. In the context of sustainability however this is a big step because it involves an in-depth understanding of the variables of ownership and occupation across a wider spectrum than previously expected. The sustainability debate requires solutions that do not just rely on formulae or report templates.

Summary

Corpra were seeking to achieve shareholder value and help to create a sustainable enterprise (economically and environmentally) through aligning real estate with business structure and enterprise. The approach was generic and not specific to achieving sustainability goals. However, this is a good example of creating value and reducing the organisation's carbon footprint.

As a firm of consultants Corpra have sought to instil the idea that client organisations need leadership together with empathy to deliver effectively. Knowledge needs to be shared with passion, especially when the going gets tough. Through a series of case studies, Corpra have gathered primary data that they have modelled into their five dimensions of real estate. The model is particularly relevant to the workplace (the inside of the building), as property is the only work artefact that we can walk inside and try to make our home or identify our community, cave, enclosure, fortress or our physical manifestation of our power. Managing this requires a deep knowledge of organisational change and the real estate environment.

13 Introduction to the big conversation

....

Introduction

The AAT case study in the previous chapter highlighted two important issues. First, an organisation may believe that they have a real estate issue that needs resolution whereas in fact it is an organisational problem that has a real estate realignment as part of the solution. In the process, the organisation was also able to address efficiency, sufficiency and social productivity. The second issue is that the organisation was not able to identify the problem for itself. This was, partly, because its members were too close to it. However, more significantly, as a professional body, its whole fabric depended on the symbols that it had encased itself in. To break free from this, the organisation needed someone to provide a key to enable it to unlock the alternative view. BCO (2010) suggests that this type of situation can relate directly to the issue of carbon reduction and the whole sustainability question in the commercial office sector in the UK. The research undertaken for their report, 'Towards Zero Carbon Offices', sought to understand the context, content and processes of organisations that use offices. The result of this process was the Big Conversation, which forms the basis of this chapter.

The Big Conversation case study

Background

Business life is not a series of transparent professional conversations each ending with a sound logical and mathematical conclusion. They are invariably wrapped in a web of politics, personalities, personal priorities and hidden agendas.

This case study, based around the aspirations of achieving a zero carbon office, examines the role played by corporate real estate in contributing to competitive advantage and the way it influences the behaviour of staff, suppliers, partners and customers. Opinions were gathered from people who actually develop, own, occupy and manage buildings, which revealed insights that were deeply rooted in real situations and problems of corporate and administrative life specifically around the issue of sustainability.

By learning and analysing individual sustainability journeys, it was possible to establish where these companies and institutions were, what they aim at in the future and how far along the journey towards zero carbon offices they had travelled. Members of the BCO have a unique opportunity to help close the gap between aspiration and reality.

Extracts from conversations with over 130 UK and global office user organisations have been taken from the final report and are presented here in the framework of a journey towards zero carbon. These show a progression through the four common typologies of response to change, i.e. 'head in the sand', 'trinket behaviour', 'carbon is cash' and 'first class'.

This hopefully illustrates some of the issues encountered in earlier chapters and helps to inform a way forward towards not just the technical intelligence of a zero carbon office but the sustainability literacy that will underpin emotional and spiritual intelligence in the workplace. The message seems to be 'consume less, regulate sensibly but rigorously and consistently, use technology thoughtfully and change behaviours permanently'. The way in which buildings are used essentially affects relationships between landlords and tenants, it affects the environment and the financial bottom line.

The Big Conversation

Big Conversation scenario

You have just been appointed as Head of CSR in a large corporate firm in the City and the CEO says he is keen to meet you.

You are perched in the plush leather seat opposite his desk, whilst his secretary who you sometimes see in the canteen is handing him papers to sign and lists of people to call. You are balanced between being rather flattered at being in the office of such an important person and at the slight unease as to where to put your empty cup and saucer.

Eventually, a few phone calls later and some stagey eye-rolling from the boss, he turns round and outlines your brief.

'Zero Carbon office blah blah, we must all do our bit, blah blah, turn those light bulbs off, blah blah, cycle rack in the garage, blah blah but can't get excited by all this stuff about paper – it's only trees isn't it? blah blah. Well, late for my meeting good luck, bye...'.

Slightly confused but still rather elated, you leave the office, glance at the secretary from the canteen who ignores you as usual and settle down in your new office with your name on the door and get down to work.

Six months later and it looks a little less rosy. You have heard nothing from the boss for months. Several other executives you have left messages for have apologised and keep saying they really will get back to you sometime.

Several of your project ideas have been read and, although none have actually been implemented just yet, you have written several business plans with all the cost implications noted and you are pretty sure that the secretaries took quite seriously your memo about turning off their computers when they go home. At least this seemed to be the case judging from your trawl of their desks in the evening.

A year on? Although people say that it is quite irritating, the motion sensitive on/off lighting system you introduced is working well, the paper recycling bins are always full and the fines system for not turning off your computer at night is really popular on Friday nights at the local.

The engineers have rather grumpily put in two bike racks right at the back of the underground car park in the slots that the executives' Range Rovers could never really get into anyway and your idea to offset all those flights to the Glasgow office with carbon credits was on the front page of the in-house newsletter last month, although you were annoyed it was printed on only one side of paper.

But you have still not been allocated a proper budget, you have not been able to talk to anyone about the annual sales conference perhaps being held in England rather than St Lucia, the heating system is still set at the same temperature winter and summer, and your business plan – delivered within a week of being asked for it – for a new video conferencing suite does not appear to have moved from the Head of HR's in-tray.

Oh! And the boss's secretary still has not given you a second glance even though she copied you in on an e-mail about grey water utilisation, which one of the boss's mates from the golf club had forwarded to him three weeks ago.

Conversation findings

Before 2006–07 the scenario above would have been pretty familiar to employees tasked with paying lip service to the notion of creating a carbon friendly office.

A bit of technology here – just as long as it does not cost me an arm and leg – a bit of education there, some goodwill here, some stubborn resistance there and in reality not a great deal of real change going on.

Before that, any initiatives had been spasmodic, untargeted with little or no measurement. There were often cost-driven design improvements to make buildings more flexible and lettable. Few users had carbon reduction policies and CSR was only just creeping on to board agendas.

In some cases, these were driven by economics and sometimes by regulatory frameworks, in response to public sector initiatives and procurement requirements.

At this point, suddenly, organisations started edging along the path towards carbon reduction – albeit for many, it would be a long and frustrating path.

Most experts agree that well over one-third of our carbon emissions come from the whole life use of commercial premises and another third from the people, who work from those premises and from their homes.

The following conversations are provided here to demonstrate some of the archetypal leadership responses to sustainability in commercial office environments. Here, this is represented as responses from different leaders in different organisations. However, it can also map a personal journey.

> The greening of the office space should not only reduce our carbon footprint, it should also permeate society as a whole.

Head in the sand

Management obstruction or endangered market sector presents a picture that nothing can be done. Takeover or close down are the only routes for change.

One president of a company supplying software for banks summed up the sort of 'head in the sand' attitude that is unlikely to be seen over the next decade.

The man, highly successful and in his fifties, was asked, as all interviewees were, what he had done in the past about carbon emissions, what he was doing now and what he would be doing in the future?

In the past, he said, he had done nothing as it 'wasn't my business, it wasn't a problem for primary industries'.

At present, he said, they would comply with any requirement made by the government, and in future he would do the bare minimum required of him by law. He said: 'This may not make me a good citizen but there needs to be a cost benefit for any carbon stuff, otherwise we will lose money'.

And although he wanted to float his firm in a few years, the only concession he would make was 'to do some CSR window dressing, because the advisors say it may add a bit to the price'.

Other organisations, while not quite so recidivist, were also frank in their lack of motivation to change their ingrained behaviour. The introduction of a whistle-blower policy was cleverly introduced to see if it would check ingrained behaviours.

Trinket behaviour

Initiatives that do not deal with the carbon issue but derive a PR benefit or tick a box. The existing practices are difficult to break and new ideas difficult to engage.

One leading business publisher was more aware but equally a long way away from ending his zero carbon journey.

He said: 'Why should I do anything? There is no pressure, no Government regulation and no time to do it in. I barely know my landlord and even if I did and asked for some improvements he'd probably use it as an opportunity to stuff us for more money as a result'.

'Sometimes I'm asked by people to source paper responsibly so I do and charge them a bit more. The rest of the time we use the cheapest paper'.

The publisher, whilst transparently honest, is a classic case of someone unable to take personal responsibility for climate change and simply waiting until he is forced by the government to take action. Even then he would not undergo a fundamental behaviour change but would probably shop around until he found the cheapest bit of technology or ways of offsetting his carbon – classic trinket behaviour from a small company with no budget, a very competitive market and the risk of losing out to the lowest cost provider.

Slightly further down the road were some professional services companies, all at slightly different stages along their journey to zero carbon work places.

One, a household name, considers itself firmly on the path of carbon reduction. The firm and their CSR chief regard CSR as a part of being a 'professional firm' and have been recording environmental data since 2002 although until three years ago steps to improve efficiency were 'uncoordinated', and 'done because we thought that is what the partners wanted'.

Some leading firms of lawyers have agreed a common system of measuring emissions and energy consumption and are prepared to accept what might be regarded as longer than normal payback periods on some investments on greening measures.

Some say: 'We think carefully about environmental impact and actually turn away business if it is anti-environmental. We do a business plan for each investment decision. We have a hurdle rate that filters the better projects with a three year payback. The only things that get through are new marketing initiatives and outsourcing projects'.

'I would not ever risk a low carbon project unless there was a sales benefit'.

Technological innovations introduced include energy saving light bulbs, PIR lighting and ventilation systems, lead free paint and all have a head of CSR who acts as an internal educator.

To cut down on air travel, they are introducing video conferencing hubs to allow partners to talk with colleagues in America.

However this still has its apparent flaws. Lawyers from, say Frankfurt, have to fly to a hub to have a video conference with America, while lawyers from Atlanta, say, would still have to fly to New York for the same conference.

These firms have few restrictions on business travel, as they still feel lawyers have to meet face to face with clients and colleagues and very few people – and almost no top lawyers – regularly work from home.

What some of these organisations are doing is displaying an advanced form of trinket behaviour and have not done the sort of fundamental behaviour change that will result in a serious carbon reduction; the heads of CSR are happy challenging support staff but in a firm where the partners have an old fashioned – some might say almost feudal – approach, they are less happy challenging them, for example, to travel less and use video conference more, in case they complain.

As we can see, even in the more environmentally aware professional firms, entrenched professional practices are preventing them progressing on their journey towards a zero carbon environment.

> 'Entrenched professional practices such as business travel are preventing companies from reaching the end of their journey towards zero carbon'.

At another professional services firm turning over tens of millions of pounds each year, we can again see how lip service is being paid to environmental issues rather than wholesale behavioural change being implemented.

In 2006 the firm decided 'to do something' about carbon reduction.

Declaring themselves 'very enthusiastic', about carbon reduction, they first looked into carbon offsetting. Whether they baulked at the cost or not the company decided carbon offsetting was 'cheating', and instead appointed a £55,000 a year health and safety and environment officer to reduce their carbon footprint.

They introduced an environmental competition among various offices to see who could recycle more and use less carbon, ordered security guards to check computers were turned off at night and had an office 'name and shame' policy for people failing to switch off their computers.

They used the intranet to educate staff into reducing energy consumption and switched to energy efficient light bulbs. They now have a five year plan to reduce their office square footage and increase flexible working and – in what in fairness is something of a cultural change for such a firm – instead of printing all correspondence, spreadsheets and emails as a matter of course, now they electronically store the data. It sounds obvious, but it is a major step for most professional firms. The firm sees the recession as an opportunity to change and reduce their office space ahead of the re-emergence of the anticipated demand for legal work so flexible working will be established properly by that stage. Using both climate and recession as a lever for change. Good stuff!

But it is a professional service firm; support staff and back office personnel are mainly affected, not the professionals and partners. Or as one partner said: 'Professionals don't share desks, my friend'.

As we all edge along the journey to carbon reduction and in reviewing interviews, a significant number of instances of management obstruction were found – like our fictitious CSR man in his lonely post in the City.

> 'Organisations staring on the Carbon Reduction path can either follow a proper change management programme or omit to address the problem behaviourally and fail'.

Two examples stand out.

One is an academic institution and the other a media organisation.

At the academic institution a new management team took over and decided it should collect data identifying consumption of energy and carbon emissions across the business. It has many autonomous business units for which research is key and indeed which provides a major source of funding.

They appointed a director of sustainability who tried to collect data, and at a cost of over a million pounds they invested in individual metering for individual buildings across the campus. Their stated aim was to beat any government consumption or carbon emission targets and, as a science-based establishment, hoped for full behavioural support from staff and students.

But, again, there was resistance, not from the students, who supported greening measures wholeheartedly, but from academics and scientists.

In response, astonishingly, the director then embarked on an 'out of sight, out of mind', series of changes. This allowed him to reduce the ring-main voltage slightly, saving hundreds of thousands of pounds a year. A case of a passionate executive making it happen under the radar, at great risk to his position.

A similar situation emerged after interviews at the media organisation. The organisation moved to new offices about ten years ago but used the cheapest environmental technology around at the time. There was much inertia in the organisation and obstruction from creative people, who had neither the time nor the inclination to address green issues. The head of sustainability admitted, like the man from the academic institution, to sneaking in stuff 'below the budget radar and without people knowing'.

One of the biggest costs in carbon areas was the data centre. Astonishingly, he was unable to reduce temperature by even half a degree without being in breach of his contract with the management company running the site. Heating and cooling is usually the main source of carbon emissions in this type of organisation.

Obstructions litter the journey towards a zero carbon office, whether regulatory, financial or managerial.

One major property manager and occupier said its supply side had not tried hard enough to introduce a carbon agenda because 'we expect the Government to shift the goalposts suddenly, like they did with HIPS'. Although this sounds like an excuse to do nothing, it is clearly not an uncommon behaviour-led block to achieving carbon reduction.

And two charities show, in particular, why perceived financial constraints also stop them from effectively reducing their carbon emissions.

At one, they have set themselves a target of a 23 per cent carbon reduction over 2006/07 levels in three years, and achieved 18 per cent of this in one year, mainly from reducing the amount of printed paper they use. Concerns from fundraisers proved groundless.

In another charity, a plan to ferry staff to work in electrical hybrid minibuses failed to work because staff wanted to continue driving to the site on an out-of-town business park.

The charity is in a state of environmental inertia, which it believes will only change when it manages to move offices.

One executive said: 'Frankly we are waiting to move to make an impact'.

Carbon is cash

These are businesses where fuel costs or energy costs are a major business cost, often in a commoditised sector and the benefits of reduction are clear and quantifiable.

Just as some companies fail to move towards zero carbon workplaces because they have no financial imperative to do so, like the bank software producer and the contract publisher, others embrace carbon reduction because it is wholly in their financial best interests to do so.

> 'Some companies fail to move towards zero carbon workplaces because they have no financial imperative. Others embrace carbon reduction because it is wholly in their financial best interests'.

For them the mantra 'carbon is cash' is sung loudly from the rooftops and colours every aspect of their businesses.

One example from the interviews is a logistics firm that ferries goods by truck and van around the country.

Before 2000 it did nothing actively to reduce their carbon footprint, but running the business as cheaply and efficiently as it could naturally meant they were emitting less carbon than less efficient rivals.

One executive said: 'We know about carbon and its impact and our awareness has been high for five years – it's in the blood if you like'.

'When fuel costs go up we have to react quickly; for us it was commonsense. If we want to reduce costs, we reduce carbon which is fuel'.

The firm did this with efficient vehicles, driver training to conserve fuel as well as better route planning and sending vehicles out and bringing them back again with efficient new loads.

He said: 'There is not much we don't know about the cost of running a vehicle. We put in systems to see where there is spare capacity and saved £3 million. Every gallon of diesel is carbon and cash'.

Their offices are old, but everything is recycled that can be. There is flexi-working, heating and lighting and air-conditioning saving devices in place. In the words of one expert: 'It is easy for them because of what they do. They can see carbon'!

In the future, the firm will adapt to new energy saving devices and will embrace a mandatory road speed reduction from 70 miles per hour to 50 miles per hour, which would save even more fuel and reduce carbon. Ultimately, they say, they would like to run a diesel free truck, although, of course, that is many years away.

What further emerged as we trace the path of wholesale carbon reduction in the workplace was the importance of a guiding hand gripping the initiatives.

We have seen earlier how environmental tsars in some organisations are good at tinkering with policies as long as it does not upset the executives and partners, and how middle managers in institutions sneak in changes so as not to upset the status quo.

The saying: 'If the CEO says we are going green, we go green; if the £30,000 a year CSR officer says to do it, you don't', is largely true. Interviews showed several quite high-profile organisations having no guiding hand or real leadership at all.

One insurance firm cheerfully admitted it left environmental issues to individuals; another accountancy firm has several scatter-gun green initiatives going as a result of requests from young accountants and trainees, but these were largely the result of personal initiatives and agendas.

In another case the man in charge of CSR has no power and could not introduce flexible working because of partners' antipathy and, besides, has just had health and safety added to his portfolio, which means he will have even less time to try and spearhead behavioural change in the office!

World Class

These companies do most things at leading edge practice level. Their ability to anticipate and understand their customers is ahead of the market and they have already deeply integrated sustainability into the business.

> 'Every organisation's path is unique as they battle the complexities of bringing about major change in their environmental approach'.

In contrast, when a CEO or senior executive grips environmental change, our interviews show the behaviour of the organisation changes as a result.

One industry association CEO called in management consultants and became hooked on moving towards a zero carbon workplace.

She said: 'Before, I did what I could and knew that our property was inefficient but didn't know exactly what to do'.

'Now we have "greened," the business. I cycle to work and to every meeting and try and buy as "green" as I can. We are now as green as you can get'.

A new CEO-level commitment to carbon reduction was adopted and seven office buildings (and 2,000 people) were almost immediately consolidated into a new, efficient one that was designed to be BREEAM Excellent standard.

It installed a biomass boiler, ground source heat pump, heat recovery systems and now plans to roll out the advantages and experiences they have found with its HQ to a myriad of smaller buildings and depots across its estate.

A viable argument could be made in this instance that the presence of the industry regulator Ofwat (the Water Services Regulation Authority) and its various regulations concerning carbon management influenced the organisation's 'green conversion', but there is no doubt the CEO led the process with vigour and drive – a fundamental behaviour that transformed the organisation.

Oddly, given the experiences of blocking in several organisations interviewed, the presence of a senior executive at the helm of environmental change of one London law firm was equally significant.

The senior partner set up a blog and found most of the input was from staff with environmental concerns.

In 2007, he commissioned a report on the firm's carbon footprint and recommendations for reduction and set off by means of carbon credits. He looked into carbon credits and bought credits in a methane reduction company in Germany, but staff raised concerns about buying offsets so he stopped.

He is now targeting reducing emissions by 5 per cent per year; 40 per cent of paper is recycled and, although senior staff in the 1,500-strong company have resisted some change, he is in a strong enough position to overrule them.

The firm has 30 per cent flexible working and 200 people are capable of working from home. People are encouraged to cycle to work and all offices have season tickets loan schemes to encourage them to use public transport.

In short, he has transformed the behaviour of the company, although he admits – it being a law firm after all – there is still a £1 million travel and accommodation budget he has not been able to take a chunk out of and even he cannot make his lawyers use video conferencing.

The corporate building managers' viewpoint

'Now is the time to engage at an organisational and strategic level to drive out the human behaviour and life patterns that produce carbon'.

'I am asked to reduce the energy costs and improve customer satisfaction levels. But, each time I reduce energy cost by resetting the air con and heating system, everyone gets upset and I get a bad customer satisfaction rating'.

'I warm the building up and half the staff open the doors and windows. I cool the building down and they start putting their coats on in a display of anger. It then appears in my next appraisal'.

'Then the CEO tells me that I have to put a solar panel on the roof and could I get a wind turbine up there too. Budget's no problem now'.

'This month's energy consumption still went up because everyone worked over the weekend on a major project. It was the hottest weekend of the year, lights and air con on 24 hours, cost us a blooming fortune. Still got a bad appraisal because I couldn't keep the canteen open all weekend'.

Catalysts of change

Moving from 'head in the sand' typology to 'first class' there are certain catalysts of change emerging from these interviews. These include:

- diagnosis – 'our property was inefficient';
- shared vision – 'most of the input was from staff with environmental concerns';
- consensus – 'every aspect of their behaviour is driven by social and environmental awareness';
- revitalisation – 'he has transformed the behaviour of the company';
- policies and structures – 'a new CEO-level commitment to carbon reduction was adopted';
- monitor and adjust – 'staff raised concerns about buying offsets so he stopped'.

In all cases the trajectory towards 'first class' seems to be determined by the CEO or the person leading the organisation. Where there is lack of vision, lack of direction, poor communication, poor understanding or cynicism, then there is the potential for inertia in the organisation. It is often the case that the full potential of the real estate is not recognised either by the organisation itself or its advisers.

In trying to bring the threads of this book together, the next chapters reflect on this exercise to explore how organisations can use the tools available in a creative and productive way, and the contribution that the leaders of those organisations can make to ensuring sustainable working practices in sustainable real estate settings. But first, a word from the building itself!

What would the building say to us?

'Like most other office buildings I was a fabulous state of the art office block when I was built 20 years ago. They used to call me high-tech. My occupier loved me then. The owner was proud of me too, the architects even won an award because I was so handsome.

My first occupier was my favourite. All the executives loved me and were so proud of me; they had a big opening party. They even brought their kids in during the school holidays. The owners employed someone to explain how I worked. I had so much potential. That was before all the mergers and acquisitions and changes in occupation. Now there are so many different users each with their own demands and ideas about how to use me.

I was designed to be an efficient machine but, with so much tinkering over the years, it has all gone wrong. I know the occupiers are unhappy but no one seems to realise that I can do things so much better if only they bothered to find out how. Not even the current owners seem to be that interested.

My current occupier is my fifth so far. They show me no respect at all. I can't cope most days so I just shut down.

I'm now in the news again but only because I am unlettable. I use too much carbon and produce too many CFCs. Sometimes I wish they would strip me back to my frame, crush everything for road fill and refurbish me as a block of trendy apartments. Then my occupiers might respect me again!

How can this downside be minimised? It may be that the answer lies with the business model that organisations tend to use. These are based on Newtonian principles – 'linear, predictable, controllable, isolated'. In reality, organisations are complex adaptive systems that are resilient to unpredictable and uncontrollable forces that require considerable connectivity and, often, randomness to thrive'.

Summary

The above case studies have shown the hindrances and drivers along that curve towards a zero carbon zero workplace, be they money led, frustrated by superiors or simply not considered necessary.

It is a story of frustration and, as we have seen, the path is unique to every organisation as they battle the complexities of bringing about major change in their environmental approach.

The CSR director of one of those global companies told of how she and the CEO (passionate about carbon reduction) would give a helping hand to the projects that had a major carbon benefit by dropping the hurdle rate a few points, and publicising the benefits. It is interesting that all these projects actually achieved the returns required because of higher motivation, quicker project completion and smarter management of hurdles.

One firm that largely stripped through that learning curve is a major food firm. It regards itself as always being more socially aware than any company in the world. It makes 'choiceful decisions'. Every new plant it opens is accompanied by significant help for the local population. New schools, new medical facilities, new infrastructures.

Dissatisfied with existing science and technologies being thrown at carbon reduction, and questioning its value to local economies, it conducted its own worldwide survey. The survey showed the three biggest issues in the world were *poverty*, which it was doing something about; *disease,* which it was doing something about; and *war,* which it could do nothing about.

The firm had long guided actions with the saying: 'Tread lightly on this earth'.

So it addressed the carbon agenda on three levels.

On the first level, it asked: what it could do to waste less? And the answer was: 'Don't waste water, paper and energy'.

Then it addressed sustainability. It decided to generate its own power to run its plants, deliberately overproducing so it could give free power to local communities – and, in fact, it is currently building a 40 acre solar panel farm in one country.

It turned its back on carbon trading and instead invested in helping local farmers to grow crops that the firm needed more efficiently, thus giving those farmers greater financial independence.

Finally it processed and packaged everything in a carbon efficient and sustainable way.

As a result, their thousands of employees worldwide are imbued with the message: 'I'm a planet person'. Every aspect of its behaviour is driven by social and environmental awareness.

One executive said: 'On things where we are world-class, we can change anything. We also like to do it our way, not necessarily the way regulations state in different countries'.

The firm does not accept the phrase 'carbon reduction'. It sees it only as one aspect of sustainability. In short, here is a firm that occupies the moral high ground, is world class in its field and has adapted sustainability as an absolutely fundamental behaviour, intrinsic to its business.

Section IV

Sustainability Leadership
and Reflection

14 Sustainability leadership

Introduction

This chapter draws together some of the essential skills and competencies required of a leader who will be effective in changing mindset within an organisation towards more sustainable investment, more sustainable working practices and more sustainable business tools. The chapter is divided into two parts. The first part is about learning. It looks at some basic principles of learning (and relearning). This then leads onto the second part, which concentrates on the journey of the leader through learning.

Learning

There has been a wealth of research into learning. How we learn, what we learn, why we learn and where we learn. Here, learning is not so much about acquiring knowledge. It is concerned with learning as a process of constant movement from unknown to unknown. It is understanding without the fixed points that set the mind into a rigid structure of learnt habits, behaviours and knowledge. To change this mindset is to be constantly standing on the edge of the unknown, of uncertainty and of the new. This is the position where leadership may be best able to act and lead sustainably.

According to Geddes (1991) there are three basic principles of learning. They are the foundations on which leadership can be built. Each can be seen in the models that have been introduced in this book as follows:

- *Flow*. Without flow, water stagnates. Movement is needed to generate energy. The energy of the body, the energy of the water, the energy of productivity. Flow charts are only dynamic when they are used for movement. For example, the developments of capabilities within an organisation only add value when they are used in the processes that help to develop markets and lead to sustainable profits. Profit is only sustainable when part of it is recycled into developing capabilities etc. This is the balanced scorecard tool in action. This leads into the second principle of learning, balance.

- *Balance*. In the human body, in order to find balance, muscles have to be trained. So too in an organisation, muscles (i.e. the tissue that produces movement) have to be strong to survive. Understanding alignments and exercises enables muscle movement to be used in the most efficient and economical way. Just as the body seeks balance between the in-breath and the out-breath, organisations also seek to weigh costs against values (i.e. the principles underlying the five dimensions of real estate tool). When an organisation finds its true balance, less effort (i.e. less energy) is needed for each movement.
- *Clarity*. In this book, property markets and organisations have been identified as complex adaptive systems. The final principle of learning is the ability to find simplicity within complexity. 'Finding clarity is a process of listening and learning, accumulating and discharging, experimenting, holding on to what feels right, letting go of what feels wrong' (Geddes 1991: 80). This is also the process of 'the included middle' where there is no separation. For example, the three separate pillars of sustainability are joined through the shear zones that were highlighted in Chapter 10.

In this way it is possible to see a process of learning taking place through a series of tools creating a structure for that learning. This can be both individual learning and organisational learning. In the case of real estate markets and sustainable behaviour, the flow is the ability of the property assets to ensure the productivity of an organisation and to avoid blockages. But the flow is also about the agility of mind of the real estate adviser or the organisation's property team to ensure that buildings are part of the sustainable energy flows that create efficient and sufficient use of space.

Balance is achieved through taking a long-term view and not looking for certainties or attempting to forecast concrete, immovable structures. Balance is building resilience into decision making and the mindset. Horst *et al.* (1973) identified what he called 'wicked problems' that organisations often have to face as part of the process of constant change. Wicked problems have the following characteristics:

- There is no definitive formulation of a wicked problem (defining wicked problems is itself a wicked problem).
- Wicked problems have no stopping rule.
- Solutions to wicked problems are not true or false, but good or bad.
- There is no immediate and no ultimate test of a solution to a wicked problem.
- Every solution to a wicked problem is a 'one-shot operation'; because there is no opportunity to learn by trial and error, every attempt counts significantly.

- Wicked problems do not have an enumerable (or an exhaustively describable) set of potential solutions, nor is there a well-described set of permissible operations that may be incorporated into the plan.
- Every wicked problem is essentially unique.
- Every wicked problem can be considered to be a symptom of another problem.
- The existence of a discrepancy representing a wicked problem can be explained in numerous ways. The choice of explanation determines the nature of the problem's resolution.
- The planner has no right to be wrong (of course, this can also apply to the real estate adviser who should accept responsibility for the consequences of the actions they generate).

Head *et al.* (2008) suggest that the key features of 'wickedness', as far as learning is concerned, can be grouped into two key dimensions, complexity and diversity.

Complexity relates to the difficulties in understanding the nature of the wicked problem and hence the nature of the potential solutions. These difficulties arise from 'a patchy knowledge base; complex inter-dependencies of processes and structures; uncertainties arising from the contingent and dynamic nature of social issues and processes; and the incommensurability of many of the risks and potential trade-offs' (Head *et al.* 2008: 7).

Heifetz (1994) quoted in Head *et al.* (2008) further suggests a typology of problem situations (Table 14.1). According to Heifetz (1994), Type 1 situations constitute 'tame' problems, whereas Type 3 situations, and many Type 2 ones, are 'wicked' problems.

- Type1 situations are those where a clear definition and the likely solution are apparent. These situations can generally be resolved through technical knowledge and expertise.
- Type 2 situations are those where there is clear definition but uncertainty about the nature of the solution. In these situations, some form of learning is required.
- Type 3 situations, both the problem definition and the solution lack clarity and more extensive learning is required.

Table 14.1   Situational types (Head *et al.* 2008: 8)

Situation	Problem definition	Solution	Locus of responsibility	Kind of work
Type 1	Clear	Clear	Manager/expert	Technical
Type 2	Clear	Requires learning	Manager/expert and stakeholders	Technical and adaptive
Type 3	Requires learning	Requires learning	Stakeholders/ expert	Adaptive

Needless to say, sustainability per se can be identified as having a degree of 'wickedness' in that the problem and its solution are not well understood. So on the surface, it probably fits as a Type 2/Type 3 situation. But, more than that, when considering sustainability specifically as it relates to the ownership and occupation of real estate, this adds another layer.

In Chapter 5, the nature of ownership and control was addressed. Here it is clear that there is rarely just one owner and one occupier to a real estate asset. Equally, there is rarely one party that can achieve a solution. Often it is a partnership between landlords and tenants and intermediaries, such as real estate advisers.

The second dimension is *diversity*. This embraces both actors and their institutional locations and contexts, and depending on the complexity of the relationships can cause further difficulties in identifying and defining problems.

Leadership

Leadership has a significant role to play in developing the purpose and strategic direction of an organisation. The role of leadership is to take these problems through to a resolution regardless as to how 'wicked' they might be. Leadership in sustainability in organisations is one such set of circumstances. The evidence provided in this book points to the fact that there is no one right way to sustainability. Because the term itself is so open to interpretation and understanding, there cannot be one blueprint that will provide all the answers, create all the opportunities, identify all the possible changes and their consequences. Somehow, all this needs to be filtered within the particular set of circumstances, resources and vision that an organisation might have. This is the role of the leader.

There are many qualities that could be identified as being applicable to a 'good' leader, such as vision, creativity, passion and determination. However, for the purposes of this section, authenticity will be the key. The reason for this is that authentic (i.e. the *Oxford English Dictionary* definition of 'genuine') seems to be the most important quality needed to deal with issues of sustainability.

Authenticity is particularly relevant in times of radical change or when dealing with significant and complex issues such as sustainability. In many such situations, 'there is a temptation to live "inauthentically" because change widens the moral gap between individual responsibility for freedom and autonomy and social responsibility to follow the shared norms of the community' (Kumar 2007: 13). Authentic leadership is capable of filling that moral gap because it has developed three key components according to May *et al.* (2003). These are moral capacity, moral courage and moral resiliency. These help to influence the ethical actions necessary to address business within the three shear zones (Chapter 10). A leader's moral capacity is apparent from how the leader has constructed their role, their ability to view perspective and

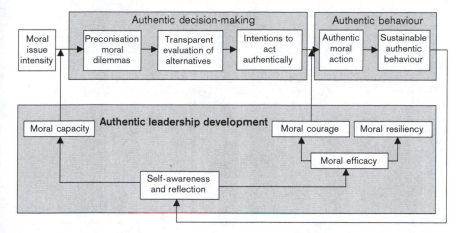

Figure 14.1

Developing the moral component of authentic leadership (May *et al.* 2003: 250)

how previous moral dilemmas have been covered. Moral courage is indicated by the leader's strength of character to convert moral intentions into actions regardless of the pressures from either inside or outside of the organisation (Figure 14.1). Finally, a morally resilient leader is one who is able to 'positively *adapt* in the face of significant adversity or risk' (May *et al.* 2003: 256).

Authentic leadership seeks an inclusive organisational culture to encourage learning and personal growth. According to Meacham (2007), such leadership can help an organisation as a complex social system to generate a wide range of forces and balances that not only maintain the status quo of that system but seek to develop its sphere of influence, as reflected through its culture. Dealing with sustainability is a multidimensional issue and 'we are in a century of complexity, with unprecedented interconnectivity, scale, novelty, unforeseen new structures with unexpected new properties, and radical innovation and transformation' (Beinecke 2009: 2).

In order to be best placed to deal with 'wicked problems' as they occur, organisations need authentic leaders. First they need to identify people who possess appropriate characteristics. Second, they need to promote initiatives to help develop such people. Table 14.2 sets out some suggestions of possible selection criteria and development initiatives (Ilies *et al.* 2005).

Looking back at the Big Conversation (Chapter 13) a 'head in the sand' or a 'trinket' approach are certainly not going to solve the problem because they are looking in the wrong direction, if they are looking at all. The alternative, 'carbon is cash', is an improvement but it, in many cases, tends to be an unbalanced approach. The cost–value axis is very often not in alignment and can over-emphasise the cost element at the expense of the longer term investment in value. The authentic leader is the 'first class' leader.

Table 14.2   Strategies for increasing authentic leadership (Ilies *et al.* 2005: 389)

Authentic leadership component	Selection criteria	Developmental interventions
Self-awareness	Positive self-concept Emotional intelligence	Multisource feedback
Unbiased processing	Integrity Learning goal orientation	Assessment centres
Authentic behaviour/acting	Self-monitoring (low other-directedness) Self-esteem	Coaching/mentoring Behavioural role modelling
Relational authenticity	Past positive relationships Past behaviour interview	Upward feedback Leader–member exchange training

The leader's journey

Leadership involves a journey, a progression from inner restlessness concerning current situations to the challenge of chaos and uncertainty. This takes the leader from the safety of knowledge to the challenge of the unknown. The creativity of leadership means that the journey repeats itself endlessly. It is part of a continuous cycle of change. However, it is not so much a process of external exploration and development as an inner journey. To be successful (and, ultimately, sustainable), leaders need to create and maintain an inner harmony. Dreher (1997) identifies the following stages in this process:

Creating inner harmony

- Stage 1 – Vocation: the first stage on the path is a feeling of restlessness about the existing business model. Probably not so much that it should be done away with completely. Simply that it seems incomplete. There is something missing. The whole process of owning and occupying real estate seems to be one dimensional based around financial return or financial productivity. There is an imbalance between these private goals and the wider social and cultural context within which real estate exists and achieves its real worth.
- Stage 2 – Crossing the threshold: here the leadership will go beyond the known environment, the safety of traditional systems, meetings, committees and agendas. There will of course be resistance – mental or physical, internal or external. Raising questions about morality and ethical positions do not fit into the standard business or real estate tools. What is the ethical year's purchase (YP) or the hyperbolic discount rate?

- Stage 3 – Initiation: freeing itself from the known, the leadership will encounter tests. Because the old familiar structures are no longer there and the leadership is in freefall (and open to ridicule) these are severe and deep tests of spiritual integrity – everything seems to fall apart and familiar patterns are no longer there to support us. Now it seems that traditional learning may not have been enough to deal with complex issues such as global finance, responsible property investing and business transformation.
- Stage 4 – Facing the dragon: now the stage has been reached where the real tests begin. How strong is the conviction? Leadership comes to confront its deepest fears in preparation for a different level of responsibility. Now is the time. Leadership finds that it is not enough just to respond to the market, that brings back the old unease. It is time to go to the market and openly confront environmental and social issues of real estate ownership.
- Stage 5 – Facing the inner dragon: having overcome the outer dragon, now it is time to go inside to explore the force of the unconscious (the Jungian shadow). It is also a time of reflection. Where does this restlessness come from? Is it trinket, just window dressing to improve the financial bottom line? Or is it something more fundamental at the spiritual level? What will be found in the unconscious?
- Stage 6 – Detachment and blending: to move on from this stage, leadership needs to experience an ego death, in order to release the energy of the whole and to allow the energy to flow. This is fatal. How can a real estate adviser live without an ego? Expanding and developing business tools to incorporate sustainability is fine. Agreeing green building designs, green leases, talking about lifecycle costings can be done. But letting go of ego and still leading?
- Stage 7 – Taking chaos: the final test of leadership 'in this world of rapid transition is how well we can 'take chaos', i.e. deal with the unexpected (Dreher 1997). How resilient is the leadership? How resilient is the organisation? How resilient is the building?

In summary, the starting point for authentic leadership is inner harmony. The seven stages identified here are a continuum of meeting changing external circumstances with an inner balance. As described above the stages relate to individuals as leaders. However, the same seven stages can be seen in the journey of organisations. The next section, therefore, uses these to explore the journey of an investing institution in its vision for sustainability.

Case study

Background

Leading organisations also take inner journeys. One such case is PRUPIM, the property investment arm of Prudential plc and one of the biggest property investors in the UK (and within the top 25 global property investors) with £15.9 billion of property assets under management. This level of investment represents approximately 8 per cent of Prudential's total assets under management. These property assets are held and managed for a variety of different client types, and include over 800 separate property holdings with individual values up to £340 million, occupied by approximately 4,000 different tenants. Approximately 85 per cent by value is located in the UK; the rest is spread across the globe.

As is the case with many UK investing institutions, residential property plays only a small part in the portfolio; the bulk of the assets are made up of properties accommodating retail, office and industrial uses. Not surprisingly, given the scale of its property investment portfolios, assets managed by PRUPIM touch many communities and have a significant environmental footprint.

The PRUPIM journey: from starting line to triple bottom line

PRUPIM is currently acknowledged as a thought leader in the field of Responsible Property Investment (RPI). In recognition of this, senior staff members in the company have chaired influential industry groupings such as the UK Green Property Alliance (UK GPA); the United Nations Environment Programme Finance Initiative Property Working Group (UNEP FI PWG); and the Property Workstream of the Institutional Investors' Group on Climate Change (IIGCC).

PRUPIM as an organisation has been engaged in a journey of learning and discovery over a ten year period to understand the requisite level and range of expertise needed to understand the implications of the interplay between the economic, environmental and social aspects of property investment, and the role its investment assets can play in changing the quality of environment and community life.

It has been a journey that has seen the company move from taking action in individual situations instinctively and incrementally, to develop a wider corporate consciousness about the potential advantage and value of managing its property portfolios in a responsible way. Broadly speaking, the journey has encompassed five stages of developing expertise and a structure necessary to work more sustainably: although this is very much work in progress on an evolving and developing topic.

Stage 1 – local creativity (vocation)

The journey began bottom up through asset managers and shopping mall teams implementing community-based initiatives, mainly through using the assets of shopping malls. The benefits that such actions reaped in terms of developing and improving relationships with occupiers in the shopping malls and with wider local communities suggested this as a form of asset management strategy with potential benefits to PRUPIM's investment portfolios, albeit at that stage intangible and hard to measure.

Stage 2 – functional and theoretical development (crossing the threshold and initiation)

These early successes from shopping malls were then collated, recorded and made public in PRUPIM's first sustainability report in 2002. Following this, the company invested resources in the creation of a bespoke function focused exclusively on exploring the potential for further business links and initiatives in the communities around major property assets. At the same time, as the environmental issue rose steadily up the political, social and investment agenda, the PRUPIM sustainability team began to look at how PRUPIM could reduce the environmental footprint of its portfolios. This began more as a quasi-technical activity, grounded in a desire to be socially responsible, rather than possessing the economic rationale that emerged later. The initial work on the environment also prompted the essential task of measuring the company's environmental footprint, so that progress could be measured against a known baseline.

Stage 3 – analysis of business implications and opportunities (facing the dragon)

As issues of environment in particular became ever more important, PRUPIM began work to try and understand what the implications of a more carbon-conscious society and property market might be for the commercial real estate markets that its funds invested in. Members of its investment team incorporated a sustainability appraisal as part of net worth calculations for assets. This helped to conceptualise and understand how increasing environmental standards might affect the value of different types of properties in its portfolios. It also showed how taking positive action to reduce environmental impact sat with the necessary fiduciary responsibilities that PRUPIM had. This work identified clear reasons why managing properties in an environmentally responsible manner could lead to good relative investment performance against the general market (see Illustration 14.1 for an example).

Illustration 14.1

Case Study 1

Case-study 1: Responsible Asset Management – Using International Standards to Reduce Resource Usage and Pollution from Commercial Real Estate

ISO14001 is a voluntary standard that promotes identification of significant impacts of an organisation's activities and drives continual improvement. The standard uses best practice environmental management and is focused on reducing inefficiency in order to optimise profitability. PRUPIM registered its first property for certification to the International Standard for Environmental Management Systems, ISO14001, in 2005. Since then, it has certified more than 50 more of its major properties to the same high standard.

PRUPIM estimates that it has directly realised the following benefits because of its roll out programme of bringing its major properties up to the ISO14001 standard:

- **6,464 tonnes reduction** in CO_2 emissions from ISO14001 properties between 2008/09 and 2009/10

- **60,728m³ reduction** in water consumption from ISO14001 properties between 2008/09 and 2009/10

- **6,937 tonnes recycled** waste averted from landfill by ISO14001 properties in 2009/10.

The operational savings of these environmental benefits in 2009/10 are in excess of £1,300,000.

Stage 4 – training and knowledge sharing (facing the inner dragon)

A continuing aspect of the journey for PRUPIM has been to spread the realisation of the benefits of operating in a TBL sustainable manner through all parts of the company since, in the past, it has tended to be promoted by individuals dotted through the company. This has resulted in major education programmes being put in place to ensure that all staff know why the company should manage real estate portfolios in a responsible way and what the most cost-effective and advantageous practices are to achieve this. The company has always been willing to share its ideas and lead debate in the industry, both in the UK and overseas.

Stage 5 – formal external consultation (detachment and blending and taking chaos)

PRUPIM has now formalised the involvement of a wider range of interested parties in helping define and develop sustainability activities by creating an expert panel of such stakeholders. The panel comprises representatives from public interest groups, occupiers, industry bodies, supplier organisations and academic institutions. The remit of the panel, which meets infrequently, is to challenge PRUPIM's sustainability strategy and reporting practices. This process, the first of its kind to be implemented by a UK property investment company, has enabled PRUPIM to develop a robust and transparent strategy that responds to stakeholder expectations.

In summary, PRUPIM's journey towards their inner harmony/sustainability can be mapped through the balanced scorecard stages. Here we can see how, as they mined through the layers (top, down) they unearthed the richness of the experience and so formed a deep structure for sustainability. Admittedly, led by sustainable profit (top line growth in income and bottom line efficiency in expenditures), they have achieved sustainable market growth (creating their eco-niche market and green building strategy) backed up by sustainable processes. In this way, they also discovered the value of sustainable capacity development not only of their own staff resources but also throughout the value chain.

Summary

In most of the examples that we have cited in this book, the reason why sustainability issues have advanced is because of leadership that is not only sympathetic to the three pillars of sustainability but also because that leadership has been able to design a way to attain a sustainable vision. This has often been achieved through the modification of models and an organisational change of mindset. The result has been more efficiency, greater resilience and socially responsible activities that help communities, encouragement of employee well-being and the provision of financial reward. Those less successful organisations (in terms of achieving green credentials) are those that seek to attach a few symbols and trinkets to their existing business model with no longer term commitment to the deeper issues that the sustainability debate raises.

This chapter has set out ideas on learning objectives in an age of complexity. These are based around the principles of flow, balance and clarity. This creative flow, sustaining balance and communication clarity are an essential part of any authentic leadership that forms the second part of the chapter. Here the qualities of authenticity have been discussed and applied to organisational leadership. The final section of the chapter, which outlines the journey that a leader might take towards resilience, shows that change is not just about knowledge. It is also about positioning, belief and inner wisdom.

15 Sustainability skills

∙ ∙

Chapter 14 identified authentic leadership within the more proactive, anticipatory approaches that can create the change environment necessary to turn an organisation into a first-class sustainable organisation. This book is about real estate and sustainable behaviour. We have tried to show throughout that real estate influences, and is influenced by, organisational culture and the people who work in and manage those organisations and their buildings. The skill of the real estate adviser, whether acting for an investing institution or a corporate occupier is to help to identify the key components of creating a balanced solution that offers both substance and agility, resilience and resonance, social, environmental as well as financial sustainability. This requires a process and tools that are predictive rather than forecasting, dynamic rather than static, anticipative rather than reactive.

The earlier parts of the book sought to open up some ideas on concepts to create a setting within which a dialogue could begin. These included identifying the knowledge and skills required of a sustainability literate person or organisation. This final chapter reflects on those skills in the light of the overall themes and discussions in the book to offer some concluding remarks.

Sustainable literacy skills and knowledge 1

An appreciation of the importance of environmental, social, political and economic contexts for each discipline

The book has attempted to introduce the notion of transdisciplinarity as part of the process of understanding and acting sustainably. By this, it is meant an approach that not only seeks to interlink disciplines, but also seeks to see no division between disciplines or, indeed, subjects and objects. An understanding of this interconnectedness of all things is fundamental to sustainable behaviour.

Real estate markets as open systems are inextricably linked with global financial markets, international institutional structures and trans-global business enterprise. This suggests *'intrinsic interconnectedness'*. There may, therefore, be a tension between the primary short-term self-interest of an individual (i.e. the client's need to know the implications of the lease terms for day-to-day operational purposes) and the inescapable interlink between the individual and the whole (i.e. the client's understanding of the wider, more remote implications of actions under the terms of the lease).

However, even where the gap in knowledge and understanding is redressed in a variety of ways it is often open to manipulation to suit the particular 'business case' requirements of the client. Somehow, the impact on community, nature and the climate needs to be factored into the professional arena at a macro, integrative way rather than just an add-on makeweight. The World Wide Fund for Nature (formerly known as WWF, the World Wildlife Fund) sees the problems in the environment as a 'consequence of rapid economic and population growth as well as the related increases in material flows and energy use' (WWF 2007: 13). This should therefore be an important issue for any property owner or occupier or their advisers.

The built environment is a significant contributor to carbon emissions and it has a major impact on community and social life. It would be reasonable, therefore, to expect professionals in the built environment disciplines to be at the forefront of seeking solutions that incorporate social costs into their analytical models. The Sustainable Property Appraisal Project, the RICS Valuation Paper No 13, CRC for Construction Innovation's report 'Evaluation of functional performance in commercial buildings' (Chapter 7) are all examples of how the real estate profession is seeking to address these issues.

This *'social stock of knowledge'* (Berger *et al.* 1976) suggests that in order to understand and confront the problems associated with, for example, climate change, a change of system provides more of the same without solution. The problem is perhaps more fundamental than that. Systems and their regulations can go so far but at the end of the day it is a behavioural issue that requires attention.

Sustainable property investment requires a new mindset that may well be entirely different from current 'best practice' in design (what you build), construction (how you build it), property investment and management, e.g. integrated sustainability assessment of property assets, objective and transparent sustainability accounting and reporting (which ought not to result in mere 'creative writing exercises'), and promoting next-generation construction approaches such as closed-loop design and the use and reuse of organic materials in order to achieve breakthroughs in energy efficiency and to create buildings that serve as utility providers rather than acting as utility consumers (RICS 2008b).

Sustainable literacy skills and knowledge 2

A broad and balanced foundation knowledge of sustainable development, its key principles and the main debate within them, including its contested and expanding boundaries

In order to act sustainably, it is necessary to have some foundation knowledge about the *what* and the *how*. This book has attempted to address both. The substantial part of the second section of the book offered the *what*. It provided commentaries on the nature of real estate markets, mechanisms and players. The third section offered a framework (including tools and processes) to help to structure how to deal with sustainable decision making and offering sound advice to a client, i.e. the *how*.

Decision makers tend to concentrate on information that they consider most important. Through a process of exploration using techniques such as dialogue, stakeholder workshops, etc., it is possible to expand the boundaries. So that, despite the complex nature of real estate and the markets within which it operates, and despite the levels of uncertainty and unpredictability in the externalities of those markets, it is possible to achieve a 'bounded rationality' in terms of advice given or decisions made. Future leadership in this complex field is going to be more effective if it builds partnerships and alliances across organisations rather than expecting knowledge to exist in one place alone. This can best be achieved through authentic leadership and anticipatory learning (Chapter 14).

By these means, it is possible to start to address the knowledge–behaviour gap. Real estate markets and their participants often have the knowledge to provide sustainable solutions but their behavioural response may focus on the short term, expeditious response. Here the notion of responsibility is important. This is the ability to respond to the 'highest capacity'. In the context of corporate social responsibility, this will relate to different criteria for different organisations (Chapter 9). In the case of Igloo Regeneration Partnership, for example, as with many other organisations, this is linked to one of their footprint themes of well-being, regeneration, environmental sustainability and urban design. The application of socially responsible investment principles in a real estate investment fund requires constant vigilance in order to ensure that the most sustainable solutions are achieved and their response to opportunities are of the 'highest capacity' (Igloo 2008).

Sustainable literacy skills and knowledge 3

Problem-solving skills in a non-reductionist manner for highly complex real-life problems

When considering a concept such as sustainability, it is ineffective to try to reduce it to its constituent parts. It has many dimensions but separately they do not provide a holistic picture. No one dimension is a 'utopian ideal' to aim for at some point in the future. They are here and now in the present being applied or waiting to be adopted by individuals, organisations, institutions; towns, cities, districts; public, private, social entities.

Furthermore, with the increased discussion around concepts such as sustainability, the message becomes more and more confusing due to its complexity. So, not only do different systems understand the issue in a particular way but, because of its growing complexity, sub-systems start to form that have their own meanings and communicate these within their sub-system and cannot see why there is a block of understanding outside of their sub-system. This leads to a range of competing interpretative codes emerging and what was one expert system turns into many experts with their own understanding and interpretation. Sustainability then becomes a concept with too many possible futures. This undermines credibility and then it tends to push expert opinions towards dogmatism. This in turn stultifies any meaningful dialogue between experts.

This is not an easy issue to resolve. However, many 'first class' organisations are taking the lead through introducing sustainable systems and working practices at the heart of their operations. Some of the case studies in the book (for example, the PRUPIM journey) attempt to show how organisations are addressing such complex issues in a non-reductionist way.

Sustainable literacy skills and knowledge 4

Ability to think creatively and holistically and to make critical judgements

In Chapter 2, Priest (2002) identified limits of thought as creating partial perceptions of the world. These limits of expression, iteration, cognition and conception are particularly relevant to any discussion about sustainability. This is partly because, at one level, there is an inexpressible nature to the process of being sustainable as a concept and partly because for humans to be sustainable requires sustainability across time and space. Sustainability exists across national borders and it exists across time, it is about seeking well-being for the future across the world. However, this is often a difficult notion to grasp because of the immediacy of thought processes.

Chapter 11 used the 'Portrait of Place' case study to show how, within a regional study, it was possible to draw out some of the critical issues existing at all levels of society to produce creative and holistic solutions and longer term sustainable programmes for development and adaptation. It is only when sustainability is integrated into the overall decision-making planning that it starts to stretch the limits of thought. That is not to say that the solutions that are eventually implemented can escape those limits. Simply to say that, through a continuous process of consultation and communication, sustainable thinking becomes part of an emerging 'collective unconscious'.

Chapter 5 highlighted the complex nature of ownership of real estate assets and drew attention to the split between ownership and control. Real estate trading has become more of a financial exercise than a physical building transaction over the last 20 years. Equally, as shown in Chapter 8, it is no longer possible simply to just feed figures into a spreadsheet or pricing model and feel comfortable with the outcome. It is now realised that the human factor in financial capital modelling is crucial. Dealings in real estate are complex and require a considerable amount of expert knowledge. However, because of the significant impact that real estate has on our lives, it is important that it is placed at the centre of the sustainability debate. Authentic leaders and their followers are crucial to the creative impetus needed to extend sustainable practices more widely.

In Chapter 3 real estate markets were described as complex adaptive systems. There are some distinguishing features of such systems. Zohar *et al.* (2004) compare these with the qualities of leaders who have spiritual intelligence (i.e. 'the intelligence with which we have access to deep meaning, fundamental values, and a sense of abiding purpose in our lives'). More specifically, in spiritual intelligence, people would often show behaviours, such as 'self-awareness, spontaneity, vision and value led, holistic, reframe, positive use of adversity, humility and sense of vocation' (Zohar *et al.* 2004: 64). Similarly, complex adaptive systems often include the following features: '1) self-organisation; 2) bounded instability; 3) emergent; 4) holistic; 5) in dialogue with environment; 6) evolutionary mutations; 7) outside control destructive; 8) exploratory; 9) recontextualize environment; and 10) order out of chaos' (Zohar *et al.* 2004: 64).

Spiritual intelligence is based around the idea of spiritual capital, which itself is defined as 'a vision and a model for organizational and cultural sustainability within a wider framework of community and global concern' (Zohar *et al.* 2004: 3). In this way, sustainable thinking becomes part of critical judgement.

Sustainable literacy skills and knowledge 5

Ability to develop a high level of self-reflection (both personal and professional)

This level of knowledge requires reflection on conscious and unconscious actions and reactions. The unconscious represents those contents inaccessible to consciousness: '[I]t is only through the rounding out of the personality through the recognition and integration of unconscious contents, a process which Jung called "individuation", that the person achieves a greater self knowledge and understanding and thus more effective social relations and adjustment' (Bowles 1990: 397–398). This equally applies to the personality of the organisation and investing institution as it does to individuals. More prosaically, Beinecke (2009: 4) sees the process of assembling effective teams as 'moving between being an active participant on the complex dance floor and pulling back to looking down from the balcony where you can see and reflect on the larger pattern of interactions'.

The participation in a dialogue was identified in Chapter 10 as a means to help individuals explore their ideas in a non-threatening way. Whilst this is unlikely, as described, to be implemented by many organisations, there should be some deep examination amongst stakeholders. Examples were used in the Brockwood case study in Chapter 10 and the 'Portrait of Place' (Chapter 11). In such ways it is possible to go through a process of self-discovery (similar to the leader's journey in Chapter 14) and reflect knowledge, attitude, behaviour and the gaps in between.

Sustainable literacy skills and knowledge 6

Ability to identify, understand, evaluate and adopt values conducive to sustainability

In order to deliver sustainable development some form of behaviour change will be needed. This is a complex subject and does not rely solely on technical information and knowledge. A whole new mindset is needed to close the so-called 'attitude–behaviour gap' (DEFRA 2005). 'Education is not merely a matter of training the mind. Training makes for efficiency; it does not bring about completeness. A mind that has merely been trained only perpetuates the past; such a mind can never discover the new' (Khare 1988: 145).

In Chapter 8, 'Decision making and sustainability', three barriers to action were identified. These were individuality, responsibility and practicality (Blake 1999). More generally, throughout the book there has been an overall theme emphasising both internal and external factors that influence behaviour. External factors have predominantly been economic, institutional and cultural or social. On the other hand, internal factors have included knowledge, values, attitude, awareness, emotion and motivation. Neither external nor internal factors should be seen in isolation. But, they should be considered together in the context of actual activities in the real estate markets whether in investor markets or in occupier markets.

Also, running through the book is the notion that whilst eco-efficiency and social productivity are aspirational in terms of organisational bottom lines, the issue of sufficiency has been stressed. At what point has enough been produced or consumed? What is a sustainable profit? How much real estate and how much return? The individual and the organisation need to consider this as part of being sustainability literate. Not only should individuals 'learn to be happy within the limits of what he has, rather than to subject himself to the perpetual increase of desires' (Khare 1998: 143), but also they should become conscious of the limits of the planet and the social fabric.

Sustainable literacy skills and knowledge 7

Ability to bridge the gap between theory and practice; in sustainable development, only transformational action counts

Throughout this book, the authors have tried to demonstrate how theoretical aspects of sustainability can be translated into practical outcomes through sustainable real estate solutions. This has ranged from real estate organisations dealing with investment (e.g. PRUPIM and RREEF) to organisations using real estate to conduct their 'business' (e.g. AAT and Brockwood). The complex nature of real estate market mechanisms, the nature of ownership and market dealings together with financial markets and modelling are covered in the second part of the book. The third part tries through models and case study examples to show how sustainability can be achieved. Organisations can be seen as part of a broad corporate system. As sub-systems, each organisation will work within and react to its surrounding environment. The level and the depth of the reaction will be determined by the resilience and adaptability, and ultimately the transformability, of each sub-system (i.e. organisation). Underlying these frameworks, models and practical examples is the simple fact that sustainable practices will be effective if there is someone to champion them. Only transformational action will count. This only comes about through authentic leadership.

Sustainable literacy skills and knowledge 8

Ability to participate creatively in interdisciplinary teams

The starting point to developing a sustainable real estate balanced scorecard is at the level of development of capabilities. This is where eco-cooperations are found and strategic alliances can be developed. There is no one organisation that holds the key. Nor is there one individual within an organisation that can create and manage sustainable practices and learning alone. These rely on team effort and partnerships. For every authentic leader there has to be a team of authentic followers. For every sustainable producer there has to be a sustainable consumer and for every sustainable professional body there has to be sustainable professionals. Part of the process of learning is to see 'how hidden values and intentions can control our behaviour, and how unnoticed differences in culture or gender can clash without our realizing what is occurring' (Bohm *et al.* 1991: 2). Use of dialogue and/or open discussion can be seen as 'an arena in which collective learning takes place, and out of which a sense of increased harmony, fellowship and creativity can arise' (Bohm *et al.* 1991: 2).

Final thoughts

So what is sustainability? Castells (2000: 118) answers this question as follows: 'A city or ecosystem, or complex structure of any kind, is sustainable if its conditions of production do not destroy over time the conditions of its reproduction'. Like many definitions, this appears, on the surface, to be straightforward – anything produced can be considered sustainable provided its production does not stop its reproduction. At the human level, being born, we are sustainable so long as we do not destroy the conditions that enabled our birth. At the corporate level, being established, an organisation is sustainable provided it does not destroy, through production or consumption, the conditions prevailing at the time it was established.

However, it may not be as simple as that. In fact the simplicity may be the problem and hence the difficulty in arriving at a meaning for the concept. Sustainability needs the future to be grounded in a past so that the present is similar. It does not take account of paradigm shifts. All it demands of the present is that it does not use up too much of its credit (future) to secure itself. But it cannot know what the future is. The future might not feed itself with what the present assumes as basic sustenance.

But it is also the social system itself, here and now, that has trouble understanding anything outside of itself. So institutional frameworks, such as the law, politics, economics, and the family can communicate within their boundaries but what they cannot do is 'directly read the other systems code'. Systems are discrete: one system (individual, group, organisation, country, ideology) can share its truths with another at one level but these may not be fully understood. No system can achieve the stranger's view of itself: a system's view of itself is, therefore, inherently partial. This makes communication across boundaries difficult and, potentially, leaves a gap where the middle should be. This is why an approach such as transdisciplinarity is important. It attempts to include the middle. Equally, a system will reduce the complexity of its environment through its selection of what is inside and what is outside.

This being the case, then a fundamental problem of understanding develops around the whole issue of sustainability. Each system (individual, organisation, etc.) can communicate the message but that message is not directly or fully understood by any other system or sub-system. Added to which the nature of the concept (i.e. sustainability in this case) is simplified using a system code. So, for example, 'green' buildings may be a code for energy efficiency, carbon neutral, zero carbon, 'smart', etc.; an investor may see a 'green' building in terms of higher sustained returns, an occupier as incurring higher rent, a corporate as part of CSR or any combination of these, etc. At the macro level we now have a split between the political, the economic and the legal systems in Western culture that accentuate the issues of communication about global issues such as sustainable environments.

'Human cultures, through language and other symbolic signals, can create an enormous range of group behavioural patterns. What is more, we can imagine *alternative* patterns and dialogue about them; we can envision *alternative* futures' (Clark 2002: 232). Real estate and the way in which it is developed, occupied and managed can play a significant role in creating an alternative sustainable future. The question is: to what extent is the real estate profession willing and able to provide authentic leadership in sustainable behavioural patterns for the future?

Bibliography

Adams, C., Frost, G. & Webber, W. (2004) Triple bottom line: A review of the literature, in Henriques, A. & Richardson, J. (ed.) *The triple bottom line: Does it all add up?*, London: Earthscan.

AECOM (2011) *Delivering a sustainable future for central Lincolnshire Portrait Of Place*, London: AECOM.

AERS (2005) *Social capital theory: A review*, Edinburgh: Applied Educational Research Scheme – Schools and Social Capital Network.

Akerlof, G. A. & Shiller, R. J. (2009) *Animal spirits: How human psychology drives the economy, and why it matters for global capitalism*, Oxford: Princeton University Press.

Amaeshi, K. M. & Adi, B. (2006) *Reconstructing the corporate social responsibility construct in Utlish*, Nottingham: International Centre for Corporate Social Responsibility.

Arrow, K. J. (1982) 'Risk perception in psychology and economics', *Economic Inquiry*, XX: 1–9.

Augier, M. & Kreiner, K. (2000) 'Rationality, imagination and intelligence: Some boundaries in human decision-making', *Industrial and Corporate Change*, 9(4): 659–681.

Bacharach, M. & Hurley, S. (1991) Issues and advances in the foundations of decision theory, in Bacharach, M. & Hurley, S. (ed.) *Foundations of decision theory: Issues and advances*, Oxford: Basil Blackwell Ltd.

Ball, M., Lizieri, C. & MacGregor, B. D. (1998) *The economics of commercial property markets*, London: Routledge.

Barberis, N. & Thaler, R. H. (2003) A survey of behavioural finance, in Constantinides, G. M., Harris, M. & Stulz, R. M. (ed.) *Handbook of the economics of finance*, Amsterdam: Elsevier B.V.

Barthorpe, S., Duncan, R. & Miller, C. (2000) 'The pluralistic facets of culture and its impact on construction', *Property Management*, 18(5): 335–351.

Baum, A. (2009) *Commercial real estate investment: A strategic approach*, 2nd edition, London: Estates Gazette.

Baum, A. & Turner, N. (2004) 'Retention rates, reinvestment and depreciation in European office markets', *Journal of Property Investment & Finance*, 22(3): 214–235.

Baum, A. & Crosby, N. (2008) *Property investment appraisal*, 3rd edition, Oxford: Blackwell Publishing.

Baum, A., Crosby, N. & MacGregor, B. D. (1996) 'Price formation, mispricing and investment analysis in the property market: A response to "a note on 'the initial yield revealed: Explicit valuations and the future of property investment'"', *Journal of Property Valuation & Investment*, 14(1): 36–49.

Baum, A., Crosby, N., Gallimore, P., McAllister, P. & Gray, A. (2000) *The influence of valuers and valuations on the workings of the commercial property investment market*, London: Education Trusts of the Investment Property Forum.

BBP (2008) *Guidance on green leases: Working together to improve sustainability*, London: Better Buildings Partnership.

BCO (2010) *Towards zero carbon offices*, London: British Council of Offices.

Beinecke, R. H. (2009) 'Introduction: Leadership for wicked problems', *The Innovation Journal: The Public Sector Innovation Journal*, 14(1): 1–17.

Belk, R. W. (1988) 'Possessions and the extended self', *Journal of Consumer Research*, 15: 139–168.

Berger, P. L. & Luckman, T. (1976) *The social construction of reality*, London: Penguin.

Birkin, F., Polesie, T. & Lewis, L. (2009) 'A new business model for sustainable development: An exploratory study using the theory of constraints in Nordic organisations', *Business Strategy and the Environment*, 18: 277–299.

Black, R. T. (1997) 'Expert property negotiators and pricing information, revisited', *Journal of Property Valuation & Investment*, 15(3): 274–281.

Black, R. T. & Diaz III, J. (1996) 'The use of information versus asking price in the real property negotiation process', *Journal of Property Research*, 13: 287–297.

Black, R. T., Brown, M. G., Diaz, J., Gibler, K. M. & Grissom, T. V. (2000) 'Behavioural research in real estate: A search for the boundaries', paper presented at RICS Cutting Edge Conference, London, September.

Blake, J. (1999) 'Overcoming the "value-action gap" in environmental policy: Tensions between national policy and local experience', *Local Environment*, 4(3): 257–278.

Bodnar, M., Kane, A., Sanchez, J. & Sharma, P. (2010) Responsible real estate: The case for retrofitting (business and the environment final paper), Washington, DC: CoStar Group, Inc.

Bohm, D., Factor, D. & Garrett, P. (1991) *Dialogue – a proposal*, London: Dialogue Groups.

Bonta, M. & Protevi, J. (2004) *Deleuze and geophilosophy: A guide and glossary*, Edinburgh: Edinburgh University Press.

Bowles, M. L. (1990) 'Recognising deep structures in organisations', *Organisational Studies*, 11(3): 395–412.

Boyd, T. (2006) 'Evaluating the impact of sustainability on investment property performance', *Pacific Rim Property Research Journal*, 12(3): 254–271.

Brandstatter, H. & Königstein, M. (2001) 'Personality influences on ultimatum bargaining decisions', *European Journal of Personality*, 15(S1): S3–S70.

Brennan, T. (2000) *Exhausting modernity: Grounds for a new economy*, London: Routledge.

Brown, G. (1985) 'The information content of property valuations', *Journal of Valuation*, 3: 350–362.

Brown, G. R. (1991) *Property investment and the capital markets*, London: E&FN Spon.

Brown, G. R. & Matysiak, G. A. (2000) *Real estate investment: A capital market approach*, Harlow: Pearson Education Limited.

Burke, L. & Logsdon, J. M. (1996) 'How corporate social responsibility pays off', *Long Range Planning*, 29(4): 495–502.

Burkitt, I. (1999) *Bodies of thought*, London: Sage Publications.

Burrell, O. K. (1951) 'Possibility of an experimental approach to investment studies', *The Journal of Finance*, 6(2): 211–219.

Camerer, C. (1995). Individual decision making, in Kagel, J. H. & Roth, A. E. (ed.) *The handbook of experimental economics*, Princeton, NJ: Princeton University Press.

Cao, A. (2000) 'The problem of chronic over-supply in China's property market: An institutional perspective', paper presented at RICS Cutting Edge Conference, London, September.

Capra, F. (1982) *The turning point: Science, society and the rising culture*, London: Fontana Paperbacks.

Castells, M. (2000) 'Urban sustainability in the information age', *City*, 4(1): 118–122.

Chan, E. & Lee, G. K. L. (2008) 'Critical factors for improving social sustainability of urban renewal projects', *Social Indicators Research*, 85(2): 243–256.

Chapman, D. (2004) 'Sustainability and our cultural myths', *Canadian Journal of Environmental Education*, 9: 92–108.

Churchland, P. S. (1989) *Neurophilosophy: Toward a unified science of the mind brain*, London: MIT Press.

Clark, M. E. (2002) *In search of human nature*, London: Routledge.

Clark, S., Hackemann, T., Mesmin, O., Roche, M. & Road, T. (2010). Progress on REIT regimes in Europe, in Newell, G. & Sieracki, K. (ed.) *Global trends in real estate finance*, Chichester: Wiley-Blackwell.

Coleman, M., Hudson-Wilson, S. & Webb, J. R. (1994) Real estate in the multiasset portfolio, in Hudson-Wilson, S. & Wurtzebach, C. H. (ed.) *Managing real estate portfolios*, Burr Ridge: IRWIN.

Corpra (2008) *Corpra case study – change management category*, London: Corpra.

CRC (2004) *Evaluation of functional performance in commercial buildings*, Brisbane: CRC for Construction Innovation.

Daniels, P. L. (2003) 'Buddhist economics and the environment', *International Journal of Social Economics*, 30(1-2): 8–33.

—— (2005) 'Economic systems and the Buddhist world view: The 21st century nexus', *The Journal of Socio-Economics*, 34: 245–268.

D'Arcy, E. & Keogh, G. (1998) 'Territorial competition and property market process: An exploratory analysis', *Urban Studies*, 35(8): 1215–1230.

Davidson, K. & Wilson, L. (2009) A critical assessment of urban social sustainability, North Terrace Adelaide: The University of South Australia.

Dawe, G., Jucker, R. & Martin, S. (2005) *Sustainable development in higher education: Current practice and future developments. A report for the higher education academy*, York: Higher Education Academy.

Dawkins, R. (1976) *The selfish gene*, Oxford: Oxford University Press.

Day, C. (1990) *Places of the soul: Architecture and environmental design as a healing art*, Wellingborough: Aquarian Press.

DEFRA (2005) Securing the future – delivering UK sustainable development strategy, Norwich: Department for Environment, Food and Rural Affairs.

Dent, P. & Temple, M. (1998) 'Economic value – a methodological dilemma?' paper presented at RICS Cutting Edge Conference, Leicester.

Dent, P. & Winter, P. (2011) 'Aligning real estate with the corporate environment', *Corporate Real Estate Journal*, 1(3): 273–283.

DeWeese-Boyd, I. & DeWeese-Boyd, M. (2007) 'The healthy city versus the luxurious city in Plato's republic: Lessons about consumption and sustainability for a globalising economy', *Contemporary Justice Review*, 10(1): 115–130.

Diaz III, J. (1990a) 'How appraisers do their work: A test of the appraisal process and the development of a descriptive model', *Journal of Real Estate Research*, 5(1): 1–15.

—— (1990b) 'The process of selecting comparable sales', *The Appraisal Journal*, 58(4): 533–540.

—— (1999) 'The first decade of behavioural research in the discipline of property', *Journal of Property Investment & Finance*, 17(4): 326–332.

Dorner, D. (1996) *The logic of failure*, New York: Basic Books.

Douglas, I. (1999). Globalisation of governance: Towards an archaeology of contemporary political reason, in Prakash, A. & Hart, J. (ed.) *Globalisation of governance*, New York: Routledge.

Dreher, D. (1997) *The tao of personal leadership*, New York: Harper Business.

Elkington, J. (1997) *Cannibals with folks*, Oxford: Capstone Publishing Ltd.

Elliott, C. (1997) 'A systems approach to the property market', paper presented at RICS Cutting Edge Conference.

Ellis, R. L. & Lipetz, M. J. (1979) *Essential sociology*, Glenview: Scott, Foresman and Co.

Ellison, L. & Sayce, S. (2006) *The sustainable property appraisal project: Final report*, Kingston: Kingston University.

Elster, J. (1998) 'Emotions and economic theory', *Journal of Economic Literature*, XXXVI: 47–74.

Engel-Di Mauro, S. (2008) 'Beyond the Bowers-McLaren debate: The importance of studying the rest of nature in forming alternative curricula', *Capitalism Nature Socialism*, 19(2): 88–95.

Epstein, S., Pacini, R., Denes-Raj, V. & Heier, H. (1996) 'Individual differences in intuitive–experiential and analytical–rational thinking styles', *Journal of Personality and Social Psychology*, 71(2): 390–405.

Eysenck, M. W. (1993) *Principles of cognitive psychology*, Hove: Lawrence Erlbaum Associates Ltd.

Fama, E. F. (1970) 'Efficient capital markets: A review of theory and empirical work', *The Journal of Finance*, (25): 383–420.

Fama, E. F. & French, K. R. (2004) 'The capital asset pricing model: Theory and evidence', *Journal of Economic Perspectives*, 18(3): 25–46.

Fischer-Kowalski, M. & Huttler, W. (1999) 'Society's metabolism: The intellectual history of materials flow analysis part II 1970–1998', *Journal of Industrial Ecology*, 2(4): 107–136.

Fischhoff, B. (1992). Risk taking: A developmental perspective, in Yates, J. F. (ed.) *Risk-taking behaviour*, Chichester: John Wiley & Sons Ltd.

Forbes, S. (1997) 'Jiddu Krishnamurti and his insights into education', paper presented at Holistic Education Conference, Toronto, October.

Forrest, R. & Kearns, A. (2001) 'Social cohesion, social capital and the neighbourhood', *Urban Studies*, 38(12): 2125–2143.

Forum for the Future (2009) *Rethinking capital: The larger lessons of the financial crisis*, London: Forum for the Future.

Fowler, H. W. & Fowler, F. G. (ed.) (1961) *The concise Oxford dictionary of current English*, 5th edition, Oxford: Oxford University Press.

Frank, J. (1999) 'Applying memetics to financial markets: Do markets evolve towards efficiency?' *Journal of Memetics – Evolutionary Models of Information Transmission*, 3(2): 1–11.

Frankfurter, G. M., McGoun, E. G. & Allen, D. E. (2004) 'The prescriptive turn in behavioural finance', *Journal of Socio-Economics*, 33: 449–468.

Frantz, R. (2004) 'The behavioural economics of George Akerloff and Harvey Leibenstein', *Journal of Socio-Economics*, 33: 29–44.

Freire, P. (1973) *Education for critical consciousness*, New York: The Seabury Press.

FSA (2009) *The Turner review: A regulatory response to the global banking crisis*, London: The Financial Services Authority.

Fuller, R. J. (2000) 'Behavioural finance and the sources of alpha', paper presented at BSI Gamma Foundation, Lugano, June.

Gallimore, P. (1996) 'Confirmation bias in the valuation process: A test for corroborating evidence', *Journal of Property Research*, 13: 261–273.

Gallimore, P. & Gray, A. (2002) 'The role of investor sentiment in property investment decisions', *Journal of Property Research*, 19(2): 111–120.

Gallimore, P. & MacAllister, P. (2005) *Judgement and quantitative forecasts in commercial property investment*, London: RICS Research.

Gallimore, P., Hansz, J. A. & Gray, A. (2000) 'Decision making in small property companies', *Journal of Property Investment & Finance*, 18(6): 602–612.

Gatzlaff, D. H. & Tirtiroglu, D. (1995) 'Real estate market efficiency: Issues and evidence', *Journal of Real Estate Literature*, 3: 157–189.

Gau, G. W. (1984) 'Weak form tests of the efficiency of real estate investment markets', *Financial Reviews*, 19(4): 301–320.

—— (1985) 'Public information and abnormal returns in real estate investment', *AREUEA Journal*, 13(1): 15–31.

—— (1987) 'Efficient real estate markets: Paradox or paradigm?', *AREUEA Journal*, 15(2): 1–12.

Geddes, G. (1991) *Looking for the golden needle*, Plymouth: Manna Media.

Geertz, C. (1973) *The interpretation of cultures*, New York: Basic.

George, B. (2004) 'Becoming an authentic leader', *Innovative Leader*, 13(1).

Gigerenzer, G. (2001). The adaptive toolbox, in Gigerenzer, G. & Selten, R. (ed.) *Bounded rationality*, Cambridge, MA: Massachusetts Institute of Technology.

Gramsci, A. (1971) *Selections from the prison notebooks, trans*. Quentin Hoare and Geoffrey Nowell-Smith, London: Lawrence and Wishart.

Greenprint Foundation (2010) *Leading real estate organizations commit to collaborative action plan for green leases*, New York: Greenprint Foundation.

—— (2011) *Greenprint foundation overview*, New York: Greenpring Foundation.

Guy, S. (1997) 'Alternative developments: The social construction of green buildings', paper presented at RICS Cutting Edge Conference.

Guy, S. & Harris, R. (1997) 'Property in a global-risk society: Towards marketing research in the office sector', *Urban Studies*, 34(1): 125–140.

Hardin, W. (1999) 'Behavioural research into heuristics and bias as an academic pursuit: Lessons from other disciplines and implications for real estate', *Journal of Property Investment & Finance*, 17(4): 333–352.

Havard, T. (1999) 'Do valuers have a greater tendency to adjust a previous valuation upwards or downwards?', *Journal of Property Investment & Finance*, 17(4): 365–373.

Head, B. & Alford, J. (2008) 'Wicked problems: The implications for public management', paper presented at International Research Society for Public Management 12th Annual Conference, Brisbane, March.

Heidegger, M. (1958) *The question of being*, trans. Jean T. Wilde and William Kluback, New Haven, CT: College and University Press Services.

Heifetz, R. A. (1994) *Leadership without easy answers*, Harvard, MA: Harvard University Press.

Hockerts, K. (2001) 'Corporate sustainability management – towards controlling corporate ecological and social sustainability', paper presented at Sustainability at the Millennium – Globalisation, Competitiveness, and the Public Trust, 9th International Conference of Greening of Industry Network, Bangkok, January.

Hoesli, M. & MacGregor, B. D. (2000) *Property investment: Principles and practice of portfolio management*, Harlow: Pearson Education Limited.

Hoffrage, U. (2004). Overconfidence, in Pohl, R. F. (ed.) *Cognitive illusions – a handbook on fallacies and biases in thinking, judgement and memory*, Hove: Psychology Press.

Hofstede, G. (1984) *Culture's consequences in work related values*, Beverly Hills: Sage.

Horst, W., Rittel, J. & Webber, M. M. (1973) 'Dilemmas in a general theory of planning', *Policy Sciences*, 4: 155–169

Huczynski, A. & Buchanan, D. (1991) *Organisational behaviour*, London: Prentice-Hall.

Hume, D. (1999) *An enquiry concerning human understanding*, Oxford: Oxford University Press.

Igloo (2008) *Footprint – world's first socially responsible property fund*, Manchester: Igloo.

Ilies, R., Morgeson, F. P. & Nahrgang, J. D. (2005) 'Authentic leadership and eudaemonic well-being: Understanding leader–follower outcomes', *The Leadership Quarterly*, 16: 373–394.

Ilmonen, M. (1996) The Finnish landscape as a social construction, IFHP Summer School, Helsinki University of Technology.

IPD (2010) *IPD environment code – measuring the environmental performance of buildings*, London: Investment Property Databank.

IPF (2004) *Liquidity in commercial property markets*, London: Investment Property Forum.

—— (2008) *Alpha and persistence in UK property fund management*, London: Investment Property Forum.

—— (2009) *Creating a sustainable property investment index*, London: Investment Property Forum.

—— (2010) *Get into property derivatives*, London: Investment Property Forum.

Isaac, D. & O'Leary, J. (2011) *Property investment*, 2nd edition, London: Palgrave MacMillan.

ISO (2004) *ISO14001:2004 environmental management systems – general guidelines on principles, systems and support techniques*, Geneva: International Organization for Standardization.

Jackson, T. (2005) *Motivating Sustainable Consumption: a review of evidence on consumer behaviour and behavioural change. A report to the Sustainable Development Research Network*, Centre for Environmental Strategy, University of Surrey, January.

James, O. (2007) *Affluenza*, Reading: Vermilion.

Jameson, F. (2000) 'Globalisation and political strategy', *New Left Review*, 4: 49–68.

—— (2003) 'Future city', *New Left Review*, 21: 65–79.

JLL (2010) *Mapping the world of transparency: Uncertainty and risk in real estate*, London: Jones Lang LaSalle.

—— (2011) *Perspectives on sustainability: Companies go green to enhance productivity*, London: Jones Lang LaSalle.

Jung, C. G. (1961) *Psychological reflections*, New York: Harper Torchbooks.

Kahneman, D. & Riepe, M. W. (1998) 'Aspects of investor psychology', *Journal of Portfolio Management*, 24(4): 52–65.

Kahneman, D. & Tversky, A. (1979) 'Prospect theory: An analysis of decision under risk', *Econometrica*, 47(2): 263–291.

Kahneman, D., Slovic, P. & Tversky, A. (1982) Preface, in Kahneman, D., Slovic, P. & Tversky, A. (ed.) *Judgement under uncertainty: Heuristics and biases*, Cambridge: Cambridge University Press.

Keogh, G. (1994) 'Use and investment markets in British real estate', *Journal of Property Valuation & Investment*, 12(4): 58–72.

Keogh, G. & D'Arcy, E. (1999) 'Property market efficiency: An institutional economics perspective', *Urban Studies*, 36(13): 2401–2414.

Khare, B. B. (1988) *J. Krishnamurti things of the mind*, Delhi: Motilal Banarsidass.

Kimmet, P. (2009) 'Comparing "socially responsible" and "sustainable" commercial property investment', *Journal of Property Investment & Finance*, 27(5): 470–480.

Kinnard Jr., W. N., Lenk, M. M. & Worzala, E. M. (1997) 'Client pressure in the commercial appraisal industry: How prevalent is it?', *Journal of Property Valuation & Investment*, 15(3): 233–244.

Kollmuss, A. & Agyeman, J. (2002) 'Mind the gap: Why do people act environmentally and what are the barriers to pro-environmental behaviour?', *Environmental Education Research*, 8(3): 239–260.

Korhonen, J. & Seager, T. P. (2008) 'Beyond eco-efficiency: A resilience perspective', *Business Strategy and the Environment*, 17(7): 411–419.

Krishnamurti, J. (2007) *The nature of the new mind*, India: KFI Chennai.

—— (2010) *Freedom from the known*, London: Rider.

Krumm, P. J. M. M. & De Vries, J. (2003) 'Value creation through the management of corporate real estate', *Journal of Property Investment and Finance*, 21(1): 61–72.

Kumar, A. (2007) *Authentic transformational leadership: Authenticity as the key to sustainable organisation change*, n.p.

Kyle, A. S. (1985) 'Continuous auctions and insider trading', *Econometrica*, 53(6): 1315–1335.

L&G (2011) *Sustainability review and strategy 2011*, London: Legal & General Property.

Langford, I. H. (2002) 'An existential approach to risk perception', *Risk Analysis*, 22(1): 101–120.

Leece, D. (2003) *Behavioural finance and urban sustainability*, London: RICS Foundation – Future Thinking.

Leff, E. (2005) 'Nature, culture, sustainability: The social construction of an environmental rationality', paper presented at Ecological Threats and New Promises of Sustainability for the 21 Century Conference, Oxford, July.

Levy, D. & Schuck, E. (1999) 'The influence of clients on valuations', *Journal of Property Investment & Finance*, 17(4): 380–400.

Lindholm, A. L. & Nenonen, S. (2006) 'A conceptual framework of CREM performance measurement tools', *Journal of Corporate Real Estate*, 8(3): 108–119.

Ling, D. C. (2005) 'A random walk down main street: Can experts predict returns on commercial real estate?', *Journal of Real Estate Research*, 27(2): 137–154.

Loasby, B. J. (2001) 'Cognition, imagination and institutions in demand creation', *Journal of Evolutionary Economics*, 11: 7–21.

Loorbach, D., Van Bakel, J. C., Whiteman, G. & Rotmans, J. (2010) 'Business strategies for transitions towards sustainable systems', *Business Strategy and the Environment*, 19: 133–146.

Loori, J. D. (2007) *Teachings of the earth*, Boston, MA: Shambhala.

Lorenz, D. & Lützkendorf, T. (2008) 'Sustainability in property valuation: Theory and practice', *Journal of Property Investment & Finance*, 26(6): 482–521.

Lotman, J. (1990) *Universe of the mind: Semiotic theory of culture*, London: I.B. Tauris.

Lützkendorf, T. & Lorenz, D. (2007) 'Integrating sustainability into property risk assessments for market transformation', *Building Research & Information* 35(6): 644–661.

MacIntosh, R. & MacLean, D. (1999) 'Conditioned emergence: A dissipative structures approach to transformation', *Strategic Management Journal*, 20(4): 297–316.

—— (2001) 'Conditioned emergence: Researching change and changing research', *International Journal of Operations and Production Management*, 21(10): 1343–1357.

MacKenzie, D. (2004) 'Social connectivities in global financial markets', *Environment and Planning D: Society and Space*, 22: 83–101.

March, J. G. (1978) 'Bounded rationality, ambiguity and the engineering of choice', *The Bell Journal of Economics*, 9(2): 587–608.

Marciano, A. (2006) 'David Hume's model of man: Classical political economy as "Inspired" Political economy', *Review of Social Economy*, 6(3): 369–386.

Marsden, P. (1998) 'Memetics and social contagion: Two sides of the same coin?', *Journal of Memetics – Evolutionary Models of Information Transmission*, 2(2): 171–185.

Matthiessen, L. F. & Morris, P. (2007) *Cost of green revisited: Re-examining the feasibility and cost impact of sustainable design in the light of increased market adoption*, Sacramento, CA: David Langdon.

Max-Neef, M. A. (2005) 'Foundations of transdisciplinarity', *Ecological Economics*, 53: 5–16.

May, D. R., Chan, A. Y. L., Hodges, T. D. & Avolio, B. J. (2003) 'Developing the moral component of authentic leadership', *Organizational Dynamics*, 32(3): 247–260.

McAllister, P., Newell, G. & Matysiak, G. (2005) 'Analysing UK real estate market forecast disagreement', paper presented at American Real Estate Society Conference, Santa Fe, April.

McGrew, W. C. (1998) 'Culture in nonhuman primates?', *Annual Review of Anthropology*, 27: 301–328.

McIntosh, W. & Henderson, G. V. J. (1989) 'Efficiency of the office properties market', *Journal of Real Estate Finance and Economics*, 2: 61–70.

Meacham, M. (2007) *Authentic leadership*. Available online: http://eaglecommunications.info/newModels/Meacham%20Authentic%20Leadership%20Article.pdf (accessed 18 August 2011).

Miljkovic, D. (2005) 'Rational choice and irrational individuals or simply an irrational theory: A critical review of the hypothesis of perfect rationality', *The Journal of Socio-Economics*, 34: 621–634.

Miller, T. R., Munõz-Erickson, T. & Redman, C. L. (2011) 'Transforming knowledge for sustainability: Towards adaptive academic institutions', *International Journal of Sustainability in Higher Education*, 12(2): 177–192.

Mitchell, P. M. & McNamara, P. F. (1997) 'Issues in the development and application of property market forecasting: The investor's perspective', *Journal of Property Finance*, 8(4): 363–376.

Montier, J. (2002) *Behavioural finance: Insights into irrational minds and markets*, Chichester: John Wiley & Sons Ltd.

Muldavin, S. R. (2010) *Value beyond cost savings: How to underwrite sustainable properties*, London: Green Building Finance Consortium.

Mulligan, E. J. & Hastie, R. (2005) 'Explanations determine the impact of information on financial investment judgements', *Journal of Behavioural Decision Making*, 18: 145–156.

Murray, P. E. & Murray, S. A. (2007) 'Promoting sustainability values within career-oriented degree programmes. A case study analysis', *International Journal of Sustainability in Higher Education*, 8 (3): 285–300.

Newell, G. & MacFarlane, J. (2006) 'The accuracy of property forecasting in Australia', paper presented at Pacific Rim Real Estate Society Conference, Auckland, January.

O'Brien, G., Brodowicz, D. & Ratcliffe, J. (2009) *Built environment foresight 2030: The sustainable development imperative*, Dublin: Dublin Institution of Technology.

Olsen, R. A. (1997) 'Prospect theory as an explanation of risky choice by professional investors: Some evidence', *Review of Financial Economics*, 6(2): 225–232.

—— (1998) 'Behavioural finance and its implications for stock-price volatility', *Financial Analysts Journal*, 54(2): 10–18.

—— (2010) 'Toward a theory of behavioural finance: Implications from the natural sciences', *Qualitative Research in Financial Markets*, 2(2): 100–128.

ONS (2011) *United Kingdom national accounts – the blue book*, 2011 edition, Newport: The Office for National Statistics.

Orr, D. W. (2004) *Earth in mind: On education, environment, and the human prospect*, Washington, DC: First Island Press.

Oskamp, S. (2000) 'Psychological contributions to achieving an ecologically sustainable future for humanity', *Journal of Social Issues*, 56(3): 373–390.

Pacala, S. & Socolow, R. (2004) 'Stabilization wedges: Solving the climate problem for the next 50 years with current technologies', *Science*, 305(5686): 968–972.

Parker, A. M. & Fischhoff, B. (2005) 'Decision-making competence: External validation through an individual-differences approach', *Journal of Behavioural Decision Making*, 18: 1–27.

Parkin, S., Johnson, A., Buckland, H. & White, E. (2004) 'Learning and skills for sustainable development: Developing a sustainability literate society. Guidance for higher education institutions', paper presented at Higher Education Partnership for Sustainability/Forum for the Future, Cheltenham, June.

Pascal, E. (1994) *Jung to live by*, London: Souvenir Press.

Pascale, R. T. & Sternin, J. (2005) 'Your company's secret change agents', *Science*, 305(5686): 1–11.

Perold, A. F. (2004) 'The capital asset pricing model', *Journal of Economic Perspectives*, 18(3): 3–24.

Pinsent Masons (2009) *The Pinsent Masons sustainability toolkit series*, London: Pinsent Masons.

Pivo, G. & Fisher, J. D. (2008) Investment returns from responsible property investments: Energy efficient, transit-oriented and urban regeneration office properties in the US from 1998–2007, Boston: Working Paper Responsible Property Investing Centre, Boston College and University of Arizona WP08-2, Benecki Centre for Real Estate Studies, Indiana University.

Plous, S. (1993) *The psychology of judgement and decision making*, New York: McGraw-Hill Inc.

Pohl, R. F. (2004) *Introduction: Cognitive illusions*, in Pohl, R. F. (ed.) *Cognitive illusions – a handbook on fallacies and biases in thinking, judgement and memory*, Hove: Psychology Press.

Price, I. (1995) 'Organizational memetics: Organizational learning as a selection process', *Management Learning*, 26: 299–318.

Priest, G. (2002) *Beyond the limits of thought*, Oxford: Clarendon Press.

Procurement Executives' Association (1999) *Guide to a balanced scorecard: Performance management methodology*, Arlington, VA: Procurement Executives' Association.

Pryke, M. & Lee, R. (1995) 'Place your bets: Towards an understanding of globalisation, socio-financial engineering and competition within a financial centre', *Urban Studies*, 32(2): 329–344.

Reilly, F. K. & Norton E.A. (1999) *Investment,*5th edition, New York: Harcourt Inc.

RICS (2007) *A green profession? RICS members and the sustainability agenda*, London: RICS.

—— (2008a) *Breaking the vicious circle of blame – making the business case for sustainable buildings*, London: RICS.

—— (2008b) *Sustainable property investment and management: Key issues and major challenges*, London: RICS.

—— (2009a) *Valuation and sale price report 2009*, London: RICS.

—— (2009b) *RICS valuation information paper 13: Sustainability and commercial property valuation*, London: RICS.

—— (2009c) *Property in the economy: Agile working*, London: RICS.

—— (2010) *Is sustainability reflected in commercial property prices: A review of existing evidence, findings in built and rural environments*, London: RICS.

—— (2012) *RICS valuation professional standards – global and UK*, the red book, 8th edition, London: RICS.

Robertson, C. J. & Crittenden, W. F. (2003) 'Mapping moral philosophies: Strategic implications for multinational firms', *Strategic Management Journal*, 24: 385–392.

Ross, S. A., Westerfield, R., W. & Jaffe, J. (1999) *Corporate finance*, 5th edition, New York: Irwin McGraw-Hill.

Royston, P. J. (2003) 'Beyond finance theory: How framing influences the behaviour of real estate investors', paper presented at 10th Annual Conference of the European Real Estate Society, Helsinki Finland, June.

RREEF (2009) *How green a recession? – sustainability prospects in the US real estate industry*, San Francisco: RREEF Research.

—— (2011a) 'update Peter Dent [1]', email (11 August 2011).

—— (2011b) *Case studies, publishing on the internet*, London: RREFF. Available online: http://www.rreef.com/sustainability/studies.jsp (accessed 18 August 2011).

Samuelson, P. A. & Nordhaus, W. D. (2001) *Economics*, 17th edition, New York: McGraw-Hill Irwin.

Sayce, S., Ellison, L. & Parnell, P. (2007) 'Understanding investment drivers for UK sustainable property', *Building Research and Information*, 35(6): 629–643.

Sayce, S., Ellison, L. & Smith, J. (2004) 'Incorporating sustainability in commercial property appraisal: Evidence from the UK', paper presented at 11th European Real Estate Society Conference, Milano, Italy, June.

Scherer, C. W. & Cho, H. (2003) 'A social network contagion theory of risk perception', *Risk Analysis*, 23(2): 261–267.

Schleich, H., Lindholm, A. & Falkenback, H. (2009) *Environmental sustainability – drivers for the real estate investor*, Deutschland: University of Regensbury.

Schwegler, R., Tuncer, B. & Peter, D. (2008) *Sustainable consumption: Consumers as trendsetters for sustainability?*, Zurich: INrate for Sustainable Investment.

SDC (2005) *Sustainable buildings – the challenge of the existing stock: A technical working paper*, London: Sustainable Development Commission.

Shalley, M. J. (2008) *Green buildings: A new paradigm in real estate*, Atlanta, GA: Institute For Professionals in Taxation: Property Tax Symposium.

Sharpe, W. F. (1964) 'Capital asset prices: A theory of market equilibrium under conditions of risk', *The Journal of Finance*, 19(3): 425–442.

Shefrin, H. (2002) *Beyond greed and fear – understanding behavioural finance and the psychology of investing*, Oxford: Oxford University Press.

Shiller, R. J. (2008) *The subprime solution: How today's global financial crisis happened, and what to do about it?*, Oxford: Princeton University Press.

Simon, H. A. (1955) 'A behavioural model of rational choice', *The Quarterly Journal of Economics*, 69(1): 99–118.

Simon, A. F., Fagley, N. S. & Halleran, J. G. (2004) 'Decision framing: Moderating effects of individual differences and cognitive process', *Journal of Behavioural Decision Making*, 17(2): 77–93.

Sitkin, S. B. & Pablo, A. L. (1992) 'Reconceptualizing the determinants of risk behaviour', *The Academy of Management Review*, 17(1): 9–38.

Slovic, P. (1972) 'Psychological study of human judgement: Implications for investment decision making', *The Journal of Finance*, 27: 779–799.

Smith, D. M. & Blanc, M. (1997) 'Grass-roots democracy and participation: A new analytical and practical approach', *Environment and Planning D: Society and Space*, 15: 281–303.

Smith, V. L. (2005) 'Behavioural economics research and the foundations of economics', *The Journal of Socio-Economics*, 35: 135–150.

Socolow, R., Hotinski, R., Greenblatt, J. B. & Pacala, S. (2004) 'Solving the climate problem: Technologies available to curb CO_2 emissions', *Environment*, 46(10): 8–19.

Soros, G. (1998) *The crisis of global capitalism*, New York: Perseus Books Group.

Spengler, O. (1980) *The decline of the west*, New York: Alfred A. Knopf.

Stacey, R. D. (2003) *Strategic management and organisational dynamics: The challenge of complexity*, 4th edition, Harlow: FT Prentice Hall.

Statman, M. (1995). Behavioural finance versus standard finance, in Wood, A. S. (ed.) *Behavioural finance and decision theory in investment management*, Charlottesville, VA: AIMR.

—— (1999) 'Behaviourial finance: Past battles and future engagements', *Financial Analysts Journal*, Nov/Dec: 18–27.

Stringer, L. (2009) *The green workplace*, New York: Palgrave Macmillan.

TCPA/FoE (2006) *Planning policy statement 26: Tackling climate change through planning: The government's objectives*, London: Town and Country Planning Association and Friends of the Earth.

Terry, V. (1999) 'Sustainability: The converging triple bottom line', *Account-Ability Quarterly*, 14(11): 16.

Thrift, N. (2004) 'Remembering the technological unconscious by foregrounding knowledges of position', *Environment and Planning D: Society and Space*, 22: 175–190.

Tschakert, P. & Dietrich, K. A. (2010) 'Anticipatory learning for climate change adaptation and resilience', *Ecology and Society*, 15(2): 11–34.

Tvede, L. (1999) *The psychology of finance*, Chichester: John Wiley & Sons Ltd.

Tversky, A. & Kahneman, D. (1974) 'Judgement under uncertainty: Heuristics and biases', *Science*, 185: 1124–1131.

ULI (2010) *New tools. New rules. Climate change, land use, and energy*, Washington, DC: Urban Land Institute.

UNEP (2008) *Responsible property investment: What the leaders are doing?*, Nairobi: United Nations Environment Programme.

UNPRI (2011) *Principles for investors in inclusive finance*, London: United Nations Principles for Responsible Investment.

Vare, P. & Scott, W. (2007) 'Learning for a change exploring the relationship between education and sustainable development', *Journal of Education for Sustainable Development*, 1(2): 191–198

Von Neumann, J. & Morgenstern, O. (1947) *Theory of games and economic behavior*, 2nd edition, Princeton, NJ: Princeton University Press.

Wall, G. (1993) *The way to save*, New York: Henry Holt.

Wang, K. (1998) *Classic of Dao: A new investigation*, Beijing: Foreign Language Press.

Weber, R. (2002) 'Extracting value from the city: Neo-liberalism and urban redevelopment', *Antipode*, 34(3): 519–540.

Werczberger, E. (1997) 'Home ownership and rent control in Switzerland', *Housing Studies*, 12(3): 337–353.

Widén-Wulff, G. & Ginman, M. (2004) 'Explaining knowledge sharing in organizations through the dimensions of social capital', *Journal of Information Science*, 30(5): 448–458.

Wilkinson, S. & Reed, R. (2008) *Property development*, 5th edition, Abingdon: Routledge

Wines, J. (1993) 'Architecture in the age of ecology', *The Amicus Journal*, Summer: 22–23.

Woffold, L. (1985) 'Cognitive processes as determinants of real estate investment decisions', *The Appraisal Journal*, 53: 388–395.

Wood, A. S. (1995) Behavioural finance and decision theory in investment management: An overview, in Wood, A. S. (ed.) *Behavioural finance and decision theory in investment management*, Charlottesville, VA: AIMR.

WWF (2007) *One planet business – the dawning of a new era in a resource-constrained world*, Godalming: WWF-UK.

Xu, Y. & Dent, P. (2007) 'CAPM and the Shanghai prime office market', paper presented at 13th Pacific-Rim Real Estate Society Conference Fremantle, Western Australia, January.

Zaleskiewicz, T. (2001) 'Beyond risk seeking and risk aversion: Personality and the dual nature of economic risk taking', *European Journal of Personality*, 15: S105–S122.

Zohar, D. & Marshall, I. (2004) *Spiritual capital*, London: Bloomsbury.

Index

accountability 113, 133, 146
accounting 59, 133, 172, 207
accreditation 126
actions 27
adaptation 199, 210, 212
adaptive toolbox 95
AECOM Design and Planning 150,
    152, 154, 155–7
aesthetics 42–3, 48
Akerloff, G.A. 101
Allendorf, G. 123
allocative efficiency 83, 107
altruism 15, 116–17
Analog Devices 167
analysis 152, 153–4
Annual All Property Total Return
    Index 63–5
anticipation 152, 155–6, 206, 208
Anticipatory Action Learning 157
anticipatory change 166, 175
arbitrage 103
artificial neural networks (ANN) 92
asset strippers 58
Association of Accounting
    Technicians (AAT) 164, 170–5,
    179, 212
attitude-behaviour gap 20, 211
attitudes 27
attractor settlements 152 152

audits 44, 130–1, 149–63, 167, 169,
    173, 177
Australia 45, 59
authenticity 196–7, 201, 208, 210,
    210–12
Authorised Property Unit Trust
    (APUT) 60, 62
auto-regressive integrated moving
    average (ARIMA) 92

balance 196
balanced scorecard 163–78, 196, 212
banks 46, 56, 60, 66, 75; big
    conversation 182, 186; decision
    making 81; responsible
    investment 120–6
Barbados 61
barriers to sustainability 126, 138
Baum, A. 43
behaviour patterns 27, 98–101
behavioural barriers 106–9
behavioural finance 6–7, 100–3, 110
behavioural studies 103–5, 111
Beinecke, R.H. 211
beliefs 27
Better Buildings Partnership (BBP)
    117, 126, 129
Big Bang 48
big conversation 178–91, 199

biodiversity 116, 151
biology 97
biomass 188
Birkin, F. 177
Blake, J. 108
The Blue Book 39
Boyd, T. 92
BP 77
brands 166
BREEAM 50, 77, 79, 188
Brennan, T. 14
British Council of Offices (BCO) 8,
    178–9
Broadgate Estate 77
Brockwood Park School 141–7
Brown, G. 82
Brundtland Report 69, 135
Bucklersbury House 75–6
Building Exchange (BEX) 123
Building Regulations 43, 48–54
Burke, L. 114
Burrell, O.K. 101
business plans 181, 183
business rates 41, 43

calculated rationality 98
Canary Wharf 48
Cao, A. 32–3
Capital Asset Pricing Model (CAPM)
    81–2, 85, 95–6
capital gains 50, 59
Capital Gains Tax (CGT) 58
capital theory 6, 14–15, 82
capitalism 25, 67
carbon emissions 4, 18, 33, 50–1,
    68–9; big conversation 182,
    184–7, 189–91; case study 151;
    decision making 108; responsible
    investment 117, 127; skills 207
Carbon Index 117
Carbon Trust 52

carbon-is-cash behaviour 180, 185–6,
    199
case studies 7–8, 76–8, 120–6,
    149–52, 171–90; shear zones 137,
    141–8; skills 199–205, 208–10
Castells, M. 146, 162, 213
Central Lincolnshire Joint Planning
    Unit 150, 152
Central St Giles 76–7
certification 121, 125–6, 128
change agents 167
Chapman, D. 11
Chicago Athenaeum Museum of
    Architecture and Design 123
China 27, 61, 123
Chinese Ministry of Construction
    123
Cho, M. 123
City of London 43–4, 48, 71–2, 74–6
Citypoint 77
clarity 196
climate change 20–2, 31, 33, 69, 107;
    big conversation 183; case study
    157; shear zones 138, 149; skills
    207
Climate Change Act 52
Climate Change Levy 50
closed-ended funds 55–6, 59–61,
    62–3
closed-loop design 207
coercion 120
cognition 16
cognitive behavioural theory (CBT)
    11–12
cognitive psychology 99
collaboration 149
collective un/conscious 11, 26, 210
commercial mortgage backed
    securities (CMBS) 65–6
commoditisation 186
Companies Act 70

company voluntary agreements (CVAs) 46
comparable sale selection 105
competitive advantage 180
complex adaptive systems 35–6, 39–41, 43, 103, 190; leadership 194–5, 199; skills 206–10, 214
computing power 75
conception 16
conditioned emergence 175
conditioning 167
confirmation bias 105
conflict resolution 177
congestion 51
conservatism 102
constraints 175–7
construction costs 50, 75
Construction Innovation 207
constructivism 97
consumption 136, 213
control 55
CoreNet 69
corporate real estate (CRE) 68–9, 119
Corporate Research Centre for Construction Innovation (CRC) 51, 70, 89, 207
corporate responsible behaviour (CRB) 110
corporate social responsibility (CSR) 7, 115–17, 117, 127–29, 162; big conversation 179–84, 187, 190; leadership 203, 205; scorecard 165; shear zones 133, 135; skills 208, 214
Corpra 163–4, 172–7, 180
cost 164–5, 174, 199
covenants 45, 54, 56, 60
credit crunch 31, 47, 57, 60, 63–6
creditors 46
crisis change 165–6, 174–5
Crown 54

culture 4, 7, 11–13, 16, 21; big conversation 184; business tools 120, 125; case study 152, 154, 161; decision making 96, 99; institutions 25–35; leadership 197–8; scorecard 167, 173, 175, 177; shear zones 134, 136–7, 141, 145; skills 211, 211–12
currency 63–4
Cyprus 61

data collection 129–28
debt 45–6, 57, 65–6, 81
debt service ratios (DSCR) 56
decision making 6–7, 9, 21, 51, 68–9; basics 93–101; investment 80–93; occupation 138–9; process 96–7; scorecard 167; skills 208, 208–9; sustainability 93–112
decision theory 95, 98
demised areas 127
democracy 146
demolition 75–6
depreciation 41–3, 79, 86, 125
derivatives 63–5
Derrida, J. 17
descriptive theory 95
design 152, 156–7
Deutsche Bank AG 120–6
dialogue 137, 140–1, 145, 148, 176; skills 208, 208–9, 211–12
Diaz, J. 105
Dietrich, K.A. 152, 164
direct investment 55, 56–7
disabled access 43
discontinuities 152, 154–5
disease 191
disequilibrium 167
disinhibition 100
diversification 121
diversity 195–6

Dorner, D. 111
Dreher, D. 200
drivers 120, 135
due diligence 41, 66

East 27
eco-niches 166, 205
eco-town standards 151
ecological rationality 97
economics 4, 7, 9, 11–18, 25; big
    conversation 181; case study
    150–1, 154, 160–1; culture 34–7;
    decision making 95, 99–102,
    103–6; investment decisions 83,
    85, 91–2; leadership 200–1;
    market mechanisms 48, 52;
    responsible investment 113,
    118–19, 122–4, 124, 127;
    scorecard 176–7; shear zones 133,
    135, 146; skills 204–5, 211,
    211–12; uncertainty 97
editing stage 98
education 4, 20–1, 117, 139, 143; big
    conversation 181, 184; leadership
    204; skills 211
education for sustainable
    development (ESD) 140
efficiency 7, 134, 138, 152, 170, 179,
    183
efficient market hypothesis (EMH)
    82–3
electronics 98
elites 107
Elkington, J. 133
Ellison, L. 86
email 75
emotional time lines 98
endowments 119
Energy Act 69–71
energy efficiency 6, 18, 33, 44, 51;
    big conversation 183, 185;

decision making 85–6; responsible
    investment 118–19, 122–3, 125–9;
    shear zones 133–5, 140; skills 207,
    214; sustainability 69–71
Energy Efficiency Scheme 51, 70
Energy Performance Certificates
    (EPCs) 51
England 62
entropy 167
environment 7–11, 14–18, 20–2, 23,
    25; big conversation 182–8, 191;
    case study 151, 154, 162; decision
    making 99, 105–10; investment
    decisions 89, 93; leadership
    198–203; measurement standards
    128; responsible investment 113,
    118–19, 121–9; scorecard 176–7;
    shear zones 133, 135, 138, 141,
    147; skills 204–6, 210, 214;
    sustainability 70, 79
Environment Code 128
Environmental, Social and
    Governance (ESG) 120
Epstein, S. 99
equilibrium 167
equity 65–7, 81
ethics 7, 13, 115–17, 117, 133–4;
    case studies 152; leadership 198,
    200; shear zones 137–8
Europe 30, 62, 89, 123
European Centre for Architecture
    Art Design and Urban Studies
    123
European Union (EU) 62
evaluation 7, 98
evolution 97, 111, 210
exchange traded funds (ETFs)
    62–3
experience 12–13
expression 15–16
externalities 50–2, 68–9

Fama, E.F. 83
feedback 105, 167
finance 6
Finance Act 59
financial crises 11, 101, 105–6, 141
financial landowners 73–4
first-class behaviour 180, 186–8
flexible working 174, 184, 186–7
flow 193–4, 201, 207
focus groups 140–1
Forum for the Future 107
foundations 119
frame dependence 98
framing effect 105
France 45
Frantz, R. 101
freehold property 40–1, 53–4, 173
Freire, P. 20
FTSE 63, 65
full repairing and insuring (FRI)
    leases 40–2
functional depreciation 42, 44
future trends 91–2

Gallimore, P. 104–5
game theory 95
Gatzlaff, D.H. 84
Geddes, G. 195
Geertz, C. 26
Germany 123, 188
Global Compact 128
Global Reporting Initiative (GRI)
    128
global warming 120
globalisation 4, 21–2, 25, 28, 34,
    120, 125
governance 14
graduates 20–1
Greek language 16
Green Building Management Toolkit
    117

Green Deal 43, 71, 76
Green Lease Toolkit 117, 127
Green Seal 124
greenhouse houses 52
Greenprint Foundation 117, 126,
    129
Guiding Principles for Sustainability
    121

Havard, T. 105
Head, B. 197
head-in-the-sand behaviour 180,
    182, 189, 199
health and safety 116, 134, 184, 187
heating boilers 50
hegemony 12
Heifetz, R.A. 197
heterogeneity 41
heuristics 16, 95, 98, 101
hidden agendas 179
Hockerts, K. 134, 167
Hope Tower 124
horizontal substitution 136
Horst, W. 196
Hume, D. 12

identification 21
identity 137, 146, 170
ideology 29, 137
Igloo Regeneration Partnership 208
illiquidity 45, 56, 82–3, 166
illusion of certainty 11–12
imagination 12, 21
implementation 129–29, 145
impulsivity 100, 102
included middle 196, 213
income streams 44–5
independent assessment 129
India 61
indirect investment 54–67
indirect vehicles 6

individual investors 56
individuation 211
industrial landowners 74
industrialisation 4, 28
inertia 98, 165, 167, 177, 184–5, 189
inflation 44, 48
information deficit model 110
initiation 201, 203
inner harmony 198–9
insider trading 44
insolvency 46
institutional framework 33–6
institutional investors 74, 120–1
institutional wealth 10, 13–14
institutions 25–35
instrumental risk 100
insurance 54–5, 74, 119
intelligence 21
interactivity 152
interdisciplinarity 17, 21, 210–11
interest rates 63–4
Intergovernmental Panel on Climate Change (IPCC) 69
International standard on Assurance Engagements (ISAE) 128
intranets 184
investment 6–7, 9, 13–15, 21, 23; culture 30, 33; decision making 80–93; indirect 56–67; market mechanisms 38–9, 41–7, 50–2; ownership 55, 57–61, 66–7; process 126–7; responsible 115–29; sustainability 70–3, 76, 79; uncertainty 95–6
Investment Property Databank (IPD) 63–5, 74, 85, 128
Investment Property Forum (IPF) 45, 104–5
investment value 84
ISO standards 123, 126

issues in regret 102
iteration 15–16

jargon 104
joint ventures 79, 127
Jones Lang LaSalle (JLL) 69
judgement 12
Jung, C.G. 23, 99, 201, 211
junk space 28
just-in-time 29

Kahneman, D. 95, 98
Keogh, G. 32, 40
Kimmet, P. 113
knowledge 4, 9–13, 18, 20–1, 24; leadership 200, 204; market mechanisms 52; skills 204–11
Kollmuss, A. 109
Krumm, P.J.M. 21

landfill 124
landlords 32, 41–3, 46, 92, 126; big conversation 180, 183; leadership 198; responsible investment 127
landowners 48, 73–4
Latin language 16
leadership 7–8, 69, 96, 117, 121; big conversation 182, 187; journey 198–9, 211; role 196–7; scorecard 167, 175, 178; skills 206, 208, 210, 210–12; sustainability 193–205
Leadership in Energy and Environmental Design (LEED) 124
learning principles 193–6, 202, 208, 213
leasehold property 7, 40–5, 55, 122, 126, 170
Leece, D. 101–2
LEED 50
Leff, E. 106

legal depreciation 41–2
Legal and General (L&G) 77, 79
legislation 43, 46, 54, 60, 63;
    responsible investment 113, 117,
    125; sustainability 69–71, 72–3,
    80
lifecycle costing 15
limitations 15–16, 34
Limited Partnership Act 62
limited partnerships (LP) 61–2
Lincolnshire Core Strategy 150
Ling, D.C. 106
liquidity 45, 55–7, 59–65, 92, 107
listed property companies 55–7, 61
Listed Property Trusts 45
listed securities 39–41, 43–4
loan to value (LTV) 55–6
local authorities 49
logic 111, 179
London Underground 51
Lorenz, D. 139
lot size 40–1
Low Carbon Retrofit Toolkit 117
Lützkendorf, T. 92

McAllister, P. 106
McGrew, W.C. 24, 26
MacIntosh, R. 167
MacKenzie, D. 34
macroeconomics 82
maintenance 41, 146
March, J.G. 98
market failure 111
market mechanisms 4–6, 11–14,
    25–53
marketing 72, 166, 170, 183
Markowitz, H. 81
Marsden, P. 100, 104
Marx, K. 14
material flow analysis (MFA) 14
mathematical models 98

Mauritius 61
Max-Neef, M.A. 17
May, D.R. 198
Meacham, M. 199
measurement standards 128
media 125, 185
memory 12, 151–3
mental accounting 102
meta-cognition 97
microfinance 107
Miliband, D. 138
Miljkovic, D. 105
Mitsubishi Estate Company 77
mobilisation 144–5
moral gap 196–7
Muldavin, S.R. 92
Mulligan, E.J. 96
multinationals 24, 28, 74

National Health Service (NHS) 167
natural capital 13
need for cognition (NC) 105
NeoGuard 124
net asset value (NAV) 57–61, 62–3
Netherlands 45
Newton, I. 190
noise traders 103
normative theory 95, 105
norms 12, 14–15, 17, 34, 162, 166,
    198

objectivity 94
O'Brien, G. 110, 162
obsolescence 42, 71–2, 87
occupation decision making 138–9
Olsen, R.A. 94, 102, 111
one-shot operations 196
open-ended funds 55–6, 59–63
open-ended investment companies
    (OEIC) 62
operating costs 40–1, 116

operational processes 134, 170
organisational change 7, 21, 147,
    165–6, 174–7, 196, 203–4
Orr, D.W. 21
Oskamp, S. 3
outreach 148
overconfidence 98
ownership 6, 21, 30, 40, 42;
    leadership 198, 201; market
    mechanisms 45, 49–51, 53;
    methods 53–68; overview 53–4;
    scorecard 173, 178; shear zones
    139; skills 210, 212; sustainability
    72; types 54–67

Pacala, S. 18
paradigm shifts 213
Pareto efficiency 83
Parker, A.M. 97
partnership 7, 61–2, 79, 92, 107;
    leadership 198; responsible
    investment 117, 128–9, 129;
    scorecard 164, 170; skills 208, 213
Paul, J.S. 175
pensions 54–5, 61, 74, 119
performance benchmarks 84–5
performativity 34
physical depreciation 42
Pinsent Masons 127
planning 47–8, 51–3, 69–72
Planning and Compulsory Purchase
    Act 70
Pohl, R.F. 12
pollution 51, 70, 86
portfolio theory 80–2
Portrait of Place project 149–64,
    208–9
poverty 13, 191
prescriptive theory 95
price 83–4
Price, I. 100

Priest, G. 15, 209
private sector 149
procurement 120, 181
professional development 172, 174
professionalism 13, 21–2
profit 11, 15, 57–8, 66, 68–73;
    leadership 195, 205; responsible
    investment 114; scorecard 167,
    170, 174; shear zones 135, 146;
    skills 212; sustainability 76, 100
Property Authorised Investment
    Fund (PAIF) 62
property characteristics 33–6, 39–47,
    56–7
property indices 84–5
Property Workstream of the
    Institutional Investors' Group on
    Climate Change (IIGCC) 202
prospect theory 95
Prudential plc 199–202
PRUPIM 199–205, 209, 212
Pryke, M. 33
psychology 4
public commitments 127–9
public relations (PR) 125, 182
public sector 149, 181

railways 51
rational interpretation 103
reactive change 166, 174–5
real estate investment trusts (REITs)
    6, 45, 57–62
recession 120, 184
Red Book 84
reflexivity 4, 20, 22, 201, 211
refurbishment 50, 73, 75–6, 79, 87;
    big conversation 190; scorecard
    165; shear zones 135
regulation 6, 34, 42–3, 46–54, 65; big
    conversation 181, 185, 188;
    decision making 107; responsible

investment 113, 121; shear zones 136–7; skills 207; sustainability 69–73, 74–5
relearning principles 195
reporting 138
representations 16
requests for proposals (RFPs) 120
Research Corporation 106
resilience tools 93
Responsible Property Investment (RPI) 14, 115–29, 202
retrofitting 42, 44, 75, 120, 122, 126–7
return 80–1, 97, 102, 111, 114; leadership 200; responsible investment 120, 126–7; skills 212
RICS 11, 52, 83–6, 207
risk 80–1, 94–5, 98, 99–103, 107; leadership 199; shear zones 139, 141; sustainability 111
Royston, P.J. 105
RREEF 120–7, 212
rule-based behaviour 102
rumours 32
Russia 61

Scherer, C.W. 103
Schneiderman, A.M. 167
scorecard 163–78, 196, 212
Scotland 62
Second World War 48
secret language 36–7
Section 106 Agreements 49
securitised loans 65–6
self 14, 99, 111, 211
shareholders 57–8, 107, 113, 178
Sharpe, W.F. 82
shear zones 7, 132–49, 152, 170, 196, 198
Shiller, R.J. 104

shopping malls 200–1
Simon, A.F. 105
skills 204–12
skills audits 167, 169, 173
small investors 56, 59
Smith, V.L. 97
social capital 13, 144, 146–8
social choice theory 95
social construction 4, 27–29
social network contagion theory 103
social productivity 7, 133–4, 138, 145–6, 152; big conversation 179; scorecard 170; skills 212
social science 4, 178
socialism 25
socially responsible property investment 51–2
Socrates 13
software 128, 182, 186
Soros, G. 100
sovereign wealth funds 56, 119
space audits 167, 169, 173
space sufficiency 136
specialists 41, 74, 87
speculators 64
Spengler, O. 34
spiritual capital 140
spiritual integrity 201
spiritual intelligence 180, 210
stakeholders 7, 107, 116, 151, 156; leadership 205; scorecard 167, 176, 178; skills 208, 211
Stamp Duty Land Tax (SDLT) 41, 63
standards 123, 130–1, 151, 188
state 50
Stern Review 69
stimulating risk 100
Stock Exchange Tower 77
stock exchanges 57–8, 63, 77

stock markets 83–4, 103
strategic processes 170
Stringer, L. 145
subconscious 144
subcultures 27, 128
subsidies 120
sufficiency 7, 134, 137–8, 144–5, 152; big conversation 179; scorecard 170; skills 212; space 136
supporter settlements 153
sustainability 3–4, 6–17, 28–9, 29, 33–4; big conversation 178–91; case study 149–63; contextual factors 120; culture 35; decision making 93–112; initiatives 122; investment decisions 86, 93; leadership 193–205; market mechanisms 39, 44, 50, 51–2; measurement standards 128; ownership 66–7; plans 116–17; reporting 118–19; responsible investment 113, 121–2, 127–8; role 68–80; scorecard 163–78; shear zones 141 132–49; skills 204–12; solutions 134–8; tools 85–92
Sustainability Council 121
sustainability literacy 4, 8, 10, 18–22, 102; big conversation 178, 180; role 111; skills 204–11
Sustainable Development in Higher Education 20
Sustainable Investment in Real Estate (SIRE) 89
Sustainable Property Appraisal Project 85–8, 207
swap rates 47
symbolism 135–6, 164–5, 170, 174, 177–8, 205, 214
synergy 143

tactical processes 170
tame problems 197
taxation 6, 40–1, 46–53, 55, 56–8; ownership 60–2, 68, 125
technology 4, 165
tenants 32, 39–42, 43–5, 71–2, 75; big conversation 180; decision making 87, 92; leadership 198; responsible investment 122–3, 126–7; shear zones 137, 138–9; sustainability 80
tenure 29
theory of constraints (TOC) 175–6
third space 136
Thrift, N. 28
time horizons 102
timeframes 31
traditional landowners 74
transaction costs 40–1, 50, 83
transdisciplinarity 4, 10, 17–18, 149, 206, 213
transfer tax 41
transparency 43–4
trial and error 98, 196
trinket behaviour 180, 181–5, 199, 201, 205
triple bottom line (TBL) 7, 89, 93, 132–4, 170, 202, 204
triple net 43
trustees 142–3
Tschakert, P. 149, 151, 155, 157, 162, 164
Turner Review 105–6

uncertainty 94, 95–7
unconscious 97, 111, 137, 165, 176, 201, 208–9
Undertakings for Collective Investment in Transferable Securities (UCITS) 62
UnileverHaus 123

unit trusts 59–64
United Kingdom Commercial
    Property Index 65
United Kingdom Green Property
    Alliance (UK GPA) 202
United Kingdom (UK) 7, 27, 39, 40–3,
    46; case study 151; decision making
    104–5; investment decisions 83–4;
    leadership 202, 202–3; market
    mechanisms 47–53; measurement
    standards 128; ownership 57–9, 62,
    63–4; responsible investment 113,
    127; shear zones 138; sustainability
    69, 71, 77
United Nations Environment
    Programme Finance Initiative
    Property Working Group (UNEP
    FI PWG) 202
United Nations Principles for
    Responsible Investment (UNPRI)
    115
United Nations (UN) 18, 128
United States (US) 42, 45, 59, 63,
    106, 183
unlisted property companies 55–7,
    61, 63
urban space 30
urbanisation 48
utility costs 123
utility theory 96

vacant property 41, 43
valuation bias 105
Valuation Papers 87, 207
Valuation Standards 84
value 4, 9–11, 13, 15, 17; culture
    30–1; decision making 83–4, 92;
    function 98; leadership 199;
    market mechanisms 44–5;
    ownership 57–9, 67; role 20;
    scorecard 164–5, 174, 178; shear

zones 140; sustainability 70–1, 75;
    uncertainty 97
value-action gap 108, 110
valuers 103–5
values 27, 29, 34, 137, 196, 208–11
Vare, P. 19
vertical substitution 136
video conferencing 182–3, 188
vocation 200, 200–1, 210
voluntarism 114, 126
Von Neumann, J. 96

war 191
Water Services Regulation Authority
    (Ofwat) 188
wealth 134–5, 162
weight function 98
West 9, 12, 27, 30, 214
wheelchair access 43
whistle-blower policy 182
wicked problems 194–7
Widén-Wulff, G. 147
Wilkinson, S. 74, 113
Wilshire Courtyard 124
Wines, J. 23
wisdom intelligence 140
workshops 151, 156, 208
World Architecture Festival (WAF) 123
World Commission on Environment
    and Development 69
world feeling 34
World Wide Fund for Nature 207
world-class behaviour 180, 186–7,
    191, 209
worth 83–6, 203

Xiwang Tower 123
Xu, Y. 85, 97

Zaleskiewicz, T. 100
Zohar, D. 140, 142, 210